MW01040520

Faithful
Companioning

How Pastoral Counseling Heals

Chris R. Schlauch

FORTRESS PRESS   Minneapolis

Cindy,
I carry your heart with me
(I carry it in my heart)

FAITHFUL COMPANIONING
How Pastoral Counseling Heals

Copyright © 1995 Augsburg Fortress. All rights reserved. Except for brief quotations in critical articles or reviews, no part of this book may be reproduced in any manner without prior written permission from the publisher. Write to: Permissions, Augsburg Fortress, 426 S. Fifth St., Box 1209, Minneapolis, MN 55440.

Scripture quotations unless otherwise noted are from the New Revised Standard Version Bible, copyrigh © 1989 by the Division of Christian Education of the National Council of the Churches of Christ in the USA and used by permission.

Interior design: Peregrine Graphics Services
Cover design: Bentley Design, Terry W. Bentley

Library of Congress Cataloging-in-Publication Data
Schlauch, Chris Richard, 1952–
    Faithful companioning : how pastoral counseling heals / Chris R. Schlauch
        p.   cm.
    Includes bibliographical references and index.
    ISBN 0-8006-2631-1 (alk. paper)
    1. Pastoral counseling.   2. Pastoral psychology.
  3. Psychotherapy.   I. Title.
    BV4012.2.S33   1995
253'.5—dc20   95-19471
                                                                    CIP

The paper used in this publication meets the minimum requirements of American National Standard for Information Sciences—Permanence of Paper for Printed Library Materials, ANSI Z329.48-1984.   ∞

Manufactured in the U.S.A.   AF 1-2631
99   98   97   96   95   1   2   3   4   5   6   7   8   9   10

Contents

Preface 1

1
The Context of Pastoral Clinical Care 6

2
Theologizing 16

3
Theologizing about Person 45

4
The Pastoral Clinical Attitude 76

5
The Triad of Clinical Activities 104

6
The Two Questions 134

Notes 153
Bibliography 192
Index 203

Preface

wo questions central to the praxis of pastoral clinical care are addressed in this book: What is pastoral psychotherapy? and How does pastoral psychotherapy heal? Faithful companioning is the root metaphor by which I characterize the answers to both questions: Pastoral psychotherapy is, at its heart, healing through the clinician's attitude, method, and presence.

My purpose, however, is less to formulate answers than to compose a conversation through which readers are encouraged to identify, evaluate, and transform their assumptions and commitments. Each of us approaches questions from a different angle of vision in light of different authorities. As a result, we need to talk about our respective conclusions; more important, we need to engage in conversation about our ways of arriving at those conclusions.

The book presents in a conversational manner a way of arriving at answers to a series of questions that emerge at progressive levels of depth. Specifying what we do and how it heals requires identifying our basic clinical activities. These activities, however, cannot be interpreted independently of the clinician and the clinical relationship and process. They are an expression—a way of operationalizing—of the clinician's attitude, which is integral to that ongoing process and relationship. Thus, describing basic clinical activities presupposes identifying the clinical attitude these activities express. A pastoral clinician's attitude reveals underlying judgments and commitments about persons, about who we are and who we shall become. As a result, describing a clinical attitude requires specifying the theological anthropology that this attitude expresses.

Because any theological anthropology is a subset of an overall the-

1

ology, characterizing a theological anthropology requires discussing what
we mean by theology and how we go about doing theology. Theology, however, emerges in a particular context, in response to particular questions
and concerns. This book develops an approach to theology that emerges
from the experience and practice of pastoral clinical care. This unfolding series of implied questions serves as the sequence of chapters.

Terms such as *pastoral clinical care* and *pastoral psychotherapy* are used in-
terchangeably throughout this conversation. Each refers to a broad range
of activities and approaches employed by a rather diverse group of *pastoral clinicians*—ministers (commissioned or ordained), pastoral counselors,
and pastoral psychotherapists.

Most readers familiar with the literature in pastoral care, counseling,
and psychotherapy will recognize how my thinking departs from traditional
approaches to the answers to the two questions, as well as customary
methods of answering. I argue that pastoral clinical care cannot be explained by elaborating on the claim that its uniqueness is solely a function
of the personhood of the pastoral clinician. I also argue that no one can
make sense of pastoral clinical care by poring over verbatim or process
notes from clinical sessions in the attempt to demonstrate that its uniqueness turns on the explicit use of religious or theological language or on the
analysis of religious issues. Furthermore, pastoral clinical care should
not be regarded as unique because the theory is expressly theological. On
the contrary, characterizing what pastoral psychotherapy is and how it heals
involves explicating the interrelation among who we are, what we do, and
how we make sense. In particular, pastoral psychotherapy presupposes that
clinicians have a pastoral identity, regard clinical care as a form of ministry, and interpret pastoral identity and ministry through theological
reflection.

Several thinkers have oriented me in particular directions and shaped
my questions and thus my prospective responses. Having studied and
digested Sigmund Freud, I take for granted that we are always in an ongoing process of becoming aware. Beneath the manifest content of our
current ideas lie latent sensibilities, of which we are unconscious, that are
yet to be formulated. These unconscious sensibilities—be they thoughts,
memories, affects, sensations—inform the way we experience and relate
to ourselves and others and to our world in general.

My depth psychology has been qualified in a variety of ways by Paul
Tillich's depth theology. In a profound sense, I have come to regard

Tillich's metaphor of being on the boundary as critical to the reflections I offer.[1] We live on-the-boundaries of surface and depth, of knowing and not knowing (coming-to-know), of past and future, being separate and connected, being sinful yet holy.

With William James, I take for granted that we live in a pluralistic universe, in which, remarkably, each person is unique.[2] Each of us pursues different "live options," answers different questions, arrives at different truths. My academic and clinical internalization of Heinz Kohut's psychoanalytic psychology of the self deepened this commitment to appreciating the uniqueness of each person and the fundamental differences among us, our questions, our truths.

Engaging in ongoing clinical care in conjunction with the thinking of both Heinz Kohut and Donald Winnicott helped me unmask our unwitting acceptance of some of the legacy of René Descartes, from which we presume that persons are fundamentally separate and isolated from one another. Through these object relations thinkers—particularly as they enabled me to recognize phenomena that I had otherwise selected out of awareness—I recognized that persons overlap. A self not only has relationships and is in relationships; a self is relationships.

A final group of thinkers has become increasingly more significant in my life and work. In different ways, Richard Bernstein, Richard Rorty, and Robert Neville have alerted me to other dimensions of our unwitting Cartesian legacy. We tend to presume a foundation to reality. We further tend to presume that understanding something involves cutting it up into component elements, such as subject and object, self and world, thought and existence. We are inclined to isolate person from community and context, experience from reflection, practice from theory.

Steeped in this legacy of Freud, Tillich, James, Kohut, and Winnicott, I concluded that my responses to the questions—What is it that we do? and How does it work?—have to take into account certain basic concerns. First, in the context of our pluralism, we need to formulate an approach that is potentially meaningful to all persons but that affirms at the same time the integrity and uniqueness of the varieties of human experiencing and theorizing. Second, that approach must take into account the contributions of various interrelated elements—the pastoral identity of the clinician, the practice of the specialized ministry of clinical care, the theory (theology) of identity and practice, and the context in which identity, practice, and theory evolve. Third, that approach should be persistently self-critical, presuming that much of who we are, what we know, and how we relate is typically outside but potentially available to our awareness and that we are responsible for identifying and critically transforming certain dimensions of our being, doing, and knowing.

Our analysis must demonstrate not only an acquaintance but also a basic fluency in several universes of discourse, particularly theological and social scientific. Our discussion needs to be *experience near,* illustrating how our reflections emerge in our experience and practice, and have some direct bearing on our (future) clinical relationships and process. There are additional demands and hazards. "Any attempt at forming a theory of therapy is bound to prove incomplete and may even involve a number of contradictions."[3] Our theory, developed from experience with but a limited number of clients, may be "more a matter of belief than knowledge."[4] Given this, I take heart and encouragement from the Talmud, where it is written, "It is not upon you to finish the work; neither are you free to desist from it" (Aboth 2:21).

Several people have been formative in my identification and response to these questions. Numerous clients in pastoral psychotherapy helped me learn through experience some of what I have tried to convey. Randy Mason, Bernie Lyon, Marie McCarthy, and especially Terry Lyon, former colleagues at the Center for Religion and Psychotherapy of Chicago, provided an attitude, method, and presence articulated in these pages. Some of the words, and even more of the ideas, bear an indebtedness to Don Browning, former advisor and teacher.

Members of my peer group at the Danielsen Institute, Jim Barbaria, Martha Campbell, and Jane Gagliardi, each read various chapters and responded in ways that expressed their clinical expertise and enhanced mine. Several students, notably Phil Bauman and Leonard Hummel, gave helpful feedback on the entire document. Numerous students in seminars on Freud, Kohut, pastoral psychology and theology, pastoral psychotherapy, and psychology of religion have, to use Winnicott's words, "paid to teach me." Many supervisees have helped me formulate my thinking more clearly, particularly Martha Monahan, who read and criticized some of these ideas in an earlier version.

My friend Bill Burrows, managing editor at Orbis Press, gave inordinately precise and helpful feedback to a draft of chapter 2. Timothy Staveteig, former acquisitions editor at Fortress Press, helped me refine the entire manuscript.

My dean, Robert Neville, took the time to read and comment upon my ideas about theology. My colleagues in pastoral psychology, Carrie Doehring and Merle Jordan, read and responded to the entire text. Merle's companioning was especially helpful in shepherding me and this work to fruition.

My children, Caitie and Christopher, and my wife, Cindy, give me life.

1

The Context of Pastoral Clinical Care

M̲ost pastoral clinicians in the practice of their specialized ministry implicitly or explicitly follow an example or pattern that has been successful in similar situations—a particular previous case or a comment or story from a conference, supervisor, journal article, or book. The following three vignettes might be typical of persons who seek out pastoral counseling. What examples or patterns are called to mind?

A man in his mid-thirties is referred by his friend. In his first meeting, he indicates that he is despondent: His wife has threatened to leave him unless he gets some help for his depression. He has felt this way on and off for several years, but somehow this time it seems different, worse. He wonders, despairingly, why God is doing this to him. Dejectedly, he admits that he really does not expect to be helped, but, as he states quite directly, this seems to be his last chance.

A woman in her late sixties calls, requesting a meeting. She appears for her initial appointment on time but seems to be quite agitated. She sighs that she is troubled about recurring bouts of memory loss and fears having Alzheimer's disease. She also mentions that this time of year is especially difficult. She is frightened and does not know whether she really wants to find out what is wrong. She asks for help.

A young woman in her twenties is frantic that she might be pregnant. Without prompting, she states that she cannot consider abortion because her faith forbids it. Unable to tell her parents, she is frightened about dealing with this problem alone. She feels paralyzed but realizes that the longer she waits, the more restricted her options and the more urgent her response. She knows that whatever she ends up doing, somebody will be hurt. She seems helpless.

Each of these persons has requested help. How should a pastoral counselor respond? What options or possible courses of action are elicited? Is each vignette within the scope of ministry, or should one or more persons be referred to a colleague for consultation? How would you diagnose what in particular needs to be changed or healed? How should the appropriate goals of care be decided? Through what process could these goals be accomplished? Knowledge of what factors would help you decide how to respond?

Notice that even when no clear exemplar is at hand, we act nonetheless. A simple response indicates that we have some basic sense about what to do. That basic sense is the theory underlying our practice.

Most of us take for granted that we are guided in our clinical practice by an underlying theory. We think of ourselves as members of a particular clinical school or orientation, such as psychoanalytic, behavioral, or cognitive; we carry on the tradition of the originator of an approach, such as those begun by Sigmund Freud, Carl Rogers, Carl Jung, or Heinz Kohut. We can elaborate on our perspective's central concepts and its interpretation of how people change. We may even keep a paradigmatic case in mind that illustrates how the typical clinical relationship should unfold.

Yet none of these constitutes an understanding of how our theory informs and is informed by our practice. In fact, for most pastoral caregivers a gap between practice and theory exists, because we do not have at hand specific responses to central questions. Consider but three questions:

- How, concretely and specifically, does your theory guide you in diagnosing what is wrong, identifying realistic goals for clinical intervention, and recognizing what particular actions should be taken?
- How, concretely and specifically, does your theory explain how change and healing take place, as well as how does it monitor and facilitate that change?
- How, concretely and specifically, does your theory elucidate how you should modify your diagnosis, your objectives, and your pattern of intervention?

To be sure, some might be able to describe, in general terms, how theory guides their practice, but more than a few would be at a loss to explain in any detail how theory informs actions in each particular clinical relationship, moment to moment. Take the depressed and despondent man as an illustration. What would prompt one to focus on certain issues and questions to the exclusion of others? Of what relevance is ascertaining, for example, any history of depression in this man's family? Why might a clinician want to explore the circumstances around his becoming so despondent, his relationship with his wife, or what he actually means by *depression?* Why might one clinician want to be active and another reserved in style? What factors might lead to an expectation that his depression will lift or not? How would a clinician judge the ongoing effectiveness of work together? How would she or he recognize when the evolving process did or did not fit the theory? What should a clinician do when the process unfolds in a way contrary to or dramatically different from the expectations implied by his or her theory?

A GAP BETWEEN THEORY AND PRACTICE

Questions that prompt us to identify—concretely and specifically—how our theory informs our practice highlight the existing gap between our underlying commitments and our actions. To shift angles, consider how an underlying theory is a set of answers to questions. Simply responding to the despondent man, the agitated woman, and the frightened young woman implies that a theory of care is present; that is, two basic questions about care already seem to have been answered, namely, What is it that I do? and How does it work? A clinician may neither have actually raised these questions directly nor responded to them systematically and critically. Nonetheless, whoever acts is, in fact, acting according to answers to these questions, even when the practice is not sound or the theory well understood.

Let us suppose that most experienced clinicians would know what to do and even how and why a course of action could be helpful. I suspect, however, that few have examined in detail how practice is informed by and informs—concretely and specifically—theory or have addressed or responded to the two central questions; that is, many, if not most, of us act according to our theories without having actually identified and critically evaluated those theories. As Richard Chessick notes, "Many practitioners of this discipline . . . seem content to drift along with clichés and half-truths learned in training, without modifying or deepening their understanding by clinical experience."[1] Whereas Chessick maintains that the ultimate loser is the patient, the clinician also misses out.

A Spiral of Isolation

Many know clinicians who believe that the gap between practice and theory is not only unavoidable but should even be encouraged. These practitioners argue that abstract concepts and categories get in the way, distract attention from the flow of the process, and move the clinician away from her heart to her head. These clinicians are prone to follow their intuitions and esteem such well-known maxims as "trust the process" or "trust the spirit." For them, theory detracts; practice counts. Suspicious of theorizing, they do their best to avoid it, assuming, because they are not self-consciously reflecting upon their actions or explaining particular instances in theoretical terms, that theory is not involved. But in this they are mistaken, because their practice is itself the expression of underlying judgments and commitments they had already made—their theory. More generally, they deny that all theorizing about clinical care emerges from practice for purposes of making sense of and enhancing practice.

The clinician who isolates clinical care from ongoing reflection and neglects to identify the connections between his practice and his theory usually pays little attention to the connections between that practice and theory and his personal experience and history; that is, he isolates practice from theory and separates that practice and theory—*praxis*—from himself. Unaware that his praxis has evolved out of his own personal history, he may not know the pivotal events and the particular relationships that led him to choose, for example, the specialized ministry of pastoral clinical care as a vocation. He may be unaware of the way his past experiences influence how he responds to others. He may not realize that his choices of certain Scriptures as central, of particular theologians as essential, and of specific clinical orientations as authoritative are a function of his own unique past.[2]

The spiral of isolation extends further. When a practitioner isolates practice from theory and her praxis from herself, she unwittingly isolates herself from others. She may fail to appreciate that every *person* practices according to underlying theory and that every person's praxis has emerged in and is expressive of her personal experience and history. Consequently, she may neglect to encourage her clients to identify and evaluate critically their own commitments and the personal origins of those commitments. In fact, by ignoring the connections among practice, theory, and personal experience and history, she implicitly discourages her clients from examining those connections. She thus enhances clients' isolation from themselves and from others.

Moreover, those clinicians who isolate practice from theory and praxis from personal experience and history unwittingly isolate themselves from colleagues. They often continue to practice in their own particular way, making sense of the care they provide in an increasingly idiosyncratic, personalized language. While alert to gaps between their praxis and that of others, they refrain from conversation that would expose their work. In doing so, they limit opportunities to enhance and be enhanced by another's praxis. They remained isolated from others and from the context in which they live and work.

The Source of the Spiral

Given the obvious costs of isolating practice from theory, person, and context, what promotes such action apart from reflection? When the relations among practice, theory, person, and context are framed in terms of asking and answering questions, an observation by Paul Tillich seems pertinent, namely, that asking a question implies that we have both partial and insufficient knowledge of it or we neither could nor would need to ask.[3] If asking a question implies partial knowledge, then not asking implies full knowledge and renders a question irrelevant or suggests too little awareness to formulate a question or know what counts for an answer. Uncomfortably sensing our limits, we are reluctant to expose our ignorance to others, even though such ignorance does not prevent action.

Several motives seem possible. First, the task of identifying and evaluating theory is deeply personal and painful. Examining our actions—our practice—and discerning an underlying theory of change and healing disclose how highly personalized that theory is. I shall do unto others what has been done unto me. When I consider, for example, my reasons for responding to this despondent man or this agitated woman or this frightened young woman in these ways, I inevitably uncover memories of having been helped when I was despondent, agitated, or frightened. In this, I shall re-experience not only my healing but also my suffering. Like all of us, I do not want to feel despondent, agitated, or frightened; once is enough. So I isolate my actions from critical reflection, knowing at some level that I am all the while isolating my praxis from my history, and me from myself.

Second, clinicians avoid the task of identifying and evaluating theory because, in our pluralistic context, no answers are absolute and final.

Care and counseling are a variety of disciplines, distinctive languages, fundamental principles, and foundational texts. Each professional community maintains its own independent faculties, departments, resident experts, certifying bodies, and representative journals. Professionals across these different disciplines of care maintain competing interpretations of what to do and how it helps. Furthermore, professionals within these different disciplines hold competing interpretations. As our literatures illustrate, few in the area of pastoral clinical care speak a common language, stand in a common circle, and wrestle with common ideas and perspectives.

Third, clinicians avoid examining and evaluating their theory because the task is complex. How do we develop a perspective that honors our personal experience and practice but that is more than the elaboration or projection of our histories? How do we take into account the fact that each person who seeks our care operates according to her implicit theory of change and healing, which differs from ours? How can we engage in complex conversation with others, exposing to ourselves and others the painful roots of our approach, the limitations and relativity of our views, the unfinished nature of our thinking?

Fourth, pastoral clinicians avoid identifying and evaluating their theories because they face the unique task of forging an intercultural praxis of care. Historically, the varieties of pastoral clinical care followed a course expressly counter to that of differentiation and specialization. Pastoral counseling and psychotherapy are interdisciplinary *bridge disciplines* that integrate resources from diverse traditions and strive to remain intercultural as well as multilingual.

Members of bridge disciplines enjoy certain advantages. We have multiple identities or multiple "citizenships."[4] We typically become fluent in the theories and languages of a variety of health care professions as well as of ministry and theology. We can participate in contemporary movements in theology and pastoral care and can incorporate recent discoveries from social scientific and medical research. Because we have no definitive resources, methods, or guidelines, we are free to approach the territory in fresh ways.

As members of bridge disciplines, however, we live with certain fundamental dilemmas. We do not have a singular culture, language, or tradition. Having no culture of our own, we may never be at home. Having no language of our own, we have a lingua franca, a hybrid language or, more accurately, hybrid languages. Having no tradition of our own, we are prone to work in institutionalized isolation from one another;

we neglect expressing our ideas to others in anticipation of not being understood, and we neglect listening to others because their culture or language differs from ours. We cannot, like our colleagues in ministry or in the secular helping professions, more or less presume that our identity and praxis are a matter of public consensus. We cannot afford to neglect key features of that task, leave crucial questions unaddressed, or provide only sketchy answers. By definition, we must engage in constructive conversation with colleagues in our own as well as in neighboring communities of scholarship.

Pastoral clinicians avoid that constructive conversation and the task of forging an intercultural praxis of care by following three standardized, almost institutionalized paths. Some pastoral clinicians fall into reductionism by choosing a singular identity and citizenship and thereby mistakenly limit their resources and communities. They may function, for all intents and purposes, as secular practitioners and are pastoral in name only. Others become inconsistent by simplistically applying theological language or scriptural passages to human situations and by neglecting to make use of sophisticated perspectives from the social and human sciences to interpret how people change. Those following a second path shift identities and perspectives, depending on the requirements of the immediate task, and thereby unwittingly function as "multiple personalities," without a clearly defined center.[5] Still others attain incoherence by failing to recognize the need to develop a sound interdisciplinary identity and praxis. They inevitably integrate various traditions and resources in a loose manner, such that their psychological perspective is fundamentally at odds with their confessional tradition.

COLLABORATIVE CONVERSATION
AS AN ALTERNATIVE

Collaborative conversation is the alternative to the spiral of isolation. When we speak with one another about our practice and theory, we are in a position to benefit from another's theory; we are also in a position to benefit from our own. Having already implicitly answered the questions, we need to consider how others have done so and how we in fact have done so. As a result, we can understand more fully: Why am I doing what I'm doing now? How do I understand how and why it will help? Toward what goals am I enhancing care? How do I choose those goals? How do I know those goals are fitting, in general and in particular? In formulating a praxis of pastoral clinical care, three issues—pluralism, unmasking our Cartesian heritage, and self-criticism—need particular attention.

Perceiving the Problem of Pluralism

Colleagues in ministry and clients continually remind us of the varieties of questions, truths, and perspectives. We usually assume, nevertheless, that people share particular basic givens, human universals. The well-known maxim illustrates this propensity: "All persons are in some ways like all other persons, in some ways like some other persons, in some ways like no other person." Being in some ways alike—sharing certain identities, experiences, processes, communities, languages, tendencies, capacities, and needs—meaningful contact, connection, and conversation are possible. At the same time, we differ: Who we understand ourselves to be, what and how we experience, the processes of our reflecting, the languages and communities through which we apprehend and describe reality, and the tendencies, capacities, and needs we have are, in some measure, unique to each of us.

Most of us take for granted that basic experiences are shared—an attitude that is commonsensical and usually functional. Acting as if we are more or less alike, we enhance our experience of harmony and safety and minimize our awareness of difference, distance, isolation, and anxiety. Sustaining a false sense of commonality and harmony, we sacrifice understanding certain dimensions of who we are. In fact, our understanding of ourselves and of one another is typically rather marginal.

Examining and disclosing uniqueness promote collaborative exploration of aspects of oneself and experience that otherwise remain neglected, hidden, or denied. Through that activity, we may potentially transform features of our knowing and relating, appropriate dimensions that enrich us, and modify dimensions that oppress us. When engaging in collaborative conversation, presuming uniqueness, and respecting questions and truths, we have the occasion to discover and appropriate something about the other and the other in us that enhances our understanding.

Unmasking Our Cartesian Heritage

Few appreciate how thoroughly our styles of experiencing and thinking have been informed by Descartes. Many persons interpret situations by means of a characteristic procedure: discriminating component parts, analyzing those parts, and integrating them into a newly understood whole. For example, consider the two questions, What is it that we do? and How does it work? Some begin with theology by examining particular classical doctrines, such as creation and the fall, and describe how a theological interpretation of human nature is foundational to any kind of ministry.[6] At the same time, however, one might neglect considering how the particular choice and understanding of relevant doctrines evolved from personal experience and practice, as well as how these doctrines concretely and meaningfully inform experience and practice. Theory is isolated from practice and person.

Others suggest that concrete procedures can be described by beginning with an analysis of clinical techniques. Those techniques, however, express a particular theory of human nature. Technique, a dimension of practice, is isolated from reflection.

Still others formulate a clinical approach that involves a discussion of person, process, and goals as a complete and nuanced philosophical perspective. Implied is that a counseling trainee has simply to learn to apply the perspective to people. This approach fails to appreciate that each of us reads, interprets, and assimilates perspectives differently. Theory is isolated from person and person from context.

Because of our tendency to employ helpful analytic distinctions between person, thing, practice, and context in ways that isolate these elements, this book is organized around bridging concepts. These concepts—theologizing, metaphor, narrative, self, and attitude—intentionally represent the underlying inseparability of person, theory, practice, and context.

3 Persisting in Self-Criticism

Pluralism and relativism make it necessary for each person to strive to make his truths more accurate and more objective. Each needs to examine carefully, in an ongoing way, how particular experiences have led to knowing or believing particular truths. Each needs to study critically the preunderstandings and prejudices that inform one's judgments. Only collaboratively can these tasks be accomplished.

Often persons who engage in persistent, collaborative self-criticism discover that some of the most foundational features of our experiencing and interpreting may be outside awareness. Because many of these features may be cultural and shared, we have difficulty gaining distance or perspective. As a consequence, when critically examining subjective pre-understandings, we should presume that features of those preunder-standings are yet hidden—features characteristic of one's gender, race, faith group, class, culture.

We should intend to see beyond and behind what we see. Thinkers have often made use of a visual metaphor to help us focus on the issue with some acuity. N. R. Hanson comments, for example, that all of us have "spectacles behind our eyes."[7] All of our observation is interpretation that reveals something about the observer. "We never see only what we see; we always see something else with it and through it. . . . We see beyond what we see," Tillich notes.[8] We need to examine how our subjectivities are em-bedded in styles of seeing. Becoming aware of spectacles and those fea-tures of those subjectivities that pattern our experiencing and relating, we are empowered to see more clearly, know more fully, and relate more soundly.

Conversation involves identifying, addressing, and responding to questions, seeking the questions behind the questions, and learning to ask better questions. "A conversation . . . is not a confrontation. It is not a de-bate. It is not an exam. It is questioning itself. It is willingness to follow the question wherever it may go."[9] Through conversation, we may be enabled to identify, evaluate, and potentially transform assumptions and com-mitments, according to which we have already been operating. "The-ologian of care"—in which healing is a collaborative activity—is offered here as a category and identity through which such a transformation can take place.

2

Theologizing

El- theology 'n ...

F or pastoral counselors, making sense of who we are and what we do is an expressly theological enterprise. But how, specifically and concretely, is theology not only relevant but also integral to explaining the identity of the pastoral clinician and the praxis of pastoral clinical care? Answering this question is especially difficult, in part because no agreement exists regarding the subject matter, methods, or purposes of theology.[1]

Most take for granted that theology has to do with God. When talking about God, we describe specific qualities and dimensions of experience by using a particular kind of discourse characteristic of a particular historical faith community. When expressing their faith, members of a community follow traditional patterns of interpretation. Thus, for example, Christians explain sin through Scripture and stories by using symbols and myths, according to time-honored ideas.

Understanding theology as a kind of language and reflection points to a second, more basic and common usage, namely, theology as a perspective, a kind of theory or discipline. In this sense, a theology is a more or less comprehensive vision of human experience. Through this characterization, some of the ways in which theology may be integral to explaining pastoral identity and the praxis of pastoral clinical care will be explored.

THEOLOGY AS SEPARATED FROM
PASTORAL IDENTITY AND PRAXIS

Pastoral clinical care is a kind of conversation. Sometimes in that conversation one or another of the participants talks about a certain problem

16

or question in a way that seems to warrant theological language. The despondent man who seeks reasons why God is making him depressed indicates that his relationship with God is central to his suffering and, by implication, to his healing. The agitated elderly woman in the midst of her grieving faces the loss of her own powers and ultimately her life. The frightened pregnant woman who cannot consider abortion because "It's a sin" needs someone to help her deal with her moral dilemma as well as support her in her emotional and spiritual pain.

As these situations illustrate, sometimes the theological language that is invoked promotes shared theological reflection. The man considering suicide to escape from what he fears will be interminable suffering talks about how his life lacks real meaning and implies that he longs for some meaning that he cannot identify in isolation. The woman fearing Alzheimer's hopes she did not do anything that would jeopardize her being with God, her husband, and the faithful for eternity. The pregnant woman needs someone to help her clarify what is right in regard to her fetus, herself, the unborn child's father, her family, and God.

By using theological language and reflection to interpret suffering and healing, the clinician and client indicate that they interpret dimensions of their life and experience in terms of an underlying theological perspective. At times their conversation may focus directly on these perspectives. The pastoral clinician, for example, could help the elderly woman recognize how she professes belief in a God of love and forgiveness and yet lives in relation to a God who punishes her mercilessly. Examining her lived theology in conjunction with her professed theology could empower her to transform her theological perspective and thereby alleviate some of her suffering.

Theology can thus be considered integral to the identity of the pastoral clinician and to the praxis of pastoral clinical care. Theology—as language, reflection, and theory—informs our understanding of who we are and what we do. Because theology is so pivotal, we should be alert to potential problems that may emerge in how we understand and use theology. Such problems can be approached from two sides: How might our understanding and use contribute to problems in our clinical care? Conversely, how might problems in our clinical care reveal underlying problems in how we understand and use theology?

One's Understanding of Theology
May Cause Clinical Problems

Recall the background situation: Many clinicians practice according to a more or less unexamined theory that is part of a spiral of isolation. Against this background, it is helpful to examine how traditional understandings of theology in relation to pastoral clinical care might reveal as well as reinforce separations between practice, theory, person, and context.

First, consider the gap between practice and theory. Using the three clinical vignettes of chapter 1 as illustrations, we might ask how theology guides the way a clinician responds to the despondent man, the agitated woman, the frightened younger woman. Many—perhaps most—of us have difficulty specifying how our theological concepts in particular and our theological perspective in general guide us in our ongoing clinical responses. Theology has to do with the big picture, painted with broad brush strokes. The language, reflection, and theory do not seem to equip us to act in any precise way at any particular moment. How, specifically and concretely, are sin and grace, faith and doubt connected either to diagnosis or to modifying one's pattern of intervention?

This lack of specificity—the disjunction between theology and practice—points to a related gap between theological praxis and person. Pivotal events and significant relationships are formative in developing pastoral identity, a vision of ministry, and a style of theological reflection. A person's choice of favorite Scriptures or theologians has biographical roots, even though that person may have difficulty specifying ways in which her theology is autobiographical. Particular critical incidents are taken for granted as having shaped what each of us believes, but probably few of us have explored in any detail how our beliefs are so thoroughly subjective. We usually act as if our gospel is *the* gospel—even when we profess otherwise. If this is the case, then our lived understanding and use of theological concepts and reflection reveal and reinforce a gap between praxis and person.

These gaps between theology, practice, and person highlight a gap between persons. People commonly think about theology as the subject matter of a select group of trained professionals: clergy and seminary professors. Many regard theology as having to do with the expression of faith of a particular community: the Christian church or particular denominations. In both instances, we differentiate between people and groups on theological grounds, either as specialist versus nonspecialist or member versus nonmember. Using theology in this way reveals and re-inforces gaps between and among persons.

Furthermore, most people—clients, colleagues in ministry, colleagues in clinical practice, pastoral as well as secular—probably do not regard the-ology as something relevant to everyday life. Some people may use cer-tain religious words in conversation or think about religious issues in passing. Rarely, however, is our use of such words or conversations about such experiences regarded as doing theology. More common is the view that theology is the language and subject matter of a select group, ap-propriate to a particular setting and meaningful in regard to specific is-sues and moments. Thus, theology is restricted to particular persons, places, and times and isolated from everyday experience.

Many act as if there were around theology a threefold fence, de-marking person, place, and time. Our attempts to understand ordinary experience theologically are often awkward and even artificial. We may sense such questions as, Why not describe or explain this in everyday lan-guage? Why use such strange words? Is some foreign terminology being used to characterize what is unfolding?

Given the liabilities of separating theology from practice, from per-son, and from context, what prompts people to isolate theology in person, place, and time? Theology historically has much to do with questions of life and death, finitude and the infinite, the meaning and purpose of life, and who we are to be and become. Raising and responding to such ques-tions provokes our becoming directly aware of our limits and failings, our finitude and death in a spectrum of existential responses including help-lessness, dependence, shame, guilt, and anxiety. As a means of disavow-ing our finitude and failings, we erect a threefold fence around theology. If theology were something that a select group of professionals do, irrel-evant to our ongoing experience, then the questions addressed would not be ours. By disowning the language and questions, we disavow the spec-trum of existential responses to the confrontation of limits.

Through our denial of death and other big questions, we seek to be less encumbered by the thoughts and emotions these issues provoke, as if by ignoring them they will go away. Instead, we become habituated to iso-lating ourselves from ourselves and one another. Whatever jeopardizes this practiced isolation and denial becomes suspect. Theology is such an en-terprise. It requires addressing the questions and issues and confronting the finitude and failings that we naturally work hard to avoid. As a result, we understand and use theological concepts and reflection with ambivalence, and we do so ambiguously. This only heightens our awareness of our limits and further promotes our denial and isolation.

Clinical Problems May Expose Liabilities in One's Understanding of Theology

Some clients may come to think, however mistakenly, that pastoral clinicians live in a world different from theirs. They may imagine our faith remarkable and theirs, by comparison, ordinary, ambiguous, and full of doubt. They may experience us as closer to God and feel diminished or judged simply by our presence. They may feel ashamed to reveal their lack of faith or to expose their seemingly childish questions about God. They may feel uneasy with our specialized training or our fluency in Scripture. In a word, they may experience us as Other. During their suffering, when they need to be cared for by someone they feel really understands and is like them, they may feel alone, apart from the Other.

Many clients feel separated or alienated from themselves, as if they live in different worlds. At times they are safe, in control, and adultlike, and they can be imaginative, playful, constructive, and generative. At other times they feel quite different: endangered, helpless, infantile, irrational. They are at a loss to connect the different selves, the different worlds. They may, at times, be unable to identify the reasons why they act as they do. They may, at times, know their motives, yet be unable to stop or change their behavior. They may sense that another cannot understand or be with them, because they cannot understand or be with themselves. They may experience not only others as Other but also themselves as Other. During their suffering they may feel alone and apart from the Other, in large part because they are more than one person, in more than one place.

Some pastoral clinicians may feel separated or alienated from their clients. Our education and training have sensitized us to features and dimensions of experience that we may feel are hidden from or foreign to the ongoing lives of many clients. We might talk theology in seminary or with other religious professionals, but when we use these words in conversation, a clinical session, or a sermon, we might lose contact with the other person. Such moments may put into bold relief the difference that is common to some relationships between religious professionals and laypersons. When in the company of people we experience as different, we may try to meet them where they are but fear their land is foreign to us. We may try to collaborate but fear that we speak different languages and do not share basic assumptions. We may sense that, in our efforts to help this different Other, we come across awkwardly, ambivalently, and ambiguously. We feel isolated.

Like our clients, we pastoral clinicians often are isolated from ourselves, as if we live in different worlds inside. We are alternatingly safe or endangered, authoritative or helpless, reasoning or irrational, faithful or skeptical. We are divided against ourselves. Like our clients, we deny—disown—our finitude and failings, our shame, guilt, and anxiety.

When viewed from this angle, we realize how thoroughly all of us are prone to experience gaps within as well as between and among us. We recognize how the ways we understand and use theology may exacerbate these problems precisely because our theology does not challenge but unwittingly accepts and reinforces these gaps as normative. We need to consider an alternative.[2]

THEOLOGY AS INSEPARABLE FROM EXPERIENCE

Theology is the human critical praxis of interdisciplinary conversation in the ever-present territory of the big questions, interpreted especially through the concepts of metaphor and narrative. In that theology is an expressly human enterprise, persons and groups are not differentiated or separated as specialist versus nonspecialist or member versus nonmember. As praxis, the interrelationship of practice and theory, experience and reflection are accentuated; the theory-to-practice, source-to-application model is challenged. As taking place in the ever-present territory of the big questions, theology and questions of finitude and failings are not limited to particular settings or moments in time.

We can make fuller sense of an experience or story only through concepts and reflection; we can make fuller sense of concepts and reflection only through story and experience. The interdependence of experience and reflection, practice and theory will be illusrated through the method as well as the content of the unfolding discussion.[3] Langdon Gilkey used to illustrate a Tillichian distinction that can serve as a point of departure. Two friends are sitting and drinking together, engaged in a relaxed yet serious conversation. Their conversation gradually shifts, and they wonder, "What's life really about?" "Why are we alive?" "What does it all mean?" "What should we be about?" This is *theology*. They reach a point where they no longer speak, yet they are communicating nonetheless. This is *religion*.[4]

The Human Enterprise of Theology

What would it be like to think about theology as something all human beings do? What would it mean to regard every person we meet as a theologian? How might our praxis change were we to regard the despondent man, the agitated older woman, and the pregnant woman as theologians and our clinical conversation as, in part, theological dialogue?

As human beings, we are born with a capacity and need to make sense of unfolding experience. Each of us naturally develops a way around, a particular style of negotiating in our world in the context of our unique vision of that world. In more formal terms, each of us develops a method of gathering and organizing significant information in the context of an overall theory of self and world. We not only live in our experience but can also reflect upon that experience. We are not only aware but also aware of being aware. We have an ability to be subjects of and in our experience and objects to ourselves in our experience.

One way of expressing this concept is to suggest that we live and function on two interpenetrating, mutually informing dimensions: experiencing and reflecting upon experience. Thinkers from a variety of perspectives—existentialism, pragmatism, psychoanalytic theory, cognitive structural psychology, philosophy of science—have regarded these two dimensions as interpenetrating and mutually informing. What and how we experience has been shaped and guided by previous reflection, which itself had been shaped and informed by previous experience.

Following Kierkegaard, our most basic and elemental level of existence is what we actually live. We reflect upon that as a way of making sense of what we are doing. Following William James, we function according to certain truths of experience. Our reflections are true to the degree to which they enable us to live and function well enough. Following Freud, our secondary process thinking is employed to enable us to adapt more adequately and satisfactorily. Only in the experience of frustration and anxiety, as we realize that our way of making sense is inadequate, are we called upon to formulate an alternative response. Following Jean Piaget, we assimilate experience into our existing schemata and modify those schemata (accommodate) only when the schemata do not fit. Following Thomas Kuhn, we live within a paradigm through which we make more or less adequate sense, undergoing a paradigm shift only when we are unable to function adequately within and according to that paradigm.

As a matter of course, we usually take for granted our reflections, our accumulated wisdom on negotiating our way in the world. We act according to previous thinking and theorizing, forced to modify how we have made sense only when we come to an impasse, have an accident, or encounter a crisis. We amend our theory and method in order to live and function more effectively and proceed more smoothly.

When we consider our capacity and need to reflect upon ongoing experience, we realize that we experience and reflect in a variety of ways. We also realize that reality, as such, can be approached from a variety of angles, in light of a diversity of questions and issues. Over the course of human history, the variety of ways of living reality and reflecting upon reality have become progressively more formally organized into specialized areas of experience and disciplines of knowledge. For example, we typically distinguish among physical, mental, and spiritual dimensions of experience; among body, mind, and soul; as well as among the so-called hard sciences, the social sciences, and the humanities. Following Tillich, I will speak about a certain domain of living and experiencing reality— *religion*—and a corresponding way of reflecting upon reality—*theology*.

Religion and Theology as Experiencing and Reflecting

Many people could identify with the conversation between friends. Each of us has, at different times and in different ways, wondered about the meanings and purposes of our life, about why we are, who and whose we are, for what or for whom we are. Some of us may have been taught to think of these questions and concerns as philosophical or in the province of meta-ethical reflection. Like Tillich, I will regard these questions as expressly having to do with religion and theology.

When we ask, Why am I alive? Who am I? we somehow sense that all human beings, at some time or another, have raised these questions. In this, we recognize our membership in the human race. Our questions and concerns are at once like those of all other persons—universal, human, yet like no other person—particular, profoundly personal, and unique.

Tillich regarded these fundamentally human questions as having to do with a certain area or domain of experience—religion—and with a corresponding kind of reflection—theology. Furthermore, he proposed that religion and theology were fundamentally interpenetrating. By formulating that understanding, Tillich not only departed from but also challenged a traditional approach to theology in a foundational way. Traditionally, theology has been regarded as reflection on God, divine matters, or faith. Furthermore, it has been understood as the reflection of a particular historical community—Christians—on the God of Abraham, Isaac, and Jacob, the Creator of all that is seen and unseen, made manifest in Jesus the Christ.[5] In contrast, Tillich (1) approached theology as a "human" enterprise and (2) challenged the idea that such reflection can, however implicitly and unwittingly, be understood apart from experience. Let me describe these two related issues further, again with reference to the conversation between two friends.

According to Tillich, the two friends were involved in theology and religion. They illustrate that human beings, as *Homo religiosus,* share an innate capacity and need for experiencing what he referred to as "the depth dimension," on the one hand, and for reflecting upon that area of experience, through theology, on the other. To be human is to experience and to reflect upon that depth; that is, religion and theology are universal categories that take particular forms or expressions, as characteristically human enterprises. In this regard, Christian faith and Christian theology are particular forms or expressions of religion and theology.

In addition to regarding theology as a human enterprise, Tillich argued that religion and theology *interpenetrate:* Experience and reflection are mutually informing. Theological reflection emerges from, and returns to, religious experiencing. Reflecting on God, divine matters, or faith evolves from and informs ongoing experience. Many theologians, however, formulate perspectives in which the connections between reflection and experience appear severed. Theology mistakenly becomes an intellectual discipline, at times isolated from religion and from human experiencing.[6]

More than a few liabilities emerge in separating reflecting from experiencing and theology from religion. First, we imply that ideas exist on some transhistorical plane and have some kind of inherent life and movement. We imply that these ideas can be isolated from the persons who created them and from the existential context in which they emerged. Second, we run the risk of functioning according to a theory-to-practice or source-to-application model.[7] We study and master ideas and then engage in the awkward and artificial task of applying these ideas to situations. Once we have isolated reflecting from experiencing, we have to recross an artificial chasm and engage in what is supposedly a distinctly different enterprise—action, or practice. Third, when we understand theology as ideas, we naturally regard it as the special province of a particular community— clergy and academic theologians—who possess fluency in a special universe of discourse. Correlatively, we presume that theology is peculiar to particular settings, such as a seminary or divinity school and sacred or holy places. Hence, specialists do theology to and for, but not with, nonspecialists. Finally, and not least significantly, when we regard theology as ideas involving a special language game of a particular professional class, we falsely presume that theology exists in an isolated domain, somehow not only distinct but also separable from other domains of experiencing and reflecting. In other words, we have mistakenly, and probably unconsciously, constructed a threefold fence around theology.

From a traditional theological perspective, then, the conversation between friends had little if anything to do with theologians or theology. In contrast, assuming that theology is a human enterprise and that we are all theologians would have dramatic implications for how we might respond and what would unfold.[8] We would hear—because we listened for—others talking, however indirectly and ambiguously, about religious experience. We would talk with them about how they make sense of those experiences, through their theological reflection. We would expect that they will do so ambivalently and ambiguously, in part trying to disown features of their experiences.

Assuming a most basic commonality between us, we would be more disposed to collaborate with than do something to or for others. We function less from within a hierarchical model of talking down than within an egalitarian model of developing with. We would listen to another's experience and reflection, and we would, in addition, engage with another in new experiencing and reflecting. Thus, even if the despondent man never mentioned God, the elderly woman never spoke about eternal life, and the pregnant woman nver used the word *sin*, we would presume that each was engaged in a process of making sense of religious questions and issues. By regarding them as theologians, we would be inviting them to speak more directly to and about those dimensions they might otherwise avoid. We could also illustrate with them how we reflect upon religious experience, equipping them to do so more fluently and meaningfully.

This view calls for a shift in language: Theology is used less as a noun—as language, reflection, or theory—than as a verb, as a doing with others. Thus, the awkward but preferable term *theologizing* is used here to accentuate the interplay of experiencing and reflecting.[9] Concerns that parallel the interaction of experiencing and reflecting have reemerged in contemporary philosophy and theology under the rubrics of praxis, practical philosophy, and practical theology. Although the concept of praxis has a long and complex history and has been interpreted in a variety of ways, focusing on praxis helps us recover the inherent, practical interaction of reflecting and experiencing.

THEOLOGIZING AS PRAXIS

What would it mean to think about theologizing as the interrelation of practice and theory? What would it mean to approach theory as evolving out of and returning to practice? How, for example, would this approach inform how we would respond and work with the despondent man, the grieving woman, the pregnant woman, or any person?

A tendency not only to distinguish but also to separate theory from practice has been noted. Theory involves thinking; practice, in contrast, is doing. Developing theory presupposes analytic, synthetic, and constructive cognitive and intellectual talents. Practice is a matter of how-to, the steps through which we apply theory in technique. Such thinking observes the usual class distinctions between professional and lay, specialist and nonspecialist: Theory development has an elite quality, whereas practice can be done by the masses.

This distinction between theory and practice "is found in all European languages"[10] and "has been central to almost every Western philosopher since Aristotle."[11] Aristotle, however, did not contrast either abstract doctrine and concrete application or thinking and acting. Rather, he differentiated among several varieties of life activities a "free man" could pursue: *poiesis* ("the productive life"), *praxis* ("the practical life"), and *theoria* ("the speculative life"). Aristotle tended to collapse this tripartite scheme to an opposition between the practical life—"the life of active citizenship, of active participation in the life of the polis" (*praxis*)—and the theoretical life," a life of detachment from political partnership," of "the philosopher who strives for the contemplation of eternal truths" (*theoria*).[12]

Historically, the distinction between *theoria* and *praxis* devolved to an opposition between theory and practice, departing from Aristotle's original characterization. But praxis always includes "twin moments—action (i.e., engagement) and reflection, but not separated from each other; it is action done reflectively, and reflection on what is being done."[13]

Each of several historical surveys of the concepts of theory and practice, from Aristotle through Plato, Immanuel Kant, Georg Hegel, Karl Marx, Jürgen Habermas, and Richard Bernstein, describes how the meanings of these terms and their relationships change depending on context.[14] In the midst of that complex evolution and variation, it has become a commonplace to oppose, if only colloquially, theory and practice. It has also become a commonplace to oppose, if only colloquially, theology (*theoria*, a classical discipline) and ministry (practice, a practical discipline).

Given the evolution and variations in meaning, any contemporary discussion of theory and practice should be situated in historical context. Stephen Toulmin recommends approaching the history of philosophy in terms of pendulum swings between theory-centered and practice-centered agendas. Practical-minded Aristotelians "will not claim universality for their views in advance of practical experience"; "theoretically inclined Platonists are willing to speculate more freely and to hazard broader generalizations."[15] The former group's agenda emphasizes the oral, the particular, the local, and the timely, whereas the latter emphasizes the written, the universal, the general, and the timeless.[16] According to Toulmin, "we are in the middle of yet another pendulum swing back, from a Platonically oriented, theory-centered style of philosophy toward the re-acceptance of more practical, Aristotelian concerns."[17] In the current "recovery of practical philosophy," one is less disposed to isolate theory from practice and more inclined to appreciate the twin interdependent moments of action and reflection.[18] *Praxis,* as used in this book, claims first that practice is informed by and informing of theory and that theory emerges from and returns to practice.[19] Second, it means that all application aims not merely to comprehend but also to change reality.[20] In sum, praxis is the interpenetration of theory and practice.

Understanding theology in light of the analysis of praxis engenders a reorientation: Theology is not *theoria*. It is not a set of ideas formulated in a series of doctrines or propositions, recorded in a book. Theology is not something that is or that one has. Theologizing is praxis—an active, dynamic process that emerges and evolves in history, concerned with application, with changing reality. *Theologizing* is the practice of—the doing of—theology. Quentin Hand puts it well: "Pastoral counseling [is] the *practice* of theology. For the practice of theology requires both knowing theology and 'doing' theology."[21] This praxis of theology requires, as Thomas Groome says, the "knowing about theology in a theoretical sense" and "being able to do theology in the context of a pastoral situation," doing theology in one's head and doing it on one's feet.[22] Theologizing is always done, as Charles Gerkin says, "in the midst of necessity of action."[23] Even the most abstract, formal, systematic, speculative theologizing should be understood as precipated by and responding to experience and practice in order to enhance future experience and practice.

Theologizing as praxis—as the dialectical interaction between religion and theology—can inform our understanding of the conversation between the two friends.[24] As they theologizie about the religion they had already known, their evolving reflection enhances and modifies their ongoing religious experiencing. Provoked by particular life events, they will act differently in light of their reflecting directly on those concrete concerns. Simply put, their doing theology presupposes prior practice and informs future practice.

How would it make a difference to appreciate that all expressly theological reflection emerges from and informs religious experience and practice? First, pastoral clinical conversation would be understood as neither practice nor theory, but praxis. Clinician and client are not involved in teaching and learning how to apply abstract theory to concrete situations; they are experiencing and reflecting, practicing and theorizing, together. In a collaborative praxis, they move back and forth, deepening experience while enhancing reflection. Thus, the grieving woman discusses what life, eternal life, and living life abundantly mean to her. She talks with shame and guilt about behaviors that are so sinful that she expects she is beyond grace and redemption. She fears eternal damnation. She helps her clinician and herself grasp what experiences have given rise to these ideas. Having her clinician's ideas, some of which differ from her ideas, contributes to her appreciation that ideas emerge from experience and that her ideas and her experience are intimately connected. Through experiencing and reflecting with another, she has the occasion both to deepen her experience and to modify her reflections. She may confront the dissonance between the merciless God she lives with and the loving God she professes. Aware of making God in the image of her own experience, she may include others' experiences to expand her understanding of God.

Second, a person's reflections—theorizing—would be understood as having been forged in previous experience and practice. Clinical care thus involves exploring the connections between past experience and the content and patterns of current thinking. The despondent man, for example, would benefit from understanding what leads him to despair as well as what leads him to seek help and hope. Furthermore, clinical care presumes persons differ in their experiences and theorizing: Convictions forged in one person's experience may have only limited relevance to another. What a clinician says or does takes root only if it is planted in the soil of the client's experience.

Third, because all praxis is aimed not merely to comprehend reality but to change it, one should be especially attentive to what a client implicitly as well as explicitly intends. One would want to understand, for example, how the pregnant young woman imagines that someone might help. What, specifically and concretely, would help look like? How would conversation, or any other response, enhance the kind of change and healing she was seeking? In this context, then, one presumes that all reflecting together was geared toward enhancing future experience and practice, that is, had as its express purpose changing her experience and modifying how she would act.

THEOLOGIZING AS PRACTICAL CONVERSATION

What would it be like to think about theologizing as practical conversation? How might our pastoral clinical care differ if we approached clinical conversation in general as holding the occasion for the practical conversation of theologizing in particular?

Because clinical care involves the spoken exchange of thoughts and feelings, regarding such care as conversation may seem self-evident. Thinking about theology as "a kind of conversation" requires a greater leap of the imagination.[25] Indeed, theologians who describe their vocation in this way use the term figuratively, referring less to actual talking between people than to an abstract dialogue between resources of various fields of study.[26] For them, theology is the interaction of, for example, existential philosophy and reflections on Christian Scripture and tradition. This theological conversation is less the engagement of persons than the correlation of and dialogue between ideas.

Clinicians and theologians share a second conceptualization, namely, the viewing of their respective projects as hermeneutic or interpretive disciplines.[27] Clinical theorists speak about counseling and psychotherapy as the process of interpretation and reinterpretation of the text. By "text" they may mean the conversation either between the two participants or within the client. Many are familiar with Anton Boisen's use and Gerkin's revival of the metaphor of client as a "living human document."[28] In contrast, regarding theology as a hermeneutic or interpretive enterprise has a more literal meaning: the interpretation and reinterpretation of texts, whether sacred or classic, usually in conjunction with one another.[29]

Whereas theorists of clinical care use conversation in a literal sense, the theologians' use is more figurative. Conversely, clinical theorists use the interpretation of texts in a figurative way, but theologians are literal in their meaning. Nonetheless, clinical care and theology can be thought of as interpretive conversations or interpreting in conversation. Bringing the praxes of theologizing and clinical care together in this way has advantages. It challenges theologians to construe their enterprise less as the dialogue between and among ideas than as interpreting persons-in-situations, a reorientation that would lessen the gaps between theory, practice, person, and context. Similarly, it challenges clinical theorists to reevaluate the nonhuman metaphor of text, which disposes us to depersonalize and dehistoricize relationships.

Conceiving theologizing as practical conversation enables us to identify pivotal features of our subject matter.[30] Theologizing is a practical enterprise, informed by prior experience and practice and informing of future experience and practice; that is, it has a past and a future, a context and a *telos*.[31]

Theologizing as practical conversation carries forward our previous conversations and the conversations of those who preceded us: Theologizing is historical. Each person theologizes in ways that express his particular history in unique ways.[32] Neither the language, symbols, purposes, and styles of theology nor the situations that demand a response are created by anyone.[33] Each person participates in theologizing further what and how we, and others, have previously theologized. In a sense, every conversation is the occasion for the convergence and extension of prior conversations.

Because all theologizing is spoken from a particular place, one's thoughts, feelings, and images are especially relevant to a particular moment. The words and symbols employed and the language used to describe experience are a function of a unique context. Furthermore, that context varies, depending on culture, class, race, and gender. Previous theologizing that informs current theologizing is itself rooted elsewhere and has only limited meaning. Presuming its accuracy and absolute relevance to the current moment exposes how much one is tethered to preunderstandings and how little one can appreciate that a partner in conversation has a different history, preunderstanding, and purpose.

The form, content, and purposes of such practical conversation are presumed to be plural. A survey of contributions to the text *The Vocation of the Theologian* serves as a good illustration.[34] Theological perspectives reflect the historical context in which they are constructed. The experiences from which theologians draw, the issues to which they attend, and the categories of analysis they employ are rooted in and reflective of a particular historical place. Indeed, in order to be appropriate—that is, practical to their time—theologians need to attend to these influences.[35]

Theological perspectives also reflect the personal experience of the theologizer. Because all theologizing is done to make sense of what is happening in order to negotiate one's way in the world, it is by definition a deeply existential enterprise.[36] As an effort to make sense, it is dynamic, evolving, in flux, modifying as situations change—an open activity of exploration more than a closed system of explanation.[37] It is more provisional and plausible than final and authoritative. It is particular, not universal, and occasional, not enduring.[38] The contemporary American philosopher Richard Rorty provides a helpful term, *redescription*.[39] In our practical conversations, we cannot help but redescribe, reconstruct, revision, translate and prior reflected-upon experience and thus modify the language and categories through which we made and will make sense of experience.

How does approaching theologizing as practical conversation, in light of these comments, inform our clinical care in concrete and specific ways? First, because clinical care and theologizing can be characterized according to the common rubrics of conversation and interpretation, the relationship between these two praxes would be described differently. As intersecting praxes, both are interpreting in conversation aimed at changing reality, in part through understanding.

Second, because every conversation is the occasion for the convergence and extension of numerous prior conversations, clinical care and theologizing could not be understood independent of historical communities and context. Suffering and healing individuals can be understood only as members of communities, as rooted in a specific situation.

Third, every conversation holds the occasion for something new. When we are engaged in a process of redescription, translation, and reconstruction, conclusions are more provisional and plausible than final and authoritative, more particular than universal, and more occasional than enduring. When meeting with the despondent man, one intends modifying his experience and reflection. He may emerge more hopeful and less despairing, and act differently. In addition, the collaborative experiencing and reflecting change the clinician.

METAPHOR AND NARRATIVE
AS NATURAL BRIDGES

What would it mean to think about our theologizing as practical *interdisciplinary* conversation? How does the modifier interdisciplinary inform our praxis of pastoral clinical care? Conversation is identified as interdisciplinary for several reasons. First, persons experience and reflect in a variety of ways, and reality, as such, can be approached from a variety of angles, in light of a diversity of questions and issues. At each moment, experiencing and reflecting are informed by a variety of perspectives or, more formally, by a variety of disciplines. For example, when the elderly woman speaks about losing her memory and fearing her own death, one listens as someone concerned about biological changes as well as about her emotional well-being, her social supports, her family and community, and her faith.

Second, regarding conversation as interdisciplinary represents a more formal way of characterizing the praxis of pastoral clinical care, which has been a bridge discipline. All theologizing presumes the interaction among diverse languages and perspectives.

Third, identifying theologizing as an interdisciplinary enterprise draws upon and extends Tillich's thinking. In this regard, no one can do theology by simply reflecting on one's respective confessional tradition in a narrow, parochial way. Choosing, interpreting, and integrating reflections in and on a tradition unfold in light of and in conjunction with other resources and authorities. Theology cannot be isolated from other disciplines and universes of discourse. Tillich provided a helpful way of understanding some of these matters. Theology is transmethodological.[40] Doing theology is integrating or "correlating" resources of the confessional tradition and secular materials.[41]

Having recognized that theologizing as practical interdisciplinary conversation involves the synthesis of ideas and methods from diverse communities of inquiry, we are faced with the task of relating varied resources in consistent and coherent ways. Contemporary discussions of both metaphor and narrative suggest important directions for elucidating the connections across different disciplinary resources. Theologians, psychologists, and theorists of clinical practice have used these concepts to describe how we experience, know, and relate and how we may help one another. These concepts provide natural bridges between experiencing and reflecting and between practice and theory, as well as across different communities of inquiry and professional enterprises. Linking the disciplines of theology, psychology, and clinical care is not dependent upon the construction of an artificial—and idiosyncratic—analytic bridge: Features of metaphor and narrative reveal innate underlying connections.

Metaphor and Narrative

Theorists in the respective fields of theology, psychology, and clinical care have increasingly been approaching their praxes as hermeneutic or interpretive enterprises and have, in addition, used the concepts of metaphor and narrative to explicate critical features of their respective projects. Although metaphor and narrative have been used in an extraordinary range of contexts, with a similarly extraordinary range of claims, basic parallel claims can be summarized in this way:[42]

1. Metaphor and narrative illumine pivotal features of what we know and how we know.

2. Metaphor and narrative lie at the root and foundation of all theories or perspectives.

3. Metaphor and narrative illumine pivotal features of who we are and how we understand ourselves; we not only have but also are metaphors and narratives.

What is needed is a way of understanding the basic meanings and uses of these concepts.

METAPHOR AS BRIDGE

Because metaphor is used in a variety of contexts in a variety of ways, what is needed (metaphorically) is a way in. *Metaphor* can be defined as "understanding and experiencing one kind of thing in terms of another," that is, understanding the unfamiliar in terms of the familiar.[43] For example, to say that "God is love" is to understand and experience God in terms of love.

Some theorists of metaphor have argued that understanding and experiencing one kind of thing in terms of another—that is, *via* metaphor—is the way we live and act. George Lakoff and Mark Johnson, for example, propose that "our ordinary conceptual system, in terms of which we both think and act, is fundamentally metaphorical in nature . . . the way we think, what we experience, and what we do every day is very much a matter of metaphor."[44] Sallie McFague puts it this way: "Metaphor follows the way the human mind *works*. Metaphor is not only a poetic device for the creation of new meaning, but metaphor is as ultimate as thought. It is and can be *the* source for new insight because all human discovery is by metaphor."[45]

A spectrum of theorists, following Stephen Pepper, have claimed that metaphors lie at the root of various kinds of theorizing: world hypotheses (or what might be called our myths), religious thinking, theology, psychology, interdisciplinary conversation.[46] Philosophical theories, Pepper has argued, are founded on root metaphors:

> What I call the root metaphor theory is the theory that a world hypothesis to cover all facts is framed in the first instance on the basis of a rather small set of facts and then expanded in reference so as to cover all facts. The set of facts which inspired the hypothesis is the original root metaphor.[47]

Pepper proposes that human beings naturally locate some commonsense fact or feature of the world and employ or exploit it as if it represented, in microcosm, a pivotal if not essential feature of all reality.[48]

Although, according to Pepper, world theories are constructed from the root upward, most persons are unaware of the fact that their world theory expresses an underlying metaphor and thus neglect to identify that operative metaphor. Pepper's ideas encourage us to approach theorizing from another angle, consider that metaphors inform theories, and engage in the task of identifying each person's operative metaphor.[49]

Numerous writers have extended Pepper's ideas and constructively understood and experienced other issues in terms of his proposal. For example, David Tracy states: "That all major religions are grounded in certain root metaphors has become a commonplace in modern religious studies."[50] Don Browning echoes these thoughts when discussing thinking and action in general and then religious thinking:

> All thinking rests on a foundation of metaphors. We start thinking about the world in metaphors and symbols long before we start making discrete propositional statements. In fact, our discursive and propositional statements grow out of and assume metaphorical levels of apprehending the world. . . .
> When it comes to speaking about the most ultimate (in the sense of most

determinative) aspect of our experience, we do it in metaphorical language. None of us knows directly the ultimate context of experience; therefore we take more familiar and tangible aspects of experience and apply them metaphorically to the intangible and mysterious ultimate features of experience.[51]

If we entertain the hypothesis that all our thinking is metaphorical and guided by underlying root metaphors, then our religious thinking—our theologizing—must be metaphorical. Think for a moment about the questions the two friends (in Tillich's story) addressed: What is life really about? Why are we alive? What does it all mean? What should we be about? These questions can be answered only metaphorically; that is, all of life must be represented in particular terms, by way of a specific image. The less-known domains of life, purpose, meaning, and responsibility are experienced and understood in terms of more familiar images. For example, life is a journey or pilgrimage, and the purpose of life is living in harmony with all of creation.

Recapitulating these unfolding ideas, we experience and reflect, in all domains and disciplines, by way of metaphor. All theories and practices—and thus all praxes of clinical care and theologizing—evolve by way of metaphor, in terms of underlying metaphors.[52] This serves as the basis for our approaching our interdisciplinary work relating different praxes, such as theologizing and clinical care, in light of metaphor.

In short, metaphor helps us appreciate the interpenetration of how we know, what we know, and who we are: the interpenetration of practice-theory-person. Appreciation of the foundational role of metaphors has led to an appreciation of the formative place of narrative.

NARRATIVE AS BRIDGE

The concept of narrative has been understood and used in a spectrum of competing ways.[53] Various authors utilize E. M. Forster's characterization: "A story is a narrative of events arranged in a time sequence; we read on in a story to find out 'what happens next?'"[54] As Hauerwas and Jones note, "The crucial appeal to narrative is not because of the significance of 'stories,' though that may be part of it; rather what is significant is the recognition that rationality, methods of argument, and historical explanation have, at least to some extent, a fundamentally narrative form."[55] That is, theorists in various contexts may use narrative as a means of identifying underlying structures embedded in how we experience, reflect, and communicate.

Although discussions of both narrative and metaphor are rare, examining them in conjunction with one another is instructive. Theodore Sarbin, for example, suggests that narrative can be viewed as a root metaphor.[56] Roy Schafer claims that metaphor must be understood in a broader context, a narrative structure involving metaphoric entailments of "mutually interactive associations."[57] These extending associations are themselves part of a self-generating web (another metaphor).

The progressively more elaborate interconnections between metaphor and narrative reveal how all praxes share fundamental features. We observe-understand-apply in and through narratives. We have foundational narratives; we are foundational narratives. Theorists have understood and used narrative in diverse ways.

(1) Persons experience in a narrative form. Theodore Sarbin, for example, suggests "the narratory principle: that human beings think, perceive, imagine, and make moral choices according to narrative structures."[58]

2. Clinicians approach and interpret others through professional narratives. Frederick Wyatt suggests that the clinician's resources, as stories, take shape in a basic orientation, a way of listening and organizing, that lies "before and above" theory—the clinician's "set."[59]

Persons live within stories. Alisdair MacIntyre comments that "man is in his actions and practice, as well as in his fictions, essentially a story-telling animal. He is not essentially, but becomes through his history, a teller of stories."[60] The story that one lives and tells is crucial to one's identity. Stephen Crites elaborates: "A man's sense of his own identity seems largely determined by the kind of story which he understands himself to have been enacting through the events of his career, the story of his life."[61] Each person's story is lived and told with others. We are all part of one another's narratives, contributing to their forming and reforming. As MacIntyre puts it, "I am one who can always ask others for an account, who can put others to the question. I am part of their story as they are part of mine. The narrative of any one life is part of an interlocking set of narratives."[62]

Clinical praxis is working in narratives. Clinicians "are workers in story."[63] "Pastoral counselors are, more than anything else, listeners to

and interpreters of stories. Persons seek out a pastoral counselor because
they need someone to listen to their story. . . . The one seeking counseling
comes asking for a fresh interpretation of what has been experienced, a new
'story' for his or her life."[64] Pastoral clinicians interpret another's stories in
light of their own stories, as well as in conjunction with the narrative
structure of the Christian story. "The pastoral counselor works self-consciously as a representative of Christian forms of interpretation rooted in
the primordial images of Christian understanding of the world."[65] As
telling, listening, and interpreting stories, theologizing will always involve,
if only implicitly, a theological language game; that is, each person sym-
bolizes what life is really about in terms of the symbols of his or her particular faith tradition. Symbolizing and making sense will always at least
indirectly presuppose, or lead to, the express articulation of experience in
theological language. At the same time, however, there are and will be moments of our theologizing that do not involve the explicit use of theological language.[66] Conversation will move across disciplinary boundaries, at
times including but not restricted to "traditional theological discourse."[67]

     Although remarkable parallels can be drawn between the meanings
and uses of metaphor and narrative, two points of divergence need to be
accentuated. First, metaphors generate as well as presuppose certain
webs of associations.[68] Narratives, in contrast, indicate as well as presuppose—in more explicit ways—the interconnectedness among stories,
that is, among persons. Second, narratives indicate as well as presuppose an underlying sense of moral responsibilities in moral relationship.

IMPLICATIONS

     What, concretely and specifically, are some of the implications of these
ideas for the praxis of pastoral clinical care? First, the perspective through
which we make sense of who we are, how we experience and practice, and
how and what we theorize is informed by many areas of inquiry, that is,
is interdisciplinary. We should strive to understand how each of the contributions to our interpretive perspective influences our presence and
action. How does a particular psychological orientation—for example, psychoanalytic—equip a clinician to understand and help the despondent man
in a particular way? Then again, what are some of the liabilities of this
perspective? How does it inhibit appreciation of other important aspects
of this man's life, suffering, and healing? At the same time, how does one's
confessional tradition enhance as well as inhibit effective care? Finally, how

are a clinician's commitments to psychological and confessional traditions competing and conflicting, as well as mutually enhancing?[69]

Second, approaching theologizing as interdisciplinary praxis accentuates the underlying connection between a person's identity and praxis and thus the need to ensure consistency and coherence. The question then arises, How might the metaphors according to which I experience and understand myself and others, drawn from different resources, compete and potentially conflict with one another? How might missing the mark compete with peeling away layers of an onion? How might *imago dei* compete with a growing seed? How might the story of the creation and fall compete with the myth of Oedipus?

Third, as workers in metaphor and story, pastoral clinicians listen expressly to how clients make meaning, guided by metaphors and stories. How does the grieving elderly woman make sense of eternal life? In terms of what does she understand and experience it? How does the young pregnant woman understand her dilemma in the context of her life story? How in the context of her story does she understand you, your role, and faith as providing the occasion for help and healing? What events in the despondent man's life have contributed to his developing a story in which God was contributing to, if not causing, his despair?

Fourth, as workers in metaphor and story, pastoral clinicians would be especially attentive to the ways a particular clinical set meaningfully and accurately expresses the stories of the communities in which they live and that they represent.

THEOLOGIZING IN THE EVER-PRESENT TERRITORY OF THE BIG QUESTIONS

What would it be like to think about theologizing as taking place in the ever-present territory of the big questions? How might our pastoral clinical care differ, were we to approach clinical conversation with this point in mind?

My discussion of a revised approach to theology opened with a story in which two friends discussed certain questions: "What is life really about?" "Why are we alive?" "What does it all mean?" "What should we be about?" Noting that all human beings address these questions, I proposed that these questions express a religious domain of human experience inextricably related to theological reflection.

The questions and answers characteristic of theologizing have much

to do with life and death, finitude and the infinite, the meaning and purpose of life, who we are to be and to become, and what is most precious
and typically private in our existence. Theologizing involves "what concerns us ultimately," that is, "that which determines our being or not-
being."[70] Theologizing focuses on "what really matters"—why we are, who
we are, how we are to live.[71] Paul Holmer says it this way: "The whole
thrust of theology has to be in the direction not of finding something out—
for that is only at the beginning—but rather of becoming something
more worthy and justified."[72]

The concept of limit helps to elucidate this dimension of theologizing. Throughout life a person is aware of various kinds of boundaries. One
can entertain the idea of the infinite or immortality, but know that death
is inevitable. One can experience freedom, yet sense being fated, destined,
or determined by forces beyond one's awareness and control. One can will
one thing, yet do another. As David Tracy explains, "All genuine limit-sit-
uations refer to those experiences, both positive and negative, wherein we
both experience our own human limits (limit-to) as our own as well as recognize, however haltingly, some disclosure of a limit-of our experience."[73]
In a variety of ways, one can become directly aware that our experiences, reflections, and very lives are finite, contingent, and transient. At
the same time, interpreting ordinary experience at times discloses "fundamental structures of our existence beyond that ordinary experience."[74]
In other words, experiences of limit point in two directions: They turn one
back on the self and the "limits-to" experience, and they reveal something
through from beyond those "limits-of" experience.

As finite beings, our theologizing is less explanatory than exploratory.
We are involved less in figuring out than in opening up, less in finding the
answers than in being in a territory where one can attempt to grasp the
questions. This state is what Letty Russell refers to as "a theology of constantly revised questions and tentative observations . . . rather than the type
of theology described by Thomas Aquinas as a 'science of conclusions.'"[75]

How do we respond to and cope with these limits? How do we deal
with the fact that we not only "have" the questions but also "are" the question?[76] Søren Kierkegaard gave a clue by observing that persons often become concerned with "the little questions of existence" in order to avoid
becoming aware of "the big questions." One becomes preoccupied with
certain concerns—such as power, wealth, or esteem—in part to distract
attention from more threatening concerns, for example, how to face
death or how to serve one's neighbor. Much of who we are and what we

do is constructed for purposes of displacing and distracting our attention. Much of what we say and do is motivated by denial and avoidance; we are denying that we have and are the big questions, that we are limited.

One expression of the attempt to avoid the big questions, as suggested earlier, is constructing a threefold fence around theology, isolating it in terms of person, place, and time. The spatial metaphor of a fence represents how one avoids something by locating it elsewhere. A second spatial metaphor is illuminative: If we are the question, we are always, if only implicitly and potentially, in the ever-present territory of the big questions. This vision of the ever-present territory of the big questions accentuates certain issues. First, theologizing occurs anywhere and everywhere. Second, theologizing is something we all do, often without realizing it. We are usually unaware of the fact that all conversation is a limit situation. We are, as a result, unaware that we are always in the territory of the big questions and, as such, are always, if only indirectly and obliquely, trying to articulate and respond to them. In a sense, then, we are always exploring and responding, in the midst of limits and failings. We can therefore readily appreciate that theologizing is intimately connected with such experiences as helplessness, dependence, shame, guilt, and anxiety. Living and conversing in the territory of the big questions, wherein all conversation is itself a limit-situation, are threatening. We disown the fact of being in the territory and the activity of theologizing.[77]

Third, experiences of limits point in two directions. They point back upon ourselves, yet disclose something beyond. In this regard, with Freud one recognizes that theologizing involves projection and more and, with Feuerbach, that it involves anthropology and more. In the territory of the big questions, we become aware of another Participant to whom we respond in conversations.

Although theologizing is a human activity, it takes place in the presence of and in response to God and God's action. We human beings are confronted by mystery in a variety of ways, including mystery "making us its object whenever we try to make it our object."[78] That mystery may confront us directly, awesomely; it may be present "within" oneself or presented in and through another; it may be present through another's actions. We have to respond to what confronts us but, in a manner expressed by H. Richard Niebuhr: "God is acting in all actions upon you. So respond to all actions upon you as to respond to his action."[79] Thus, our practical conversation in the territory is not a series of reflections and theories about God but an ongoing conversation in response to and with God.

This conversation is what James Whitehead calls "practical play"—

"interplay."[80] As Charles Gerkin notes, "It is in the intersubjective 'play' between members of a conversation or any interpretive encounter that something truly new, which transcends what each participant brought to the encounter, emerges. In the play of genuine encounter all the participants are changed."[81] Theologizing emerges and evolves in and through dialogue—*dia*, "one with another," *legesthai*, "to tell, talk." In fact, theologizing emerges in community and is a collective effort done in groups.[82]

In our theologizing we are engaged with others in light of four contributors: faith tradition, cultural information, personal experience, and God. Tradition and culture are part and parcel of every conversation, orienting us in the territory and providing us with ways of articulating and negotiating. In that regard, there is no "theology in general," only particular theologies.[83]

These observations about theologizing in the ever-present territory of the big questions influence our praxis of pastoral clinical care in several ways. First, we assume that we are always actively, although usually unwittingly, denying that we have and are the questions. Thus, for example, we should listen for ways in which the elderly woman self-guardedly focuses on certain issues, not only to solve them but also to keep her and the clinician's attention away from something more threatening. Every subject emerges for purposes of both concealment and disclosure.

Second, we approach all conversation as a limit-situation, one that reveals limits-to and discloses limits-of. Talking with the anxious pregnant woman about her becoming pregnant might lead to her exposing a wish to be special, to be taken care of. It could involve her revealing her belief that she is unlovable except as she can bring another life into the world. These conversations could provide the occasion for unwanted experiences of shame and guilt, but also unexpected experiences of grace and redemption.

Third, we assume and listen for the presence and activity of the Participant. God's presence can be heard, in the midst of the depressed man's despair, in his hope and longing for restoration. Space can be made for someone beyond both of us to speak the truth in love, to reveal the Word beyond what we could expect.

Fourth, we assume that every client is potentially and implicitly asking and responding to these questions in an ongoing way, throughout all conversations. Being aware of motives to deny and avoid the territory and apprising clients of their denial and avoidance, we invite them to participate in exploratory responding. They are partners in the shared praxis of theologizing together, directly, explicitly, and constructively with God.

THEOLOGIZING AS A CRITICAL ENTERPRISE

It might seem that regarding theologizing as a "critical" enterprise is simply adding one final, independent criterion or feature to this characterization. Nonetheless, it will become progressively apparent that this section simply renders explicit what has been implied throughout the discussion. Embedded in the previous unfolding interpretation of theologizing are a variety of moments of critical judgment. Some of the basic points in that unfolding discussion can be reread with the following sense of *critical* in mind. When critical, one is intentionally and conscientiously attempting to discern and judge unidentified features of what and how one experiences-reflects, practices-theorizes. Critical praxis involves procedures of seeing through, deciphering, unmasking, and deconstructing, through a hermeneutic of suspicion.

Theologizing has been characterized as the interpenetration of religion and theology, experiencing and reflecting, practice and theory (praxis). What and how any individual reflects and theorizes are always as a reflection of prior experience and practice in the service of subsequent experience and practice. In other words, one constantly tests and evaluates how one makes sense. Admittedly, most of us typically lose sight of the fact that we are hypothesizing, or constructing, a perspective, that our reflections are not representations that we have found and that mirror or correspond to reality, but rather descriptions that enhance commerce with reality and others.

The praxis in which we engage is not solitary but inherently social. The reflection and theory we experiment with and test are not of our own individual construction. The language and categories through which we experience—the form and content of the questions we address—are social. Thus, in our ongoing "practical conversations" we are continuously, if only potentially, amending the hypotheses of others; that is, interpersonal and intercommunity conversations presuppose an ongoing challenge not only to the content but also to the forms and purposes of our interaction. Typically, however, we fail to acknowledge that our community's representations are themselves descriptions.

In every conversation, each person draws upon faith tradition, cultural information, personal experience, and God, in particular, subjective ways. A conflict of interpretations, within as well as between participants, is thus presumed. Interestingly, however, we typically gloss over such conflict, enforce our own position, and dismiss the ambiguities involved in praxis. It is difficult to gain a distance on our own experience; it is even more difficult to achieve perspective regarding the language, questions, and ways of being and knowing that are peculiar to one's particular community. We are motivated to deny the need for such distance, to deny the limit-character of not only our praxis but also our very selves.

Identifying that our practical conversation is inherently interdisciplinary enhances our appreciation of the inherent complexity and ambiguity of interaction. In every conversation each participant is testing individual hypotheses and community hypotheses in terms of conflicting authorities, with others who are testing, in a complex, interdisciplinary manner.

The concepts of metaphor and narrative have been particularly instructive and illuminating in this regard. These concepts designate ways in which how and what we experience are intimately of a part with how and what we reflect. How and what we practice are intimately of a part with how and what we theorize. Our praxis is intimately of a part with our person. And, finally, our praxis and person are intimately of a part with another's praxis and person.

Thus, theologizing as described in this chapter has presupposed and indicated some of the ways in which theologizing is and must be critical; that is, theologizing is an inherently critical enterprise. Gordon Kaufman notes,

> Theology (like philosophy) is a *reflexive* activity. Unlike disciplines such as chemistry or biology or music, which study objects other than themselves, theology and philosophy in studying their objects must develop theories of themselves as well as of their objects—because they are themselves included within the objects they are trying to understand.[84]

In a more recent article, he writes about critical theology:

> Theology that is done with full attention to, and is thus an expression of, critical consciousness is what we are looking for: theology that opens itself willingly to severe criticism from outside perspectives (as well as from within). Theology that is formulated through the exercise of critical judgment with respect to all pertinent evidence and arguments (what we can quite properly call *critical theology*) has an important and distinctive role to play.[85]

We must proceed critically, that is, thoroughly aware of our methods and presuppositions and willing to amend our approach under certain conditions.[86] The literature in practical theology provides a variety of such critical methods. Don Browning, for example, outlines four steps of practical theological action: (1) experiencing and initially defining the problem; (2) attending, listening, and understanding; (3) critically analyzing and comparing; and (4) deciding and strategizing.[87] This outline, Browning acknowledges, extends the Whiteheads' three-stage method—the stage of attention or listening, the stage of assertion, the stage of decision—which he regards as lacking a "concrete method for actually controlling the critical and comparative task."[88]

THE PARADOX OF THEOLOGIZING

Theologizing involves praying as if everything depends on you, while working as if everything depends on God.[89] At the heart of our faith, our actions, and our theologizing lies a fundamental paradox. When praying, we negotiate our way in the territory of the big questions, discerning how we are to respond, presuming that "everything depends on us." At the same time, we presume that God is an active Participant in history, that "God is faithful," that "everything depends on God."

When appreciating our human differences, the limits of our abilities to understand and relate, the helplessness and anxiety that dispose us to deny our differences and the limits of our abilities, and the distortions that emerge in the context of this self-deception—in the face of these, the possibility of meaningful practical conversation seems miraculous. Indeed, this is precisely the point. Theologizing takes place not because of our remarkable abilities, but despite our remarkable limits. Theologizing is a gift.

Paul Holmer aptly acknowledges the nature and limitations of theological research:

> Theology is taught to us in an "about" mood, as a kind of third-person thought and language of Apostles, prophets, and our Lord himself. But to use it supposes that we translate from the third-person mood of being their knowledge and language "about" God to becoming my language "of" faith. . . . Theology is not done best in scholarly forms and artifacts of the learned. At best, the theological research that goes on does not quite issue in real theology—instead it prepares people a bit, at the most, for appreciating the real thing. It is like logic in respect to thinking and grammar in respect to writing prose.[90]

3

Theologizing about Person

Traditionally, theologians characterize human nature and experience in ways that are universal, not limited to particular times or cultures. They often employ formal, abstract jargon. They diminish and disguise how their reflections are rooted in particular, subjective, personal experience, as if that would jeopardize the objective validity and universal applicability of their ideas. In the end, however, this approach distorts their efforts. Articulating universal conditions, a theologian loses touch with particular situations and sacrifices connections to felt experience and practice.

Theologians acknowledge but rarely explore how theology is informed by its author's life experience, gender, race, ethnic heritage, socioeconomic class, and choices about relevant questions or answers. Nevertheless, every theology is praxis: It expresses the theologian's attempt to make sense of experience, in light of previous practice, for purposes of enhancing future practice.

In this chapter I attempt to make sense of the practice of pastoral clinical care in order to enhance it. My comments orient more than explain.

HOW TO THEOLOGIZE ABOUT PERSON

Consider various ways to talk about person: personality, self, subjectivity, human nature, individual, creature, human being, identity, character. Each elicits different associations and is situated in a different context. *Individual,* for example, casts person in the singular and provokes associations to group or collective. *Character,* in contrast, elicits associations to literary terms such as *narrative, plot,* and *theme* and to philosophical-ethical ideas such as virtue and the good person.

Consider, further, the impact of both the grammatical structure and the semantic structure on what and how we experience. We carve up the ongoing flow of experience into discrete elements by using words as conventions that name various things, events, and actions and categorize that flow according to things, events, and actions. A language provides conventions, governs the delineation of things, and marks out the boundaries within our everyday experience.[1]

Compare English with Chinese. English discriminates between things and actions. Numerous Chinese words represent both nouns and verbs, "so that one who thinks in Chinese has little difficulty in seeing that objects are also events, that our world is a collection of processes rather than entities."[2] English is constructed by linking letters together to form words and linking words to form sentences: joining independent units together in a linear fashion. Chinese written language, in contrast, although linear, may be "a little closer to life than spelled words because they are essentially pictures and, as a Chinese proverb puts it, 'One showing is worth a hundred sayings.'"[3] The Chinese are less disposed to experience reality as atomistic units that can be connected, externally, for instrumental purposes, in a linear fashion.

Consider another example. The English language has two voices: The speaker is active or passive. "I write this sentence" (active voice); "this sentence is written by me" (passive voice). English has no middle voice to express self-reflexive actions, and instead it relies upon constructions such as "I am doing this to myself." But the grammatical structure organizes experience in such a way that differentiating *I* and *myself* implicitly enhances experiencing person as a duality, as I and me.[4]

Language also informs praxis through its semantic structure. Words function to carve out from the flow of future experience particular features we are prepared to recognize. Eskimos use different words for snow, depending on whether they are building, sledding, or falling.[5] A person's ability to differentiate among fear, apprehension, anxiety, and angst depends on having this vocabulary.

Recall the elements of metaphor and narrative. Metaphor is a way or method of knowing and of changing; a metaphor lies at the root of every theology, every psychology, and every interdisciplinary theory of care; formulating an interdisciplinary theory of care should involve the identification and conversation of root metaphors; metaphor lies at the root of every self; therapeutic conversation involves the engagement of selves and their root metaphors.[6] Likewise, narrative has been employed in a number of ways: Narrative is a way of knowing and changing; narrative is at the foundation of a theology; narrative is at the foundation of every self; therapeutic conversation involves the engagement of selves and their narratives.[7] The purpose for considering these constructions is that metaphor and narrative help identify elemental features of how we are, change, and know.

Further Notes about Metaphor

Metaphor has been understood in two contrasting ways: On the one hand, those beginning with Aristotle who hold the substitutable view believe that metaphor has to do with syntax. Experience can be described in a variety of equally satisfactory ways. Metaphorical descriptions can be represented in other linguistic forms without any loss of meaning. On the other hand, those holding the unsubstitutable view regard metaphor as having to do with semantics or meaning. Nothing else can do what metaphor does.

Some who hold this second view assert that metaphor is the way thought and language work. Lakoff and Johnson, for example, claim that "the way we think, what we experience, and what we do every day is very much a matter of metaphor."[8] Sallie McFague says that "metaphor follows the way the human mind works. Metaphor is not only a poetic device for the creation of new meaning, but metaphor is as ultimate as thought. It is and can be the source for new insight because all human discovery is by metaphor."[9] She continues that "metaphor . . . is the human method of investigating the universe" (p. 59). James Olney refers to metaphor as "a way of knowing," coining the apt phrase "metaphorizing process." He writes, "This is the psychological basis of the metaphorizing process: to grasp the unknown through the known, or to let the known stand for the unknown and thereby fit that into an organized, patterned body of experiential knowledge."[10]

This view seems helpful. "Grasping the unknown through the known" or "understanding and experiencing one kind of thing in terms of another,"[11] the essence of metaphor and the metaphorizing process is the way the mind works. Metaphor mirrors the basic comparative structure and movement of human knowing: grasping the unknown in conjunction with or through the known.[12]

Consider this example: Walking in a strange land, one observes a rather massive animal, with four legs, a tail, a mane, and black and white stripes. One cannot recognize (re-cognize) what it is. It is "a horse but not a horse." Through comparison and contrast, the unknown is understood in light of and in conjunction with the known.

M. H. Abrams describes the situation well:

> Any area for investigation, so long as it lacks prior concepts to give it structure and an express terminology with which it can be managed, appears to the inquiring mind inchoate—either a blank, or an elusive and tantalizing confusion. Our usual recourse is, more or less deliberately, to cast about for objects which offer parallels to dimly sensed aspects of the new situation, to use the better known to elucidate the less known, to discuss the intangible in terms of the tangible. This analogical procedure seems characteristic of much intellectual enterprise. There is a good deal of wisdom in the popular locution for "what is its nature?" namely: "What's it like?" We tend to describe the nature of something in similes and metaphors, and the vehicles of these recurrent figures, when analyzed, often turn out to be the attributes of an implicit analog through which we are viewing the object we describe.[13]

Consider becoming aware of something, such as experiencing a sensation or feeling. Putting the experience into words may be difficult. By observing that "this feels like such and such," one draws a comparison to something already known. Consider these questions: How would you describe your friend? What is it like to feel *tranquil?* How does hot differ from cold? Each response is probably comparative: She's like the woman you told me about, namely, determined. Tranquil is a feeling of not being in any danger, like floating on water without any waves. Hot differs from cold like burning pain differs from numbing pain.

The metaphorizing process suggests that a self is binary in both its understanding and judgment and in its being. Elizabeth Sewell captures it this way:

> "As a man thinketh, so is he." It is an old dry nut of a saying; but hold it in the hand [or mind], turn it over, warm it a little, and it begins to come to life. As we think, which is Method, and what we are, which is Man, stand in an "as-and-so" relation to one another, a relation of resemblance and of cause and effect.[14]

Further Notes about Narrative

Narrative, like metaphor, involves elemental features of human being and knowing. To understand something is to recognize it in context. Observation is "theory-laden"[15] or "blik-laden."[16] Experience makes sense or comes to make sense as it is fit into an existing schema or as a new schema is formed.

Theorists have alluded to features of experiencing-in-context as the "narrative quality" of experience. Experience is "itself an incipient story."[17] Stephen Crites suggests that

> our common *Lebenswelt* contains what we encounter in immediate experience and deal with in our practical activity, to which narrative locution is our most direct linguistic access. When we speak to or of what is immediately real to us we tell stories and fragments of stories. "Ordinary language" is largely made up of the sorts of locutions we employ in telling stories. What we ordinarily recognize as real and attempt practically to cope with is what can be put in narrative language.[18]

Crites continues, "In stories we meet what is concrete in experience, in the most concrete language we have. We employ abstract language to interpret it."[19]

AN EXERCISE IN PRACTICAL INTERDISCIPLINARY CONVERSATION

A Clinical Vignette

A man in his early thirties seeks help. He is feeling depressed and "empty." He has been feeling this way on and off for most of his life, noting periods when he felt considerably better, usually when he was in a good relationship. He feels rather isolated, wondering whether his pursuit of a vocation in Christian ministry is truly right for him. He feels as if God is not there; he no longer experiences God's presence and support. He mentions, as an aside, that the only remnant he feels of God's presence is in a cross he wears all the time, given to him as a child by his mother.

As he describes his current situation, he reports some conflicts with his superiors. He is troubled by how disappointing they are, not worthy of the authority they have. Periodically he has gotten into arguments; he has been convinced that he is right and amazed that they fail to see the error of their ways. A recent series of arguments with his formation director has led that director to suggest he seek help. Although he sensed that this suggestion was intended as a sign of support, he was more aware of feeling pushed away, hurt by the insinuation that something was wrong with him, and angry that they did not realize that they were the ones who needed help.

The clinician suggests that it would be appropriate to try to understand him and his suffering more fully and to take the time in a couple of meetings to place what is happening in some historical context. The man reports that he has had other experiences of being sent for help by a male authority figure because of conflicts. His previous experiences of help were also disappointing: The supposed professionals with whom he met never really understood him. This history has led him to be less than hopeful about the prospect of help.

He talks about being an only child. He remembers his mother as at times wonderful, sitting and talking to him for hours, and at other times being preoccupied with how she looked and with what she was going to wear. During those periods, she was off in her own little world and did not even know he existed. His father was a sad case. He gave orders but rarely listened. His parents fought all the time. That was so different from life as he recalled it as a small child, when his father seemed so big and strong—his idol.

The clinician gradually became aware of certain features of the man's presentation and certain emotional responses. A kind of snide quality was present in the man's voice, as if the clinician was probably another one of these supposed professionals who gives the appearance of being able to help but will probably only take his money. Several times the clinician offered an observation about what the man was saying and experienced him to be rather jumpy, as if he had been hurt. This reaction seemed to be inconsistent with requests he made while walking out the door: What should I do? It was as if he needed and wanted an authoritative view, yet left little space for contributions; what was offered he found lacking. He could, at times, talk for long stretches, almost without taking a breath and without leaving any opportunity for comment. The clinician felt somewhat bored, almost depressed, and even a little angry. These data complemented and enhanced the clinician's understanding of the man and his suffering.

During their meetings the clinician became aware of a fleeting

thought: My clinical theories provide me with a feeling of safety, without
which I would be lost, anxious, and unable to find my way.

Making Sense as Four Related
Features of Experiencing

Although making choices moment-to-moment, we usually operate in
a seemingly automatic mode. We do not scrutinize features of each situation before deciding to act; we apprehend and respond out of habit. By
doing so, we remain unaware of much of what is happening. Only when
confronted by the unexpected—a crisis, perhaps—are we unable to con-
serve energy in habit and are forced to take a second look.

Consider some features of making sense that are usually outside of
awareness. Two visual analogies help. Imagine watching events as if
through a video camera, with the opportunity to pause as well as replay
before proceeding, or imagine viewing a situation under a microscope and
being alert to a variety of details. Four related features of experiencing—the metaphorizing process, the narrative quality of experience, internal translating, and interpersonal translating—can be noticed.

As this man reports his unfolding experience, he often speaks as
though he already knew what he was going to say, as if everything already
made sense and he was simply narrating the facts like a newscaster reading from a TelePrompTer. At other times, however, he does not already
know what he will say. He understands his statements only as he says them,
or after the fact.

He relies, as does everyone, on past experience. He forms ideas hesitatingly, as if to say, "This is like . . ." or "this reminds me of. . . ." He is
making sense of the unfamiliar in conjunction with the familiar. When
asked to describe what he means by feeling empty, he responds, "It's just
an expression. I'm not sure what I mean. . . . It's like I can't really say, or
put my finger on it. . . . Sometimes it feels as if there's nothing there inside. Kind of like . . . like if I were an onion: if I keep on peeling away layers, there's a point when there's 'nothing' inside."

To articulate what he means by feeling empty, he uses the familiar
image of an onion. The onion provides associations through which he describes his experience as "peeling away layers," "bringing tears to my eyes,"
and hoping to find something different, to find "a core," but finding layer
after layer that look regrettably identical to what he has seen before. This

man illustrates a metaphorizing process, experiencing something yet to be known in part *as* something.

Making sense of the unknown involves experiencing in context. One interprets something new through categories or schemata brought to the experience: Whatever has caught attention in the foreground is understood against an existing background. For example, when this man reports that he is not particularly hopeful about meeting, he reports a history of contact with professionals. He indicates that the clinician is experienced in a story that preexists their meeting.

The metaphorizing process and narrative form of experience expose how sense is as much made as found. Participants in conversation describe to themselves and another what they are experiencing. For example, this man felt in his gut something that would not go away. He refers to it as haunting, intruding. He reports difficulty putting sensations into words because he is not experiencing in words. Practicing the linkage between sensations and verbal description, sensations become experienced through those words. Nevertheless, he notes slippage between felt experience and word description.[20] He is aware of recasting experiences into another form.[21] In other words (as this double entendre now illustrates), he is constantly involved in *internal translation.*[22]

Both participants are also involved in a parallel procedure of interpersonal translating. The clinician does not truly know what the haunting, intruding experience in the man's gut is. The clinician asks, What might I be feeling, were I to find this description accurate? While the man is putting experience into words, the clinician is using the other's words to orient her own experience and translating what the other says.

Metaphorizing, narrative quality of experience, internal and interpersonal translating—these point to inherent complexity and ambiguity in conversation. Making sense in an interdisciplinary way further illustrates this complexity.

An Interdisciplinary Approach to the Clinical Situation

Experiencing and reflecting are informed by a variety of perspectives, more formally, by a variety of disciplines. For example, one cannot interpret an event or situation from a singularly theological or psychological point of view. We naturally and inevitably make sense of something through many perspectives, in an interdisciplinary way.

Approaching a situation expressly from the vantage point of the

Christian tradition highlights particular questions, issues, and images, such as, for example, Where is God present and active in this event? How is God revealing God's self in this place? How are persons denying God's presence, functioning as if they were God? Approaching that situation expressly from the vantage point of a psychological perspective involves different questions, issues, and images, such as, "How have past experiences of painful events—'primitive agonies'—contributed to a person's unique way of experiencing self and others?"[23]

Regarding a situation from both confessional and psychological vantage points enhances our understanding in several ways. Figuratively speaking, one looks in more than one place and in the same place, although in different ways.

Understanding through both confessional and psychological perspectives is preferable in the simple sense that two angles of vision are better than one. Thus, for example, one may examine both an individual's experience of and relationship with God, as well as ways in which past experiences have influenced his personality, character, and relationships. In fact, however, in understanding, the perspectives interact. One explores how God was present and active in this person's past experience of primitive agonies and in his current ways of experiencing himself. Examining persons' ways of experiencing themselves, as a function of the past, enables us to appreciate the ways in which they can and cannot recognize God's presence and action.

When theologizing in a practical interdisciplinary way, one does not interpret situations through a sequence of independent perspectives, one after another, but brings the various ways of making sense into conversation with one another. Two different things emerge: First, one becomes equipped to ask questions that take into account both perspectives simultaneously; second, one becomes alert to the particular ways in which each approach guides inquiry and how each perspective is limited and selective. Thus, for example, were one to interpret a situation solely in light of confessional resources, the person's history and patterns of experiencing and relating might be mistakenly ignored. Employing only psychological questions would neglect the sacred, the holy, God.

Approaching Situations in Light of the Christian Tradition

Christian theologians approach situations by presuming the past and current action of God in human history and by utilizing the stories, symbols, and images of the Bible and other sources in the Christian tradition to guide observing, interpreting, and responding.

Consider some orienting questions: How do this person's experiences reflect the tension or conflict of, for example, belonging to or being estranged from herself, from others, or from God? How do they reflect being created good, in the image of God or being fallen and sinful, or being justified by grace through faith or being justified by works, or being nature or being spirit? How do the experiences convey an awareness of, and relation to, what might be called depth, ground, Unconditional, ultimate, the sacred, the Holy? These questions might take a form that reflects the themes of creation, the fall, and redemption: Where is God acting in and through this event? How is God making God known? Where is the burning bush, the revelation of God's presence? In what ways is this person aware or unaware, responsive or unresponsive, oriented toward or away from God's presence and action? How are this person's ways of making sense of and responding to this event oriented in a manner that not only excludes an awareness of God, denying God, but also assumes God's place, replacing God? In what ways is this person receptive to a transforming gift of acceptance, love, and forgiveness that comes from beyond herself, in spite of herself?

Approaching the clinical situation in light of these basic questions can sensitize us to a number of things. The man's crisis is, in part, a crisis of faith: The God who had called him to Christian ministry is absent. His prayers for help have gone unheeded. As he decides on his own, he betrays a sense of omniscience, as if only he knew what was happening. He acts as if he were God. He describes others as turned away, yet he comes across as having turned away from them. Although he hurts because he is isolated and needs others' support, friendship, and guidance, he also states angrily that he does not need anyone, that he is safe only in relying on himself in deciding what to do. It is difficult to know whether he is receptive to anyone's love or care, including the clinician's. He aggressivly alienates others, including the clinician, seemingly unaware of his complicity. He disguises his influence in his life in general, and his suffering in particular. He fails to recognize how his presumption that there is no God, that he is beyond God's love and grace, paradoxically represents his idea that he is more powerful than God, that God's existence is contingent on his experience and belief, and that God's irresistible grace is within his power to resist.

When we see that his railing against an absent God is an expression of his faith, we realize his desperate search for, yet failure to recognize ever-present revelations. His only glimpses are signaled by the cross he wears. He needs some kind of sign, burning bush, miracle, or disclosure. He yearns for an experience of love and acceptance that appears to have consistently been beyond his grasp. He conveys that none of the persons in his life has been a sustaining presence mediating the gift of God's love and forgiveness. He is unable to experience the Christ within himself and within others.[24]

B. Approaching Situations from Psychological Points of View

Some important features of three related psychological points of view—a classical psychoanalytic approach, the self psychological approach of Heinz Kohut, and the object relations approach of D. W. Winnicott—will be examined here. These ideas were called forth by the exigencies of practice and are relevant and meaningful only to the degree to which they enhance our abilities to grasp more fully and intervene more therapeutically.

A CLASSICAL PSYCHOANALYTIC APPROACH

A clinician trained in a classical psychoanalytic orientation would take for granted a series of basic assumptions: Human beings are organisms who function according to the pleasure principle, seeking pleasure and avoiding pain. All thinking and action are expressions of two fundamental instincts, sexuality and aggression. All psychopathology is interpreted in the context of the oedipal complex, the nuclear complex of the neuroses. This oedipal complex emerges during the oedipal stage of human development. Psychic development unfolds according to a single-axis model, in which the personality matures from a stage of autoerotism to and through a stage of narcissism into an oedipal stage of object love. Development from one phase to the next means growing beyond or past earlier styles.[25]

A classically oriented clinician would look for parallels and themes underlying this man's current and past relationships and his relationship with the clinician. The clinician would also be mindful of how these relationships expressed conflicts in his sexual and aggressive drives with others. For example, the clinician would notice resemblances in his experiences of certain people. Some objects—mother, God, some past friends—appear available, present, contributing to his feeling wonderful when they are there, but then seem uncontrollably absent and unavailable, leaving him isolated, hurt, and angry. He ambivalently turns to some objects—father, God, superiors, or the clinician—for guidance, support, and strength, but then combatively demeans and ignores what these disappointing people provide. He appears to alternate between a competitive oedipal relationship and a withdrawn, narcissistic stance.

The clinician would be prepared to observe *transference phenomena,* those situations in which a patient relates to a clinician in the present as if the clinician were, in part, someone from the patient's past. In those instances, something would be inappropriate in the quality, intensity, or duration of the person's experience of the other. In addition, the clinician would anticipate that transference reactions would have to do with sexual and aggressive impulses, precisely because these impulses are the sole, fundamental instincts underlying all thinking and behavior. Thus, for example, she might consider several aspects of this man's presentation as conveying potential transference reactions: the snide quality in his voice; his comments about the clinician probably being another one of those supposed professionals who gives the appearance of being able to help but who will probably only take his money; his being jumpy, as if the clinician might or had hurt him; his requests, while walking out the door, to be told what to do; his talking for long stretches, almost without taking a breath and without leaving any opportunity for comments. In addition, the clinician would pay attention to her experiences of at times feeling somewhat bored, almost depressed, even a little angry.

Initially the man alternated between being provocative, competitive, and hostile and being withdrawn, isolated, and preoccupied with himself. As work continued, he became progressively self-absorbed. Often a major part of a clinical hour was spent in his reciting a narrative of events that had occurred during his time since the last session. He would provide almost a step-by-step accounting of what he had said and done, as though his recitation were spellbinding. He would rarely pause to ask if the clinician understood. The clinician felt talked at rather than spoken with. It seemed that what was most important was simply to tell, presuming the importance of whatever was told.

The psychoanalytically oriented clinician would wonder, in conjunction with these unfolding events, whether the man's behavior were symptomatic of an underlying characterological problem. She would consider the possibility that he was narcissistic. Presuming that all thinking and behavior that were not directly or manifestly sexual or aggressive were derivative and defensive, the clinician might have wondered aloud in therapy about how the man used the time. She probably would have suggested that more intimate and personal relationships threatened him and that he had to be rather insulated and absorbed, in part to defend against engaging another (in this case, the clinician) more fully. It would be assumed that he was threatened by the prospect of sexual and aggressive impulses being expressed in their relationship.

The clinician is trained to interpret what is happening in a particular way. This man is thought to be exhibiting a disturbance of narcissism in which, like the central character in the myth, he betrays a preoccupation with himself and his own image at the expense of attending to others. Persons with primarily narcissistic pathology are invested in themselves and unable to invest in others, that is, unable to develop classical transference reactions. They are, as a consequence, unanalyzable. Indeed, this man seemingly confirms this assumption in how he terminates, saying he thought he had gotten as much as he could. The clinician had indeed fulfilled the man's prophecy.

Given the psychoanalytically oriented clinician's theoretical commitments, *narcissism* is understood as the libidinal investment in or cathexis of the self. A narcissistic person is essentially someone who is preoccupied with or invested in herself or himself. In a technical sense, narcissistic people invest energy in themselves rather than in others. A person would manifest these narcissistic phenomena as an expression of being caught or fixated in a pre-oedipal phase of development. Persons with this kind of pathology are stuck or caught in that phase for primarily defensive reasons: They are unable or unwilling to give up their investment in and preoccupation with themselves and move to investing in others, because of an anticipated danger. Following Freud, one assumes that energy is directed either inward or outward, toward self or toward other. The relative amounts of investment were thought to be of inverse, reciprocal proportions: The more narcissism, the less investment in objects; the more object relations, the less narcissism.

In many ways, the clinician might have found this perspective extremely helpful in making sense of this individual. His terminating without really having benefited from therapy only served to confirm the theory's validity. At the same time, how troubling it is that this man—and many like him—seems to be beyond help.

Suppose that discomfort provoked the clinician to wonder about his clinical expertise, as well as about the perspective that seemed so valid and empowering. We might imagine the clinician reading psychoanalytic essays that refuted the claim that narcissism and object relations were related in inverse reciprocal proportions. This pivotal observation—the man *was* engaged in object relations—appears to contradict the theory, which stated that narcissism and object relations, investment in self and investment in others, were mutually exclusive or at least inversely proportional. Somehow the theory seems vulnerable. In addition, the clinician might wonder about how the man seemed to get into a stable pattern of relating. Although having explained his narcissism as *defensive*, as a withdrawal or regression to narcissism as a defense against an oedipal transference, his way of engaging in that narcissistic state resembles classical transferences. Indeed, it seems transferencelike: He was relating in a somewhat distorted manner. Furthermore, several narcissistic clients presented that kind of transferencelike reaction: They talked as if they wanted only to be seen and heard.

A SELF PSYCHOLOGICAL APPROACH

One might imagine the clinician examining the writings of Heinz Kohut, a psychoanalyst who specialized in the treatment of patients with narcissistic disorders. Kohut seemed to be observing and interpreting in a new way. First, he was committed to the claims that psychoanalysis has an essence and that this essence is methodological. According to him, introspection and empathy "define the field of vision" of psychoanalysis.[26] "Introspection or empathy can never be absent from psychological observation, and . . . may be present alone."[27]

One brief explication might go like this. Psychoanalysis is a field whose concepts and theories were constructed to make sense of the psychic processes of suffering individuals. In the process of psychoanalysis, an analysand was instructed to *introspect*, that is, pay attention to and report her or his own unfolding internal experiences. In conjunction with this, the analyst attempted to make sense of the analysand's experience through empathy, or *vicarious introspection*, introspecting as if he or she were the analysand. Most importantly, according to Kohut's perspective, all concepts and theories must derive from, be examined, confirmed, and amended through introspection and empathy. Psychoanalysis, then, is observing and understanding another via introspection and empathy, and observing and understanding another via concepts and theories that were constructed through introspective-empathic observation. In this approach, theorizing is tentative.

After reading Kohut, the clinician might reconsider the clinical data from an introspective-empathic approach and judge that he was not experienced as a person or self, but as some thing enabling this man to see and hear himself. The clinician had been doing something for the man, as if performing or executing a psychological function. In order to try to understand, imaginatively, what the man might have been experiencing, the clinician free associates:

> He needs to be seen and heard. He must really need this because he's almost totally oblivious to the fact that I'm here. I don't feel here. In his experience, I'm not really or fully here, except as I'm keeping some eye contact and nodding to signal I'm listening. I'm not a self. He's talking to himself. He's investing himself with energy, not me. But, in some strange way, I seem to be included in the loop, if you will. It's as if he has to talk to me, or through me, to talk to himself. Maybe when I feel like an eye, or an ear, I'm seeing or hearing something on his behalf. Maybe he needs to be seen and heard, but can't do that for himself. Maybe he's experiencing me, or part of me, to be doing that for him.

The clinician would be important for the man only in a particular, restricted way. Continuing the imaginative reflection:

> He appears to be investing only himself with energy, to be preoccupied only with himself. Yet it is also true that energy seems to come through me, or through my providing something for him. It seems as if I'm a part of him. I'm an eye to look at him that may be missing in him; an ear to hear him that may be missing. In some sense, then, I'm not a separate self; I'm a part or extension of his self. I provide a function that seems to be needed, even required. As "part of the loop," I seem to "mediate" some capacity through which he feels somehow better, restored, stabilized. Something comes "through" me.

This way of trying to describe some of the experiential phenomena could leave the clinician in a quandary. What does it mean that something comes through the clinician, that he mediates something important in being part of the loop? What does it mean that the clinician is not a self with this man? What does it mean to be a part of his self, that from his point of view only one self, namely, his was in the room?

Notice how this quandary is connected to a basic language assumption that a self is coextensive with the body, that two bodies in the room mean two selves. But data derived via introspection and empathy suggest that that is not a given. In this case, two bodies are in the room. From the point of view of his internal experience, however, there was but one self!

What is a self? What does it mean if a self understood via introspection and empathy is potentially different from a self understood colloquially?[28] What does it mean that a self can include another self in it, or a part or function of another self? What does this say about human nature, about theologizing about person? Is there another way of conceptualizing self, of constructing an anthropology?

Kohut worked with patients whose patterns of experience and engagement were similar to the individual described here, that is, people who exhibited characterological narcissistic pathology. He observed how numerous people experienced and related to him in a distorted, inappropriate way, as if he were a person (or a feature of a person) from the past.[29] They engaged him as if he were a part of their selves, as if they invested in themselves through him. Kohut began to conceptualize these recurrent forms of engagement as narcissistic transferences.

In the Freudian perspective, transference meant the transfer of sexual or aggressive energies from one object to another object. Conflicted sexual and aggressive wishes amalgamate with preconscious, secondary process material. Crossing the repression barrier, these wishes seek pleasure and avoid pain. Transference is by definition (1) repressed, (2) sexual or aggressive (3) wishes, (4) seeking pleasure (5) with objects.[30] Narcissistic transference is a contradiction in terms: One cannot transfer sexual and aggressive energy while investing oneself with narcissistic libido. But Kohut would not resolve the contradiction on the authority of theory.

Kohut observed how narcissistic transferences had a tone quite different from classical transferences. Repression was not an essential constituent. The experience was neither sexual nor aggressive, but narcissistic—having to do with the maintenance of self-esteem. Although these transferences did appear to have the character of expressing wishes (and

Kohut for much of his writings employs the classical term *wish*), he later termed them *developmental needs*. The person was not pursuing the fulfillment of drives in the experience of pleasure but was seeking reassurance. The analyst was not experienced as an independent object but as a part or extension of the person of the analysand. Kohut could not properly refer to narcissistic transferences as *transferences* in the classical sense but as *transferencelike*.

One of Kohut's primary motives for continuing to examine and work with people manifesting these narcissistic clinical phenomena was his recognition that these phenomena appeared in recurrent forms. He had inferred that the appearance of such phenomena in several persons may reflect more general (quasi-universal) qualities about personality functioning. Kohut labeled the recurrent patterns in which narcissistic transference emerged *idealizing* and *mirror* and later added *alter-ego* transference. In the idealizing transference, the analyst is experienced and related to as ideal, as perfect. In the mirror transference, the analysand experiences herself or himself as ideal and perfect. In the alter-ego transference, the analysand experiences both herself or himself and the analyst to share common fundamental experiences, perceptions, and values.

Narcissistic transferences have several traits. First, the analyst is experienced as the self, or a part or extension of the self, of the analysand. Second, the analytic relationship is sustaining, reassuring, and soothing, as long as the analysand experienced the analyst to fulfill the required psychic functions. These analytic relationships have less to do with pleasure and unpleasure and more to do with well-being, equilibrium, cohesiveness, and self-esteem. Third, when engaged via an introspective-empathic approach, narcissistic persons develop transferencelike reactions that were worked through.

In Kohut's efforts to make sense of the clinical process and conceptualize what was happening in psychoanalytic language, he continued to work as much as possible within the traditional perspective. He retained the classical definition of *narcissism* as the libidinal investment of the self but realized that the self was different from the views of either Freud or ego psychologists. The commitment to the introspective-empathic approach required that he redefine both *narcissism* and *self*.

Self, understood from the inside via introspection and empathy in an experiential, phenomenological way, is not inherently coextensive with the body. A person may experience that her self extends to include other persons or shrinks when, for example, she experiences being driven.

The traditional psychoanalytic approach, following colloquial language, presumes a self as coextensive with the body. It presupposes a subject-object model of persons as essentially and ultimately separate from one another. Although appreciating that the psychic boundaries within and between individuals are remarkably fluid, this fluidity is viewed within the context of a subject-object model.

Traditional psychoanalytic language, like colloquial language, frames experience in terms of a Cartesian, subject-object model. Experience is collapsed into two basic categories that have to do with a subject and a separate object. Phenomena that stand on the boundary, or between subject and object, are reduced to fit within one or the other category or simply excluded from consideration.

In all of Kohut's psychologizing about the self, he appreciated that

> the self . . . is, like all reality . . . not knowable in its essence. We cannot, by introspection and empathy, penetrate to the self per se; only its introspectively and empathically perceived manifestations are open to us. Demands for an exact definition of the nature of the self disregard the fact that "the self" is not a concept of an abstract science, but a generalization derived from empirical data."[31]

All theorizing was derived from empirical data. For some of those data, Kohut created the novel and brilliant concept of *selfobject,* a conflation self and object.

When, in a narcissistic transference, the clinician is experienced as a part of or extension of the self of the client, we say that that clinician is or serves as a selfobject for the client. The term conflates two vantage points. From an internal point of view, a selfobject is experienced as a part of the self of the client: self and selfobject are psychically one. From an external point of view, a selfobject is observed to be independent of the self: self and selfobject are physically separate.

Recognizing and speaking accurately about the nature of the selfobject and its relation to the self are difficult, because these kinds of phenomena are typically approached in terms of a subject-object model. One imagines the self of the client—the self coextensive with his body—having a part of the clinician—thought of as a separate person—be a part of himself. When imagining the experience from the inside, along the lines of the client's actual experience, the traditional boundary does not exist: Phenomenologically, the self includes the function of the other. More precisely, the self is the client and the function as a totality.

Using this concept of selfobject, Kohut recast narcissistic transferences as *selfobject transferences*. Certain selves needed to be recognized, noticed, appreciated, and affirmed. In order to attain a sense of basic value and goodness, they needed the function of mirroring to be supplied or performed by another. Hence Kohut spoke about mirror selfobject transference. Other selves needed to be connected to someone powerful, firm, and good. In order to attain a sense of basic value and goodness, they needed that ideal to be supplied or performed by another, hence the idealizing selfobject transference. Other selves needed to be connected with others who shared their basic experiences and values. In order to attain a sense of basic value and goodness, they needed the function of confirmation of the basic rightness of their experience to be supplied or performed by another, hence the alter-ego or twinship selfobject transference.

How might the man have required the clinician to be the attentive, appreciative listener who prized his experience in a way that he could not? How might he have needed the clinician to be like his father had been when he was small, the idol who had not and would not fall from grace, as had his father, God, his "superiors"? How might he have needed to experience the clinician sharing in an enduring way in his ongoing experience, with questions, values, and goals akin to his, unlike friends who seemed to be doing so only fleetingly?

Kohut's analysis of selfobject transferences led to a revised psychology of the self that included theories of therapeutic change (cure), psychic development, and psychopathology. Kohut observed that consistently immersing himself in the dynamic interior life of the self of his analysand promoted therapeutic movement toward a cure. He viewed that naturally unfolding movement in developmental terms and inferred that curative change was analogous to natural psychic development. Conversely, he inferred that pathology had to do with a blockage, fixation, or arrest in natural development. Furthermore, health, cure, and pathology involved empathy.

Kohut approached his clients via introspection and empathy precisely because he regarded empathy as a primary tool of observation, a pivotal vehicle or instrument through which he could gain access to their interior unfolding experiences. He gradually came to understand his functioning as a selfobject for a person as fulfilling a psychic need. It was as if the client were saying, not in words but through the relationship, I need you to do or be certain things on my behalf that I cannot do or be for myself. Furthermore, I am not aware (conscious of the fact) that I need you in this way but will simply experience and engage you in a way that might enhance your doing or being that.

Every self that entered analysis or therapy would at some point develop a transference relationship. By being attentive to the selfobject transferences that would evolve, Kohut would infer in what ways he was being engaged to fulfill a psychic need on behalf of the client. The client would include him in the loop, and through his mediating something to the client that client would experience some sense of stability, cohesiveness, and restored esteem. As he gradually observed the unfolding experiences of the client and the particular ways in which the client needed him, he observed how the client underwent positive change; that is, observing the dynamic, developmentally evolving selfobject transference was the occasion and vehicle for working through that transference.

Kohut expanded his understanding of empathy. Initially, empathy was a tool of observation, the primary vehicle through which he could gain access to the interior life of the self of another. He came to appreciate, however, that empathy was, in addition, a kind of psychological bond: When relating to another empathically, he was fulfilling a selfobject function.[32] The bond was, in other words, a selfobject attachment. Furthermore, he realized that empathy also provided a psychological nutriment: It was not only a means to an end, an instrument of observation, but also an end in itself, an agent of change. Engaging the patient in a consistently empathic manner was itself the mechanism promoting psychic development.

Kohut gradually developed a more refined sense of various aspects of this overall picture. First, he came to appreciate that, while this outlook provided a general or somewhat universal vision of all selves, development and growth were enhanced precisely by being attuned to an individual self in her uniqueness. Each self unfolds; yet, each self unfolds in its own unique way, according to what he termed its own *programme*. That unfolding, understood developmentally, he referred to as taking place through transmuting internalization. In transmuting internalization, the self takes something that is external to her self and brings it inside to make it internal to, a part of, the self. Through this internalization process, the self is transmuted.

Change in the self is effected when the self is met with adequate empathic, "optimal frustration."[33] Returning to Freud's famous discussion of the nursing infant in *Interpretation of Dreams,* Kohut (with Philip Seitz) ar-

gued that the clinician must engage the client in a manner similar to the
way in which the mother should engage the nursing infant. The clinician-
mother is needed to respond in a manner that neither gratifies too much
nor frustrates too severely.

The process of optimally frustrating the emerging developmental
needs of a self presupposes an empathic connection between the selfobject and the self. In other words, in order for development—that is, transmuting internalization—to occur, the client must experience developmentally optimal frustration. Furthermore, in order for developmentally
optimal frustration to occur, that client must experience empathic attunement: empathy. Thus, at the basis of growth, cure, and development is the experience of empathy.

Kohut proposed that the self refers to the basis of our sense of being
an independent center of initiative and perception, integrated with our
most central ambitions and ideals and with our experience that our body
and mind form a unit in space and a continuum in time.[34] Working from
an introspective-empathic attitude contributed to discovering a new orientation, way of theorizing, and corresponding way of working, with a different quality and tone. Furthermore, it contributed to helping identify implicit features of a standard orientation of which many are unaware.

The most basic aspect of an anthropology built upon this foundation
is that the self is not only always in relation but also the self by definition
is relation. Throughout life, a self unfolds in and through relationships;
a self is the unfolding, transforming relationships. The more fully and
deeply we appreciate the intersecting, overlapping nature of all selves, the
more we realize that interpersonal relations are actually intrapsychic relations.[35] One is, literally, a part of an other's self or, more precisely, of others' selves.

Understanding the role of selfobject highlights awareness of self-esteem, particular expressions of narcissistic needs, and expressions of
those needs in selfobject relationships. Several basic premises regarding
theologizing about person can be outlined in light of this psychological
approach.

1. In order to know, understand, or relate to a self, one must engage it from
the inside, attending to the other's experience of her self. One should not
approach the other with detached objectivity, with neutrality, as if that person were an object, but should relate with respect and humility to the other
as a subject.

2. Each self is unique. Each pursues the fulfillment of her own programme.

3. Each engagement between persons is actually a series of concurrent, overlapping relationships.[36] In some ways, persons are separate; in some ways, they are intersecting and overlapping.

4. Each relationship between selves is, in part, an intrapsychic relationship: We are intersecting, overlapping. A self is in relationship and also is relationship; a broken self is in and also is a broken relationship. We thus have direct and immediate impact on the well-being and esteem of others.

5. Each relationship involves self issues of equilibrium, cohesiveness, firmness, and well-being and narcissistic issues of mirroring, idealization, and twinning.

6. Empathy is crucial in the ongoing sustenance and creation of the self.

There are, in addition, at least two implications for clinical care. First, one can interpret, in part, a self's relationship with her God from this perspective. God, in part, can be experienced and engaged as a separate subject. At the same time, God can be experienced and engaged as a selfobject. Second, professional care, of whatever kind, presupposes an appreciation of transmuting internalization, itself presupposing optimal frustration and, behind that, empathic attunement.

AN OBJECT RELATIONS APPROACH 3

Donald Winnicott, like Kohut trained in classical psychoanalytic theory and practice, discovered and confronted clinical data that led him to construct an alternative object relations approach. The parallels are instructive. Kohut's commitment to a methodological essence of introspection and empathy led him to clinical empirical data that did not fit classical psychoanalytic concepts and theory: Self is not coextensive with the body or separate from or exclusive of it but intersects and overlaps with other selves. To account for these phenomena, Kohut formulated a revised concept of self and a concept of selfobject and selfobject relationship.

Winnicott's careful observation of different empirical data led him to similar conclusions. Self is separate from, exclusive of, other selves. Through the related concepts of transitional object, transitional phenomena, and transitional space, Winnicott accounted for territory between selves that could not be reduced to having to do with a subject or an object.

A few features of the clinical situation illustrate Winnicott's thinking.[37] The man's suffering involves being isolated from others and God; the man notes feeling better when in relationship. He retains some experience of his relationship and connection with his mother and with his God by the cross he wears. The clinician realizes that his clinical theory gives the clinician a sense of safety. Through that theory, the clinician is related to and connected with the theorist, teachers, supervisors, and colleagues. The client's cross and the clinician's theory are important symbolically, as they provide some sense of safety and security by connecting them with others.

These data are irrelevant to the classically trained psychoanalytic observer and the self-psychologically oriented observer. In the former perspective, religious imagery and the symbols might be interpreted as unconscious attempts to cope with helplessness by expressing wishes and illusions and, as such, revealing a neurotic inability to face the dangers of nature and fate with maturity. The orthodox analyst presumes that religious beliefs need to be worked through, eventuating in a mature, scientific approach to reality. The self-psychologically oriented observer might interpret these images and symbols as expressing the self's needs and presume that the truth of each self's images, symbols, and beliefs is evaluated subjectively. That observer would appreciate that both client and clinician experience the need to be connected with others in the face of danger and anxiety.

The following brief outline of Winnicott's "Transitional Objects and Transitional Phenomena" will serve as a basis for redescribing the clinical data and amplifying our revised vision of person.

Winnicott suggests that a study of the relationship between two developmentally related events—an infant's sucking her fingers and later cherishing a special object—will be profitable. He studies the relationship with that special object—say, a teddy bear or a security blanket, the first "not-me" possession—and labels it a transitional object. He then attempts to explain his terms:

> I have introduced the terms "transitional objects" and "transitional phenomena" for designation of the intermediate area of experience, between the thumb and the teddy bear, between the oral erotism and the true object-relationship, between primary creative activity and projection of what

has already been introjected, between primary unawareness of indebtedness and the acknowledgment of indebtedness.[38]

The psychoanalytically oriented Winnicott interprets phenomena developmentally, presuming a relationship between prizing a treasured object and sucking one's fingers. Because both occur during a transition involving profound psychic changes when the infant becomes aware of a distinction between what is me and what is not-me, Winnicott referred to the prized object as a transitional object and implied that its special quality derived from its origin in this transition.

Winnicott made two shifts in categorizing phenomena, initially examining a kind of object and inferring that specialness has to do with psychic transition, subsequently identifying a range of phenomena whose shared identity revolved around their relation to this transition—illusion, art, religion, culture, play, creativity, and symbolization—and concluding that the special quality of both object and phenomena involved a unique style of engaging reality, a distinguishable area of experiencing.

Winnicott was hardly the first psychoanalytic thinker to examine the processes involved in the infant-child's confrontation of the boundary between inner and outer, me and not-me. Traditional psychoanalytic theorists claimed that qualities of early objects are registered as features of object representations; qualities of self-experience are registered as features of self-representations. Winnicott adds a third option: Qualities of intersubjective experience of being in transition between inner and outer become internalized. These qualities are registered not only as the content of distinct memories but more important as structures and patterns of perception and relating. They serve as forerunners, precursors, or *anlagen* of adult symbolizing and symbolism.

This third area of experience is neither internal nor external but both, or comprised of contributions from both. The adult observer recognizes a separation between the child and the transitional object. Although the child does not regard this possession as herself, the first not-me possession is not entirely separate from herself. As Winnicott expresses it, "The transitional object is never under magical control like the internal object, nor is it outside control as the real mother is."[39] "Of the transitional object it can be said that it is a matter of agreement between us and the baby that we will never ask the question: 'Did you conceive of this or was it presented to you from without?' The important point is that no decision on this point is to be expected. The question is not to be formulated."[40]

Parents thus lend to the child a way of experiencing that intentionally does not require the child to become objective. Parents do not, for example, ask the child whether the teddy bear really needs to be with the child under the covers or really likes to sleep with the light on. Even more emphatically, parents tutor the child, in actions as well as words, by omission as well as commission, in a style of experiencing that intentionally requires the child not to become objective. Parents neither ask the child, for example, whether the God to whom they pray watches over them while they sleep, nor explain in objective terms what God really looks like or where God lives.

Winnicott assumes that "the task of reality-acceptance is never completed, that no human being is free from the strain of relating inner and outer reality, and that relief from this strain is provided by an intermediate area of experience."[41]

Winnicott's most fundamental category is neither transitional objects nor transitional phenomena nor even transition itself, but the intersubjective domain, a third intermediate area of experience that is internalized as a style of structuring experience, modeled, and tutored by parents. Related to transition, this intersubjective domain has to do with both acquiring and learning something new, as well as with loss of fantasied omnipotence. The infant-child experiences strain in relating outer and inner, losing omnipotence, and becoming new and different. Illusion provides relief from this strain. All persons negotiate this transition; subsequent experiences of transition recall the patterns and tone of this earliest transition, a domain of engaging reality, an illusionistic world.[42]

Against this background, some potential meanings of data in the clinical vignette become available. In part because this man's suffering is related to his being isolated from others and from God, he especially needs relationship, if not directly, at least symbolically. The cross functions as a transitional object, connecting him to his mother and his God. Through that symbolic connection, he retains a sense of safety in negotiating his way through life, particularly when he is most acutely and painfully aware of their absence. The images of the mother and of God[43] themselves function as transitional objects. For clinicians, theory functions as a transitional object, connecting us with teachers and supervisors and providing a sense of safety in facing anxiety-arousing situations in which we are otherwise alone.[44]

Behind the cross and his God is faith and religion; behind our theory is the play of therapy. Behind or beneath these transitional phenomena is transitional space. These objects and phenomena are pivotal because they express an underlying domain of experience, a style of experiencing that is intentionally not entirely objective.

The idea of a third area of experiencing contrasts markedly with the subject-object model embedded in classical psychoanalysis and colloquial language. The concepts of transitional objects, phenomena, and space have significant implications for our understanding of person, relationships, and the practice of care.

Winnicott's psychology expresses what Don Browning terms a *positive culture*, "a system of symbols and norms which guides a society or group by providing general images of the nature of the world, the purpose of life, and at least some of the basic principles by which life should be lived."[45] Psychological concepts—such as a third intermediate area of experiencing, illusion, and transitional object—can be regarded as having the status and function of religiotheological concepts. This point can be illustrated by contrasting the respective cultures and implicit theological visions embedded in Freud's and Winnicott's psychologies.

Freud expresses his passionate antipathy toward religion by defining it as pathological, defensive, and derivative.[46] Whether in the form of obsessional neurosis, wish fulfillment, illusion, delusion, or a private or universal neurosis, religion is competitive with reason and must be worked through, outgrown, and transcended. At the heart of this critique is the assumption that religion is illusory, a distortion of reality.

Counterposing religion and reason stands within a philosophical orientation that Richard Bernstein refers to as objectivism. The objectivist believes that when determining questions of truth, knowledge, and goodness, he can appeal to an ahistorical foundation, a permanent matrix.

> An objectivist claims that there is (or must be) such a matrix and that the primary task of the philosopher [or, in Freud's case, the psychoanalyst cum philosopher] is to discover what it is and to support his or her claims to have discovered such a matrix with the strongest possible reasons. . . .
> In modern times objectivism has been closely linked with an acceptance of a basic metaphysical or epistemological distinction between the subject and the object. What is "out there" (objective) is presumed to be independent of us (subjects), and knowledge is achieved when a subject correctly mirrors or represents objective reality.[47]

Stephen Toulmin's idea of modern science elucidates features of this position:

> (1) The classical (or modern) scientist was required to adopt a stance of detached objectivity toward the phenomena that were his subject matter: he

sought to minimize the effect of his observations on those phenomena, so that his results should be real, not observer created. (2) He also took care to study nature in a purely factual manner. To this end, he was required to avoid letting values and other subjective considerations affect his investigations, for fear of being caught in the same trap as the alchemists.[48]

Freud's position can be described succinctly in terms of these premises: "There is a world of objective reality that exists independently of us and that has a determinate nature or essence that we can know."[49] In this framework, "either there is some support for our being, a fixed foundation for our knowledge, or we cannot escape the forces of darkness that envelope us with madness, with intellectual and moral chaos."[50] Either we seek the potentially attainable truth of reason—with detached objectivity—or resign ourselves to living with and under the power of illusion. In this context, illusions are vital lies. While they enable us to cope with the blooming, buzzing confusion of life, with the anxiety of standing over seventy thousand fathoms, they impede facing life head-on, rationally, objectively. Religion as the sine qua non of illusions stands in an adversarial relationship to reason, science, and truth.

Winnicott's ideas, like Kohut's, are located in a different culture, "beyond objectivism and relativism," illustrating postmodern science. For Winnicott, no foundational separation exists between subject and object. The "intermediate area of experiencing" is a special kind of intersubjective space, another world that exists and evolves throughout one's lifetime. This, "the place where we live,"[51] is comprised of elements from both the subject and the objective world. The term *illusion* in this context does not refer to a distortion of objective perception but to imagination and play.

Paul Pruyser notes that even though the word *illusion* has acquired the connotations of deception and being unreal, it has other meanings.

> Etymologically it stems from the Latin verb *ludere* (to play) and the noun *lusus* (play, game) augmented by the prefix *in*, which here denotes intensiveness. A free rendition of these etymological origins is intense or serious play, or playing hard at. In the theater actors produce illusion by playing their roles, which is by no means taken as malevolent deception. When a child makes a train with his blocks, no trace of deception is involved. The root-meaning of the word suggests playing rather than deception.[52]

The contrast between objectivist and postmodernist cultures can be drawn in terms of their respective normative visions of being human. For

Freud, one should pursue the rational understanding of ourselves, our environment, and life with detached objectivity. We should become emancipated from the autistic world to live in the realistic world. For Winnicott, one should pursue the imaginative, playful relationship with ourselves, others, and life, in cocreating ourselves and our world. We should move fluidly among the autistic, realistic, and illusionistic worlds.[53]

INSIGHTS FROM KOHUT AND WINNICOTT

Kohut's and Winnicott's ideas contribute to a positive culture different from classical psychoanalysis and from much everyday thinking. Rather than presuming that *person* refers to a freestanding, autonomous, isolated individual, separated from others by a chasm or empty space, each person participates in an intricately intersecting-overlapping tapestry of selves. Well-being and illness, growth and stagnation are understood to occur not within an isolated individual, but in the in-between, in the relationships that are the person. Although the physical body is a convenient marker, the primary residence of the psychological self is not coextensive with the body. The space between bodies is not a vacuum for the transport of energies between and among independent selves; it is the space of intersecting-overlapping.

Part and parcel of a new culture is an attendant attitude. In a subject-object orientation, one approaches a separate other from the outside, seeking objectivity; in this alternative orientation, one approaches a connected other from the inside, seeking appreciation of subjectivity. The former orientation implies that God is to be understood somehow (analogously) along the model of a separate object. The intersubjective model offers alternative considerations: Our relationships with God can be approached in light of the concepts of selfobject relationship and transitional objects, phenomena, and space. This culture expresses a normative vision of human nature, not unlike philosophies and theologies. Because psychological perspectives implicitly function as philosophies and theologies, they can be brought into conversation with the kinds of issues and questions the theologian brings from the Christian tradition to amplify how we might understand who God is with and for us, as well as who we are with and for God.

CONCLUDING REFLECTIONS

The Christian tradition posits a Participant in the ongoing historical process of unfolding events, of whose presence we lose sight. We mistakenly presume the wisdom, authority, and responsibility to act independently of that Participant as if we were the sole authors of our existence, as if we were self-created and self-creating. By the same token, we lose sight of other participants and act independently of them. We place ourselves in the center of unfolding events, presume we are at the center, and lose awareness of other participants, including the Holy Participant.

A narrative from the book of Hosea captures some of this:

> When Israel was a child, I loved him,
>   and out of Egypt I called my son.
> The more I called them,
>   the more they went from me;
> they kept sacrificing to the Baals,
>   and offering incense to idols.
>
> Yet it was I who taught Ephraim to walk,
>   I took them up in my arms;
>   but they did not know that I healed them [that I was their healer].
>   (Hos. 11:1-3)

A psychological perspective can conflict with as well as enhance a confessional interpretation of this issue. A clinician strictly following a classical psychoanalytic approach would not presume the presence, action, and participation of God and, in fact, would interpret that presumption as a problem to be solved. For the Christian, this hubris and self-deception is an expression of sin. At the same time, the clinician who follows a classical psychoanalytic approach would be particularly attentive to ways in which we subjectively distort our experience and relationships through transference.

The clinician who follows a self psychological approach does not presume the presence, action, and participation of God, yet is not antagonistic to that vision. From the point of view of the Christian tradition, the self psychologist's focus on the individual runs the risk of being most thoroughly self-deceptive and self-absorbed, illustrating and reinforcing the sin of placing ourselves at the center. Then again, the self psychological perspective can provide an important corrective within a Christian frame of reference.

As we mistakenly and perhaps unawares place ourselves at the center of the universe, we lose sight of others, of God, and finally of ourselves. Christian theologians have traditionally presumed that any exaggerated attention to or love of self only illustrates and exacerbates the problem. The antidote to such self-absorption was self-sacrifice. But this presumed antidote itself illustrates and exacerbates the problem. Love of others can proceed only from a self who has internalized the love of others in a firm capacity of love of self.

Self psychological theory also amplifies issues central to the experience of Christian faith. The God whose face shines on us, who mirrors our goodness and value, is, at the same time, worthy of our idealization:

> Who has measured the waters in the hollow of his hand
>   and marked off the heavens with a span,
> enclosed the dust of the earth in a measure,
>   and weighed the mountains in scales
>   and the hills in a balance?
> Who has directed the spirit of the LORD,
>   or as his counselor has instructed him?
>
> (Isa. 40:12-13)

Two passages from Scripture capture essential insights of this approach: "You shall love your neighbor as yourself" (Matt. 22:39); "For as in one body we have many members . . . so we, who are many, are one body in Christ, and individually we are members one of another" (Rom. 12:4-5).

The clinician informed by Winnicott's writings neither presumes nor is antagonistic to the presence, action, and participation of God. Like the self psychologist, the object relations theorist focuses on the self as part of a dyad,[54] challenges the notion of objectivity, and appreciates that the place where we live is the area of play, illusion, imagination, and cocreation.

In its deep appreciation for an intermediate area of experiencing, of the imagination, without reducing those capacities to childishness or pathology, Winnicott's approach provides a way of interpreting how certain dimensions of religious belief and experience fit within the broader range of our functioning. In addition, it contributes to our understanding of the notion of presence.[55]

We can draw these various contributions together into a theological vision of person: Persons are created in such a manner as to have a fundamental tendency, inevitable but not necessary,[56] to misorient and exclude from awareness who we are and who we are to become. We misportray and misidentify ourselves, as if we are the center of the universe, separate from and independent of all others, rather than appreciating that we are each part of an intricate, dynamic creation that is in a process of ongoing creation. Rather than define ourselves as God's, we deny God, replace God, and repeat patterns of perception, expectation, and engagement. We have a resistance to the awareness of the fact of sin and a resistance to the awareness of our acts of sin.[57] We remain caught in a cycle in which, to use Tillichian language, the structure of finitude becomes the structure of destruction.[58] We experience brokenness, pain, suffering, guilt, and shame. We misidentify who we are, who we are to become, and how we might get there. We mistakenly rely on ourselves, our wisdom, or our resources. We experience brokenness. Healing involves recognizing the cycle and how it is founded in a fundamental misidentification, as well as an open pursuit to reidentify who we are.

Several metaphors are embedded in and expressed by these ideas. To speak about person is to speak about person in/or as relationships. This evokes an image of a web or a body or a dynamic tapestry. Each of the selves in the tapestry is in the process of weaving and being woven. As the weaving/being woven takes place, connections and selves become broken, split, isolated, and cut off from growth. Restoration presupposes that the Weaver reconnects the self within the tapestry.

Self cannot be spoken of apart from the relationships in which it exists or apart from the Weaver who created all selves, the selves through whom the Weaver enables reconnection and restoration.

{In track. is 1½ pages (54f.)
+ psych. is 17 — in a chapt
about Θ !

4

The Pastoral
Clinical Attitude

good chapter -
esp beginning & end.

P eople rarely take time to reflect upon some of the underlying commitments and judgments according to which they function on a day-to-day basis. What makes a person a person? What is human nature? Many are less likely to ask, What is my own understanding of person, of human nature?

We are characteristically inattentive to the fact that we are guided by an underlying vision of person, an anthropology that is in large measure a unique convergence of our sociocultural context—ethnic, racial, religious, class—familial background, and personal history. Occasionally something provokes a second look. Although most persons probably value the examined life, identifying one's operative anthropology is more than likely beyond our grasp. The notion of attitude facilitates self-examination. Consider the following illustration.

Søren Kierkegaard's writings are difficult, because the language is not easy to follow and because the ideas are at times beyond reach. Most readers envision a man who felt passionately, was convicted by the truth he had come to believe, and was deeply committed to imparting that wisdom to others. In ways beyond or through words, Kierkegaard communicated passion, conviction, and commitment about contributing to others. Even a reader who gets lost in the words can discern an underlying attitude.

This chapter examines how and why understanding attitude is crucial to the praxis of care. Some of the underlying narratives and metaphors that are operationalized in my own pastoral clinical attitude are used as illustrations. The root metaphor of "faithful companioning," drawn from New Testament passages, is related to that of "collaborative translating," taken from studies of clinical care as a hermeneutic activity. *Faithful companioning* refers to the pastoral clinician's fundamental commitment to be present with and to the person in her experiencing, regardless of what unfolds.)*Collaborative translating* represents the pastoral clinician's recognition that all of what unfolds in the ongoing process of care will be experienced and interpreted by the participants in different ways and that meaningful conversation is the participants' ongoing process of translating one another's interpretation of what is happening in a collaborative way.

WHAT IS ATTITUDE?

Attitude refers to a basic style, posture, stance, cast of mind, or mode of being-in-the-world—a way of seeing things. It is a person's habitual way of approaching and participating in unfolding experience—an underlying style that is more characterological, invariable, and enduring.[1]

Attitude is an inferred structure, a gyroscope or lens through which a person guides and shapes his characteristic way of experiencing.[2] It organizes our commitments about what a person is, how a person should act and relate, what a person should know and value, and who a person should be or become. Thus it expresses essential features of our vision of person—our anthropology. One's anthropology is operationalized in his attitude. That attitude expresses one's unique root metaphors and foundational narratives. Consider a brief illustration.

A person suffering from abdominal pain consults a physician. The physician asks detailed questions, focusing expressly on the chief complaint and the history of the chief complaint. The person experiences both being taken care of and yet, curiously, ignored. The physician seems less concerned about the person than about the symptoms and the pathology; the physician does not care to know who the person is, but only what is wrong. Although neither the person (now patient) nor the physician traditionally reflects upon or discusses the physician's attitude, that attitude deeply informs what does and does not happen.

Although neither exploring nor identifying the physician's underlying anthropology, one may infer from her patterns of care and presence the physician's stance or way of seeing things. One recognizes that this attitude conveys something fundamental about the physician.

Why Focus on Attitude?

The concept of attitude is helpful in a number of different ways, as the extending of the example illustrates. One might infer that the physician were expressing, although indirectly, some of the following:

> I will be most helpful to you if I can get an accurate and objective picture of the complaint. How you and I feel about that complaint, or about each other, is not only not particularly relevant, it may be distracting, even contaminating of my ability to be objective. I will deal with that complaint in isolation from other variables, in an effort to modify the factors that contribute to its presence.

The person seeking help is represented as the patient, the host of some pathology. The physician as the incisive diagnostician and skillful technician will identify and remove the alien "germ," the source of the pathology. Care proceeds through the physician's attitude that regards person as patient as organism.

This attitude is a style of knowing and relating. It informs not only what the participants will come to know and not know but also how they will relate. An attitude indirectly designates the respective roles, the relationship, the process, and the goals.

In this regard, attitude is truly a bridging construct. Most studies of the praxis of care discriminate among several elements, such as the characteristics of the client (for example, diagnosis, severity of maladjustment, personality traits, motivation, demographics, expectation); characteristics of the clinician (such as level of professional experience, standard therapeutic behaviors, personality traits); the relationship between client and clinician; and the matches between psychopathology and therapeutic orientation and between psychopathology and therapeutic modality.[3] Attitude, in contrast, captures something of *all* of the following: the person of the clinician the quality of relating and relationship, and the process and technique of the clinical care. It does not presume the separability of theory and practice, of clinician and client (as object and object), and of being and doing but represents the actual intersection of what one, for purposes of analysis, tends to differentiate.

Moreover, attitude is at the heart of care in indirect, yet deeply influential ways.[4] Everything the clinician says or does, observes, analyzes, and interprets is informed and guided by her attitude. It is a frame that orients and through which the clinician selects what is salient. For example, consider what happens when one puts on a pair of prescription sun-glasses. One is selectively attentive to what is visual and visible; other data may be comparatively less relevant. In selective attention or selective inattention, one reduces data to certain qualities and excludes data that do not have those qualities.[5]

Several authors have acknowledged the pivotal role of the clinician's attitude. David Shapiro writes:

> My teacher, Hellmuth Kaiser, once expressed a dilemma to me about the teaching of psychotherapy. He said it was no use teaching what to do or what to say because the significance and effect of what the therapist did or said depended on the attitude with which it was expressed. With the right attitude on the part of the therapist, he thought, all else would follow easily.[6]

The attitude with which anything is expressed or, more precisely, from or through which it is expressed is most formative.

Hans Loewald indicates, if only indirectly, the influence of the clinician's attitude. In response to the question, How does treatment help? he writes,

> Instead of addressing such [a] question head on, I shall try to give a general picture of various facets of the therapist's impact on the patient. Psychotherapists, if they are worth their salt, have certain characteristics in common with professions of a different cast, with priests, rabbis, ministers, the old-fashioned doctor, who at their best function also as significant models of steady convictions, whatever their content, and of compassionate concern and dedication. Therapists blend in with aspects of the conduct of the good parent, teacher, educator, or lover.[7]

Roy Schafer also concludes that the core of psychoanalytic practice is the attitude of the clinician. Behind such key concepts as metapsychology and clinical technique lies the attitude of the practitioner.[8] This attitude remains in the background, behind the scenes, shaping all of what unfolds. Although typically outside awareness and thus not a matter of discussion, the clinical attitude directly bears on all of the therapy relationship and process. Schafer, for example, examines how the psychoanalytically oriented clinician attempts to be neutral, avoids either-or thinking, consistently analyzes, aims to be helpful, provides an atmosphere of safety, has an appreciation for the client, and seeks to be disciplined, empathic, and confident.

Furthermore, attitude is deeply influential in a more direct manner: The client may be influenced not only by what is conveyed through the clinician's attitude but also by the conveying and learning of the attitude itself. Heinz Kohut puts it this way:

> I teach the patient an attitude toward himself. I create an atmosphere—not artificially, however, because it truly is mine—in which a broadened understanding for oneself is encouraged. My own interest is in what is going on in the patient—not only in what he experiences, but also in how he experiences and relates to his difficulties. This is in essence an attitude of an expanded self-empathy—an expanded capacity to be empathic with one's own past, and with aspects of oneself that one really does not own, or does not own fully, including even aspects of oneself that have not yet expanded—in other words, one's future possibilities.[9]

Most significantly, Kohut extends Shapiro's, Loewald's, and Schafer's assertions by recognizing that a client may be influenced by the conveying and learning of the attitude itself. The client learns by identifying with the clinician, internalizing features of the attitude through which the clinician engages her. The client comes to relate to herself in a manner similar to that in which she has experienced the clinician to have related to her, a feature of an intrapsychic relationship.[10]

Recall for a moment going to a physician because of pain. We may have experienced the physician's care through his exploration of our experience, perhaps almost exclusively of our pain. Probably as a consequence of that conversation, we acquired the habit of subsequently asking ourselves similar questions when that or a similar pain appeared. We became our own doctor. We unwittingly relate to ourselves (now focused expressly on the pain) in a manner that parallels our experiences of how the physician related to us. Simply put, we have acquired features of the physician's attitude.

Few may be aware that we have acquired features of the physician's attitude or the particular features of that attitude: Our acquisition or learning took place outside our awareness, unconsciously. Identification is an unconscious process; internalized functions are caught more than taught because teaching that attitude may not have been intentional. Given this fact alone, clinicians should be more critically aware not only of their actual attitude but also of how their attitude—of which they are in part unconscious—is being appropriated.

Although informed by particular theories and self-consciously expressed through certain techniques and skills, a clinician's attitude expresses
her personality, history, and professional education and training. Thus, the
pastoral clinician's attitude bears the imprint of her ministerial-voca-
tional identity and confessional-traditional context.

The incredible diversity among pastoral clinicians regarding basic clinical attitudes can be attributed not only to differences in personality and
history but also to the broad range of psychological perspectives and
confessional traditions. As a consequence, there can be no definitive pastoral clinical attitude.

Before proceeding, an important caveat needs to be noted. Schafer
observes that

> Something so important [as our clinical attitude] should be formulated in
> a relatively concise, complex, and generally acceptable way, yet we have
> no such formulation. . . .
> Could it be that what stands in the way of a satisfactory formulation of the
> analytic attitude is a [fundamental] problem . . . ? Analytic pedagogy sug-
> gests that there is such a problem. It has become pedagogical commonplace
> to acknowledge that, as a rule, students learn more about the analytic at-
> titude from undergoing their own personal analyses and the supervision of
> their own clinical work than they do from case seminars, more from case
> seminars than from didactic courses on technique and the theory of the an-
> alytic process, and more from these didactic courses than from indepen-
> dent reading. . . . Consequently, the project of presenting a definitive set
> of generalizations about the analytic attitude cannot be undertaken very
> hopefully, for these generalizations will serve only as the roughest of guide-
> lines for sorting out, one from the other, the full, the compromised, and the
> failed analytic attitude.[11]

The following roughest of guidelines are intended to focus attention and
elicit such conversation.

ONE APPROACH'S NARRATIVES AND METAPHORS

Each person has favorite scriptural passages, stories, and statements
that articulate something particularly meaningful and helpful. It may be
Psalm 23, a song of comfort and inspiration; the Sermon on the Mount,
a vision of the kingdom; John 3:16, a testimony of God's love; accounts
of the exodus; or the road to Emmaus story. These passages have a spe-

cial power to speak something particularly meaningful as we carry on day to day.

The following scriptural passages have such meaning for me and my ministry. They have no special theological status, although they function as my canon within the canon. As these passages and implicit metaphors are examined, the reader is encouraged to identify his own pivotal passages and metaphors.

Mediating a Gift

Paul writes regarding a gift: "For I handed on to you as of first importance what I in turn had received: that Christ died for our sins in accordance with the scriptures, and that he was buried, and that he was raised on the third day in accordance with the scriptures" (1 Cor. 15:3-4). Paul's statement of the kerygma conveys several significant points. First, something of utmost importance has been delivered to him, which he has been called upon to receive and to deliver to others. This is a gift regarding Jesus Christ, who has died for our sins and been raised again. In receiving and delivering this gift, he bears witness to the fact that something of first importance, forgiveness of sins, has been given. Paul thus understands himself to be mediating a gift.

Elsewhere, Paul exhorts readers, "Be imitators of me, as I am of Christ" (1 Cor. 11:1), to follow his model, as he imitates Christ. As imitators of Paul, we are to receive and deliver the gift of forgiveness. Paul notes, however, that his and our mediating are modeled on Christ.

Through Holy Regard

Paul describes how we are to witness, to mediate:

If then there is any encouragement in Christ, any consolation from love, any sharing in the Spirit, any compassion and sympathy, make my joy complete: be of the same mind, having the same love, being in full accord and of one mind. Do nothing from selfish ambition or conceit, but in humility regard others as better than yourselves. Let each of you look not only to your own interests, but to the interests of others. Let the same mind be in you that was in Christ Jesus,

>   who, though he was in the form of God,
>   did not regard equality with God

as something to be exploited,
but emptied himself,
taking the form of a slave. . . . (Phil. 2:1-7)

We witness and mediate God's gift in and through Jesus Christ by being of the same mind, having the same love, doing nothing from selfish ambition or conceit but in humility regarding others better than ourselves. We mediate the gift given to us through who and how we are. We deliver something that comes through us by our participation in the Spirit. We mediate the gift by following the model of Christ, by emptying ourselves, taking the form of a slave, and looking to others' interests as well as our own. Indeed, it is precisely in emptying himself—in becoming transparent to God and thereby mediating between God and persons. In following this model of mediating by emptying ourselves, we express God's incarnation fully in Christ and God's presence in us. As Paul expresses it, "I have been crucified with Christ; and it is no longer I who live, but it is Christ who lives in me. And the life I now live in the flesh I live by faith in the Son of God, who loved me and gave himself for me" (Gal. 2:19b–20).

We mediate the gift by having the same love, by following Christ's example: In emptying ourselves, it is Christ who lives in and through us; it is God and God's love that lives in and through us. "From now on, therefore, we regard no one from a human point of view" (2 Cor. 5:16a). We no longer regard ourselves and others as merely human but rather as being mediators and bearers of the gift—the Christ in each of us. Ours is a holy regard precisely because it is the Christ in us (and through us) that regards and relates to the Christ in (and through) the other.[12]

We are called to regard—to experience—an other as Christ. Consider this illustration. Souvenir shops sell postcards that have a peculiar plastic gloss on the surface. One image is seen when the card is viewed directly, and another when the card is regarded from an angle. One can have this imaginative gestalt switch with people. They can be experienced as they are in themselves, in all their human fullness with their typical features, behaviors, and traits. Yet they can be regarded from another angle, with a disciplined awareness or perceptual set, as if they were Christ.

These passages express how we are given the gift of life that we receive, confirm, and give by emptying ourselves, by taking the form of a servant, by looking to others' interests as well as our own. As imitators of

Christ (1 Cor. 11:1), we are willing to be the good shepherd, through whom others are known by God and know God, through whom they are loved by God and love God.

When we mediate this gift through holy regard, we participate in the Spirit who works through us. What comes through us to another may be carried in and through our words, our actions, and our person, not given directly but indirectly.[13] Persons do not experience God's love and forgiveness simply by being told that God loves them; words are empty unless made manifest in deed. These words have to be incarnated in us, so that God's love and forgiveness are shown through us.

We mediate the gift given to us by our way of being with people, by being with them genuinely and consistently. Our holy regard is constant, ever present. Even as they go through the valley of the shadow of death, even as they descend into hell, they can know that nothing can separate them from the love of God in Christ Jesus. They know that, as Ruth said to Naomi, "Where you go, I will go." "God is faithful" (1 Cor. 1:9a).

In Faithful Companioning

These sacred stories arise from, as well as generate, various symbols and metaphors. We mediate a gift through holy regard by incarnating that gift in the quality and nature of our presence. We mediate God's presence to the other through the holy regard of the other as Christ. These various aspects of Christian identity and ministry are extended through the metaphor of faithful companioning.

The others whom I meet suffer in part because they are alone in that suffering. They may have lost or never had the experience that they are loved and accepted and therefore that they are lovable and acceptable. They may have lost or never had the experience that suffering may be sustained in a different way when one is accompanied. They may have lost or never had the sense that God is present and faithful in that suffering, whether or not they experience it, trust it, or accept it. In this sense, in being faithfully companioned they have the opportunity to experience being lovable, acceptable, mediated through our being faithfully present to them, regardless of how deep their pain, how alienating their brokenness.

The others who are with me suffer in part because they may have lost or never had faith in the other. Their past and present may be peopled with individuals who have injured them by neglect, disregard, selfishness, or abuse. They may have learned that others hold the power and opportunity to hurt them, that they require vigilant protection from that likely prospect. In being faithfully companioned, they have the opportunity to experience faith in others, in the goodness and lovableness of others.

The others who are with me suffer in part because they may have lost or never had membership in a sustaining community that holds and supports them. They may have not felt a part of anything, but have remained isolated and apart from others. In being faithfully companioned, they have the opportunity to experience the faithfulness of a community, the sustaining presence of a shared vision that helps make sense of the past and provides a context for making sense of the future.

The others who are with me suffer in part because they may have lost or never had hope in the future. They may prepare for what is to come not as being full of sustenance, redemption, or healing but as holding future primitive agonies from which they have to protect themselves. They may have lost or never had the sense that they have authorship of their lives and future, that they can contribute constructively to what will unfold. They may have lost faith in their future. In being faithfully companioned, they have the opportunity to experience that faith and hope in their future.

The others who are with me suffer in part because they may have lost or never had faith. In being faithfully companioned, they have the lived sense that the other who is present with and to them shares their brokenness, doubts, agonies, and struggles about lovableness, acceptableness, and hopefulness. They have a sense that despite and because of that authentic known appreciation of such unfaith, the other brings a sense of courage and hope. They have the opportunity to experience faith that embraces unfaith. They are lent an appreciation that suffering can be taken up into care, despair into hope, doubt into faith, brokenness into redemption, loneliness into community, and alienation into acceptableness. They live in the presence of and are lent faith that can become appropriated.

One embodies these metaphors in ways that vary depending on context and relationships. Faithful companioning takes on a particular sensibility given the unique context of the ministry of pastoral psychotherapy. It is a theme on which there are variations.

PILOT AND COPILOT–FLIGHT INSTRUCTOR

Pastoral counseling can be compared to flying in an airplane, with the client as the pilot and the clinician as a flight instructor or copilot.[14] The path and pace of the flight (or flights) are determined in large part by the pilot but are influenced by the particular style, skills, and experience of the instructor-copilot. Before these pilots can depart, considerable care has to be given to preparation. They have to determine whether the client is a viable pilot, capable of sustaining the stress and perils of the flight. Will they get to a destination worthy of the investment of time and energy? Can they work together as a team, collaborating in different ways at different times, depending on the unique demands in various moments in flight? Do they agree on a destination, recognizing that because neither has ever been there before, the most they can do is fly in a particular direction and constantly reshape the contours of their joint understanding of the destination? Do they agree on the pace and direction of each aspect or leg of the flight? Do they fly only in daylight? What do they do if storms emerge? How quickly can they expect to get where they are going? Are they willing to fly back in order to move forward, to fly temporarily away from their designated destination before resuming their direct flight? And so forth.

Not unimportantly, they have to pay considerable attention to the vehicle in which they are moving. Is the plane—the container—well cared for? Can the plane sustain the kind of flying they are intending? Does it provide adequate controls for the copilot? Can it sustain carrying the various persons of the client's (and the clinician's) history, and the other baggage? Does it have procedures for taking on and letting go of some of the passengers and some of the baggage?

Finally, do pilot and copilot have sound connections with control towers? Are radar and radios working? Are they in contact with supportive people on the ground? Although the journey is taken by two people, they bring many people along with them, as well as supplies, both of which may enable as well as encumber the flight. In addition, the flight takes place in a network or community, such that the pilot and copilot periodically return to ground, touch base, reaffirm connections, and resume flying.

The metaphor of flying conveys the potential danger inherent in the process of care. Ideally the trip reaches its intended and constantly reevaluated destination. Often it reaches a new but possibly only temporary goal. At times, the trip might result in flying around but getting nowhere, not only expending costly and limited resources but also confirming a pilot's fear that she cannot get anywhere. Sometimes, the trip ends in disaster. Much is contingent on the accurate assessment of the pilot, the plane, the relationship, the journey, and the destination.

Care as an unknown journey into uncharted territory is an anxiety-arousing enterprise that requires courage and trust. The clinician and client are collaborators on a journey. The clinician, as copilot–flight instructor, is a participant-observer, a faithful companion, faithful to the process, to the other, to himself, and to God. Although it is important to reach the destination, the goal of the care is as much learning how to pilot as it is arriving somewhere new. The journey is itself the goal.

Collaborative Translating

Many theorists have come to regard psychotherapy as an interpretive hermeneutic process. Arnold Goldberg, Roy Schafer, and Donald Spence in psychoanalysis; Arthur Kleinman in psychiatry; and Don Browning, Donald Capps, Charles Gerkin, and John Patton in pastoral care and counseling have considered how hermeneutics is relevant if not central to their respective praxes.[15]

These theorists appreciate that the person seeking help and the professional providing care approach their joint enterprise from diverse contexts, by way of dissimilar universes of discourse. The prospective client has a unique way of describing himself and his suffering, and the clinician has a different way of identifying and making sense of what is presented. The clinician sees and hears something *as* something else.

Arthur Kleinman expresses this particularly well, differentiating between *illness* and *disease:* "Illness refers to how the sick person and the members of his [or her] family or wider social network perceive, live with, and respond to symptoms of disability."[16] Sick persons present their suffering through explanatory models that enable them to order, communicate, and thereby symbolically control symptoms. The illness narrative is the sufferer's unique, more or less coherent but disguised biological, psychological, cultural, ethnic, religious account of what hurts. Practitioners listen to and attempt to understand the patient by way of their own technical concepts and explanatory models. "Disease is what practitioners have been trained to see through the theoretical lenses of their particular forms of practice" (p. 5). Diagnosis is a semiotic act transforming lay speech into professional categories. The practitioner creates another entity when transforming illness into disease.

Both parties in the collaborative enterprise are constantly translating what they see and hear. Participants presume that their conversation is meaningful and constructive and disavow that misinterpretation is the order of the day. They typically collude to endow the professional with special powers and responsibilities of taking the pain away.

Regarding the activities of care and therapy as in part or essentially interpretive processes unmasks the all too common tendency to endow clinicians with special wisdom, power, objectivity, and responsibility at the expense of the integrity, uniqueness, and responsibility of the client. It exposes the need for humane, respectful collaboration. At the same time, however, the focus on care as interpretation is not without liabilities.

This perspective has drawn criticism from psychoanalytic theorists who challenge replacing history by story, truth by coherence, objectivity by usefulness. As Daniel Stern describes it,

> The story is discovered, as well as altered, by both teller and listener in the course of the telling. Historical truth is established by what gets told, not by what actually happened. This view opens the door for the possibility that any narrative about one's life (especially one's early life) may be just as valid as the next.[17]

If that is the case, truth is relative to each particular story, relationship, and context. The philosopher Robert Neville articulates the heart of the problem: "The outcome of the imperial triumph of interpretation is that reality cannot measure our claims to truth. The only measure seems to consist in what survives future interpretation."[18]

This perspective also engenders clinical problems. Focusing on the narrative distracts us from the narrator's experiencing. When intent on deciphering the story, one misses the storyteller. The sufferer and the clinician focus on the meanings of the report, at the expense of ongoing experiencing of two persons trying to relate and communicate in the midst of pain, confusion, and anxiety.

The pastoral clinician as collaborative translator appreciates that the client is making sense of what she is grasping by placing something unknown in conjunction with something known (the metaphorizing process) within a context (the narrative quality of experience). The clin-

ician can attend to how the client conveys fundamental features of her self
by way of images and root metaphors.

Pastoral Clinician as Practical Theologian

At the heart this pastoral clinical attitude is the deep appreciation of
how each person and each relationship may be experienced, observed, understood, and interpreted from a variety of angles of vision. The pastoral
clinician has a manifold professional identity, having been trained to
function as psychologist, theologian, and ethicist.

A BRIEF ARGUMENT

Every human being constructively formulates ways of making sense
of her interior life, the interiority of others, and her behavior, motives,
habits, and tendencies. Every human being is, in a functional sense, psychological—a lay psychologist.

Every human being constructively formulates ways of making sense
of her life in certain ways; organizes her life according to fundamental values, myths, and purposes; and has a sense of who God is and what is
sacred, holy, and meaningful. Every human being is, in a functional
sense, religious—a lay theologian.

Every human being constructively formulates ways of making sense
of her responsibilities and the responsibilities of her communities in certain ways. Each has some at least implicit sense of what she is supposed
to do, of who she is supposed to be or become. Every human being is, in
a functional sense, moral—a lay ethicist.

Each relationship between client and clinician may be recast as the
engagement between psychologist-theologian-ethicist and psychologist-
theologian-ethicist.[19] Together they examine collaboratively what is happening and what to do from several vantage points.

INTROSPECTION AND EMPATHY

The pastoral clinician attends to the ongoing experience of two different persons through dual concurrent processes: introspection and empathy. On the one hand, the clinician introspects, that is, pays careful
attention to her own ongoing inner experience. The clinician monitors

what she is becoming aware of—thoughts, feelings, and sensations. The clinician at the same time pays attention to the experience of the other. Through empathy or vicarious introspection, the clinician introspects as if she were the other.[20]

The introspective-empathic attitude may be characterized by way of a series of polarities: self-experience; subject-object; separate-connected; surface-depth; doubting-believing; sinful-righteous.[21] These pairs of terms help to articulate "certain imaginative modes of comprehending the form and content of human situations and the changes they undergo."[22] They are heuristic devices used to discriminate features of a process that is ongoing and dynamic, more circular than linear.

The Polarity of Self-Experience

The clinician's attention to both self and other is bifocal. The clinician wants to identify the subject who is experiencing and the nature of the unfolding experience. The clinician wonders, Who is the self who is having and reporting the experience? What is the experience that the self is reporting? Thus the clinician tracks the self and the experience of her self (via introspection) in conjunction with tracking the self and the experience of the other (via vicarious introspection).

The clinician develops a fuller sense of the client and his experiences in several ways. The clinician can infer what the client is experiencing by attending to the sensations, feelings, associations, fantasies evoked—by imagining oneself saying what the client says, by generalizing from contact with others in similar situations, and by formulating ideas from readings, studies, and training.

The clinician also wonders, Who am I as I am experiencing? And what am I experiencing as I listen to the other? What sensations emerge as we speak? What is my baseline or norm in this kind of moment? In what ways am I departing from that? What are my own tendencies, strengths, weaknesses in this kind of situation?

Self and experience are mutually informing dimensions. One can only understand an experience as a particular person's experience and a self through that self's experiences. The following expands upon the ways in which self and experience of both participants interpenetrate.

The Polarity of Conversing-Companioning

All forms of clinical care share one basic feature: Each is a sophisticated kind of conversation in which the participants talk to one another in a particular way, in the expectation and hope that certain positive therapeutic changes eventuate. Because change takes place through conversation, the clinician must attain a special appreciation for and mastery of the meanings and functions of words. This task is, however, highly ambiguous, because words conceal as well as reveal, confound as well as illumine. At times words may be empty, transport little, or connect only tangentially. Indeed, words often miscarry, misorient, and serve to disconnect.

A recurring clinical experience reveals how words have a mixed track record. A client reports, for example, that she has felt considerably better this past week and traces the improvement to the previous session. She remarks that a comment the clinician made has been pivotal. When asked what had made such a difference, she states something that the clinician not only cannot remember having said but almost could not imagine having said. She attributes considerable influence to particular words that may never have actually been spoken!

Events like these contribute to skepticism about how central words are to the actual therapeutic enterprise. We confront a paradox: Clinical care is a fundamentally verbal activity; the question remains open, however, as to how pivotal the words themselves are to therapeutic progress. We are led to look through, beyond, or behind the words to consider what else may contribute to change.

The comments are intentionally suggestive. Recall some familiar maxims: One picture is worth a thousand words. Might an image or picture inform the process? Actions speak louder than words. Additional maxims distinguish words from actions and regard the two as competitive. The parent or teacher who remarks, "Do as I say and not as I do," reveals that doing may be a more powerful teacher. One may exhort another to practice what you preach.

Even though words have influence, actions that support or communicate may influence more deeply. Some of our most formative ideas, feelings, and beliefs are codified and transmitted in our behavior. A parent who overindulges in social drinking is distraught to discover how his daughter has ignored his well-intentioned, repeated admonitions against drugs. A parent who overzealously punished his child out of misguided love despairs at how his son physically abuses the next generation and repeats the chilling statement, "I'm doing this because I love you. This hurts me more than it hurts you." A clinician is troubled when her client terminates prematurely, complaining that the clinician was inconsistent. She discovers the accuracy of the client's indictment when realizing that although she had taken considerable care to try to establish a clinical contract with a set time and fee, they had in fact been meeting irregularly, often at times that were inconvenient for the clinician, and the client had not paid her.

These scenarios illustrate not only a disjunction between words and actions but also the influence of action: How we are is a powerful vehicle of communication. One conveys something essential, something basic about oneself through ritual behaviors. Stylized patterns of behavior reveal most directly who we are.

One contributes to change in a variety of ways. The words used in observations and interpretations may provide the other with a different angle of vision, a new way of thinking, a reframing of events and experiences. Actions convey, more indirectly but possibly more significantly, a still deeper sense about how one understands and about what one values. The words and actions themselves may enhance change, may be influential, not only for what they are in and of themselves—for what they convey directly—but for what they may represent—for what they convey about something that lies behind or beneath them. Words and actions may say something about who we are, about our person, our character. Implied in this differentiation among words, actions, and character is a hierarchy: Actions may speak louder than words, but character may speak loudest of all. Finally, we may be less influential in what we say and do than in what we are through our words and actions.[23]

Change is caught more than taught. Words and actions influence most profoundly when they convey the self, one's character. Skills and techniques are important, but secondary. Theories are themselves important, but also secondary. As a consequence, when we provide care and teach how to provide care, our attention should focus less on technique, skills, and theory than on the self and attitude of the participants.

Every conversation is a complex, fluid interplay of what the participants say and do and who and how they are. Conversing-companioning represents this interplay among words, actions, and character. This can be expressed in a number of ways. Arnold Goldberg observes, for example, that "the ability to connect has become more important that the ability to know."[24] Edgar Levenson captures this rather poetically:

There are two very striking clinical effects all practitioners note. The first I shall call "the message in the bottle" effect. It deals with the flow of data from the patient. The second I shall call the "laying on of hands." This latter effect deals with the impact of the patient's experience of the therapist. This distinction is roughly akin to [the] . . . polarities of insight and relationship.[25]

Henri Nouwen notes the importance of companioning, of being present with and for the other:

> The word care finds its roots in the Gothic *Kara* which means lament. The basic meaning of care is: to grieve, to experience sorrow, to cry out with. I am very much struck by this background of the word care because we tend to look at caring as an attitude of the strong toward the weak, of the powerful toward the powerless, of the have's toward the have-not's. And, in fact, we feel quite uncomfortable with an invitation to enter into someone's pain before doing something about it.
>
> Still, when we ask ourselves which persons in our lives mean the most to us, we often find that it is those who, instead of giving much advice, solutions, or cures, have chosen rather to share our pain and touch our wounds with a gentle and tender hand. The friend who can be silent with us in a moment of despair or confusion, who can stay with us in an hour of grief and bereavement, who can tolerate not-knowing, not-curing, not-healing and face with us the reality of our powerlessness, that is the friend who cares.[26]

The Polarity of Subject-Object

Westerners typically frame relations with others as well as with themselves in subject-object terms. What is needed is closer attention to how we approach others, as well as ourselves, subjectively and objectively, considering the related polarity internal-external, making sense from the inside-outside, as understanding-explanation.

SUBJECT VERSUS OBJECT

Arnold Goldberg notes that "most of us were born into a world of assumed dichotomies: inside-outside, subject-object, up-down. We were taught to organize the world that way, and so we see it as naturally so and 'given' to us. We think of things in linear, causal ways, and we thereupon see the world as filled with things that act upon one another."[27] "Practically speaking, people use the integumentive theory, which asserts that a person ends at his or her skin."[28] Goldberg observes that psychiatric theories of development and pathology presume an underlying subject-object model—indeed, as if we are subject and they are independent objects.

Westerners tend to organize intrapsychic relating according to this same frame, being both subject and object with and to ourselves. While I write, I focus on expressing an idea. At the periphery of awareness is a sense of being the writer trying to say something. That peripheral awareness can be foregrounded. While writing, my sense of my self was irrelevant; when I observe myself as writer, I become at once subject and object in my own experience. *Introspection* presupposes that one can be both subject and object to oneself and function as experiencer and observer. Ego psychologists speak about the capacity of the ego to split into an experiencing ego and an observing ego.

The clinician working from an introspective-empathic attitude extends this capacity to be at once subject and object in several ways. First, one presumes that the self of the client who reports her experiences is at once subject and object with and to herself, that she demonstrates a capacity and shares a quality of subjectivity, split between experiencer and observer.[29] Second, one draws from and builds upon that understanding of what it means to be subject-observer and object-experienced and imaginatively share in her experience. Because I have a sense of what it is like to observe myself as I am experiencing, I can imagine that I know some of what it might be like for her to observe herself as she is experiencing; that is, I imagine what it may be like for her to tell me how sad she is (as experiencer), as well as to feel somewhat embarrassed and protective as she says it (as observer).

SUBJECTIVE-OBJECTIVE AS A FRAME OF KNOWING

In one of its most basic senses, the term *subjective* refers to being on and grasping from the inside, and *objective* refers to being on and grasping from the outside. Philosophers and psychologists have for a long time drawn upon the metaphors of internal and external. Most Westerners distinguish between events that take place inside a person (in the mind) from events occurring outside a person (in the external world). *Internal* refers to something private, known only to a subject (the person); *external* refers to something available to public observation.

Many liabilities are embedded in this way of thinking. These metaphors might be understood, as if literal, to refer to two separable spatial locations. One may mistakenly separate mental from physical and mind from body, as well as isolate person from person, creating an essentially unbridgeable chasm between selves. Despite these liabilities, the terms *internal-external* are instructive because they identify features of everyday experiencing.[30]

During every conversation, one processes information from a variety of sources in a variety of ways. Like behaviorists, we are alert to physical appearance, clothing, posture, gestures, facial expressions, pace of speech, and tone of voice and interpret behavior available through extrospection.[31] Like psychoanalysts, we infer from public behavior a person's feelings, motives, and unspoken ideas. We are active on two interrelated fronts, receiving signals that are sent publicly while imaginatively conjuring some sense of the subject who sends the signals. The clinician working from an introspective-empathic stance is simply intentional about drawing from these two interrelated sources of information. One makes ongoing judgments and develops hypotheses about these complementary sources, how they do and do not fit together; one shapes and reshapes hypotheses in deciding how and when to intervene.

For example, one seeks to appreciate the sadness, despair, and longing that a man is experiencing and expressing, drawing from the content of his words, the pace and tone of his comments, his drooping posture, his infrequent eye contact. While one is gathering data, the primary vantage point from which to monitor a self's unfolding experience is from the inside. The self to whom one addresses comments and with whom one relates is that self grasped and pictured from within.

Engaging another through this attitude influences the kind of conversation that will unfold. When particularly attentive to external behavior, one might observe,

> As you talk about being depressed, your shoulders droop, you look away, your voice lowers, you speak slowly, almost imperceptibly. I wonder if it wouldn't be helpful to practice an entirely different set of behaviors—like sitting up, retaining eye contact, speaking forcefully. You can act your way into a new way of thinking and feeling.

In contrast, when one is bifocal in attending and addressing the agent of these behaviors, one could observe, "Your words as well as your actions give me a sense of what it is like to be experiencing this sadness. Help me understand more fully."

While attending to and relating with the self of the client, one is also making ongoing judgments about oneself and experience, tracking feelings, words, posture, and mannerisms through introspection, yet remaining aware of the client's responses. Imagine conveying concern, a willingness to understand, and a basic sensitivity but being experienced as disinterested, aloof, and cold. These responses reveal something about the other; they are also about the clinician, potentially revealing something outside the clinician's awareness. Thus one should monitor information about oneself that is available externally as well as internally.

In this way, the polarity of internal-external captures the various mutually informing, fluidly interrelated sources of data, inside and outside both participants, which are available to the clinician and the client. In addition, the polarity establishes a context in which to specify the internal vantage point from which the clinician in the introspective-empathic attitude proceeds: attending to and relating with the imaginatively constructed self of the client's ongoing experience.

The subjective-objective polarity has another invaluable connotation. Regarding the other as a subject disposes one to appreciate that other as a Thou. Regarding the other as an object, in contrast, disposes one to appreciate that other as an object (Buber's It).[31] Conversely, one can be regarded by the other as Thou or It, and our regard for the other can influence which frame the other utilizes.

The introspective-empathic attitude of being subject and object to and with a client is conveyed, in part, through the parameters of the relationship. A grieving woman requests a meeting for an initial appointment in her home; she cannot bear being seen coming to an office and would feel better understood where she lives. In respecting her as a Thou, her request should be taken seriously. In taking into account one's professional needs and judgments, one might conclude that such a meeting would need to occur in an office.

Interpreting from the inside and outside involves the interrelated procedures of understanding and explanation. Most considerations of these terms pay at least passing attention to William Dilthey's contributions. Dilthey, a nineteenth-century philosopher and literary historian, argued that knowledge could be attained through two fundamentally different, mutually exclusive enterprises. The sciences of the human spirit, *Geisteswissenschaften*, pursue understanding the human. The sciences of nature, *Naturwissenschaften*, pursue explaining the natural. Writing more than a half century later, philosopher Michael Polanyi argued in support of this contrast:

The most important pair of mutually exclusive approaches to the same situation is formed by the alternative interpretations of human affairs in terms of causes and reasons. . . . You can interpret, for example, this essay in terms of the causes which have determined my action of writing it down or you may ask for my reasons for saying what I do. But the two approaches—in terms of causes and reasons—mutually exclude each other.[33]

Steven Kepnes provides a helpful illustration of the interpenetration of understanding and explanation:

Suppose two individuals, Bob and John, are having a conversation on a film which they both saw. Bob makes a statement about the movie and John agrees. The two understand one another, statement builds upon statement and creative dialogue, rich in intuitive understanding, ensues. But then John says something that seems odd to Bob and Bob asks John for an explanation. John then moves to a discussion of the structure of the plot in which he refers to theories of emplotment in film. He compares the plot to other films of the same director and then, when Bob still does not follow, he compares the film to a novel and finally to an event which occurred in his office at work. At this point the message gets through. Bob says "I understand," and the conversation proceeds forward.[34]

Understanding and explanation are two angles on a common project, two interpenetrating activities. Understanding a self means grasping from the inside who the client is and what the client is experiencing as she experiences. Explaining a self involves reflecting upon one's ongoing experience with and understanding of the other through formal theories, including theories of personality, development, therapy, and psychopathology. One organizes hypotheses about who the client is, where she came from, where she is going, and how one can intervene effectively.

The Polarity of Separate-Connected

The polarity of separate-connected is crucial to the introspective-empathic attitude.[35] Clinicians write and speak about connection and relation but often presume a fundamental separateness of persons. Writings in feminist psychology have taken a complementary tack, presuming that selves are fundamentally in relationship, connected.[36] Mary Belenky and her colleagues, for example, distinguish between two different epistemological orientations, two different kinds of relationships between knowers and the objects (or subjects) of knowing (which may or may not be persons).[37] Connected knowers presume a connection or relationship between themselves and the known, whereas separate knowers stand apart from or over and against the known. Belenky and her colleagues suggest that one or the other orientation may be dominant in a person's being in the world. The polarity *separate-connected* emphasizes that in the introspective-empathic stance, therapist and client are at once apart from and a part of one another.

Contemporary psychoanalytic self psychologists have observed how the clinical relationship may be comprised of two contrasting subjective experiences, or two domains of relatedness. A client may experience the clinician as a separate self, an object, having an independent center of initiative and continuity in space and time. The other is the object of an aggressive drive—the target of object love. A client may experience the clinician as a part of or extension of the client's self, a selfobject, as a function used by the self of the client in the service of equilibrium, cohesiveness, and reassurance. In the former, the client experiences a relationship between two separate selves; in the latter, a relationship between two connected selves (or better, a self and its extension).

In their discussion of separate and connected epistemological orientations, Belenky and her colleagues argue that one orientation may be dominant, even though typically they coexist. Similarly, when analyzing the relationship between client and clinician, the clinician may discern that the client's experience is predominantly one of object love or of selfobject relationship, yet typically there are elements of both. A person may experience another as at once a separate self (as an object) and as a part of the self (as a selfobject) with whom one is internally connected.[38]

The polarity of separate-connected provides a helpful corrective to tendencies to regard polarities as dichotomies. As inheritors of Cartesian dualism, we are prone to contrast and separate inside from outside, subjective from objective, subject from object. We unwittingly presume that the other with whom we sit and talk is finally an other from whom we are ultimately separated and disconnected. In part because both everyday and technical languages typically do not capture other features of relating, we fail to recognize how persons are fundamentally interconnected as well as separate.

Clients experience clinicians to be both connected and separate. As a client experiences attunement to him in his ongoing inner experience, he senses connection. In moments of "mis-attunement" he realizes separeteness. The client who experiences the clinician's consistency is sufficiently safe to examine moments of disconnection. Experiencing moments of not being understood within the frame of being subsequently understood—that is, empathy with breaks in empathy—he can resume exploring safely. In addition, he has endured and registered another experience of being (potentially) understood and connected, despite momentary misunderstanding and disconnection.

The polarity of separate-connected informs the introspective-empathic attitude in another extremely important way. In some ways, we are fundamentally separate from all other persons, living a life that is unique to ourselves as individuals. In some ways, we are fundamentally connected to all other persons, living a life that is shared with others as individuals. Kluckhohn and Murray captured this concept as follows: "Everyone is in certain respects (a) like all other people, (b) like some other people, and (c) like no other people."[39] The clinician respects the other as fundamentally unique and qualitatively different from all other persons and affirms the other as fundamentally like all other persons.

Indeed, were there not a fundamental connectedness and continuity across persons, were we not in some fundamental ways alike, attempts to understand another in light of one's experience would be grossly misdirected and futile. One must presume that the experience of the quality of being both subject and object to and with oneself is common to human experience and is thus shared, potentially, by clients.[40] Were there not, by contrast, a fundamental separateness and discontinuity across persons, were we not in some fundamental and significant ways different, our efforts to understand another in conjunction with and in light of our own experience would be redundant and irrelevant.

The Polarity of Surface-Depth

Readers pay careful attention to what an author directly intends while also reading between the lines for another dimension or level of communication. One listens for what is stated directly, denoted, and what is implied by the speaker and inferred by the listener, connoted. The denoted is acceptable; the connoted is somehow hidden and disguised. Something is at the surface, illumined, available to be seen and heard, and something more or other is in the depths, beyond the light.

Knowing and relating to oneself and another reflect the tension and paradox of attending to both surface and depth. The manifest will be in competition and potential conflict with what is latent. Consider, for example, when a client wants the length of meetings to remain flexible, depending upon his moods. He might feel understood were the hour extended when he felt depressed and shortened when he felt okay. He could become anxious and troubled when the clinician does not accede to his wishes.

Knowing and relating at both surface and depth mean appreciating what is experienced and reported consciously while at the same time appreciating what is dimly sensed and implied preconsciously (unconsciously). It does not mean being attuned to a person in her conscious awareness and experience. Nor does it mean being simply attuned to the person in the moment, as if the moment were out of time.

Being with another in surface and depth is therefore being with her across time. One understands the other's conscious experience of the moment in conjunction with, in the context of, the other's unfolding life history, in her developmental context.

The pastoral clinician as theologian approaches depth in different ways. Gabriel Marcel has written about the difference between a problem and a mystery.[41] In the former, something is potentially available to be solved or rendered intelligible. In the latter, something is fundamentally beyond our comprehension. Although one respects problems, they are opportunities for knowledge and mastery. Mysteries, in contrast, evoke awe and fascination. Depth-as-problem warrants one working unflaggingly to the limits of one's capacities. Depth-as-mystery encourages respecting the limits of one's capacities and appreciating that at most one can be in the presence of something beyond the self. "Our first task in approaching another . . . is to take off our shoes for the place we are approaching is holy. Else we may find ourselves treading on another's dream. More serious still, we may forget . . . that God was there before our arrival."[42]

The Polarity of Doubting-Believing

Taking seriously that all communication involves commerce across different levels—some intended, others unwitting, where messages may be not only ambiguous but also conflicting—one needs to accept, take for granted, believe what is said and simultaneously wonder, be curious and skeptical, even doubt what is said.

Peter Elbow characterizes two basic games to play in trying to find the truth.

The doubting game seeks the truth by seeking error. Doubting an assertion is the best way to find an error in it. . . . The truer it seems, the harder
you have to doubt it. . . . To doubt well, it helps if you make a special effort to extricate yourself from the assertions in question. . . .
In the believing game the first rule is to refrain from doubting the assertions. . . . We are trying to find not errors but truths, and for this it helps
to believe. . . . To do this you must make, not an act of self-extrication, but
an act of self-insertion, self-involvement.[43]

The clinician who believes and doubts applies what Paul Ricoeur referred to as "a hermeneutics of suspicion and a hermeneutics of restoration."[44] A client, for example, describes his sadness. By the end of the conversation, the clinician is exhausted, wishing she had had a cup of coffee
before meeting with him. Although the client says that he wants to tell her
everything so that she can do something, she realizes that she has strug-
gled to put words to his experience and that he has, in fact, disclosed little. She must believe in part what he says in order to understand, and she
must doubt in part the accuracy of what he says in order to understand.

Doubting-believing characterizes one attitude in knowing and relating to ourselves as well. We proceed, most naturally, to believe and trust
the accuracy of our own experience, taking for granted what we understand. By the same token, however, we must bring the same doubting attitude to ourselves and our own experience as we do to and with the
other.[45]

The Polarity of Sinful-Righteous

Theologians and religionists have used a variety of terms to represent
the interpenetration of different orders, realms, domains: sacred and
profane, divine and human, unconditional and conditioned, infinite and
finite. Christian theologians, in particular, have written about a different
but not unrelated set of interpenetrating domains: grace and nature, sinful and righteous. These religious-theological dimensions are an integral
feature of an expressly *pastoral* clinical attitude and deserve greater treatment than can be afforded here.

All of what unfolds in the clinical relationship and process participates
in the fact of sin.[46] Even though we seek to promote and can understand positive growth, movement, or development, none of these changes
signals our transcending the conditions of sin: Regardless of our healing
or sanctification, we remain sinful. That is, developmental models should

be viewed in the context of *simul justus et peccator* (justified [before God] and sinner at the same time). Whatever healing does unfold, however ambiguously and fragmentarily, is an expression and gift of the Other beyond our sinfulness. All of what unfolds is fallen and broken yet open to the transformative influence of the Other. Something other than and greater than who we are and what we can do is present and active in our relationships and processes.[47]

Healing of persons involves the presence and gift of something (someone) beyond the conditions of sinfulness, that (who) participates in part through us. The pastoral clinician in companioning and collaboratively translating simultaneously represents her self as well as something greater than and other than her self. The pastoral clinician is called and empowered to companion and collaborate precisely because she experiences the companioning and collaboration of the Other, which is greater than she. In that sense, the clinician as companion and collaborator presumes the presence and action of the Other with and through what she says, does, and is.[48]

Both clinician and client are at once human yet mediating the participation—love and forgiveness—of the Other. Both are sinful, broken human beings, yet potentially ambassadors on behalf of something (someone) greater.[49] Healing takes place both in spite of as well as because of the clinical relationship and the clinician's participation. Clinicians contribute to healing less because they are perfect, ideal, or fully analyzed than because they are authentic and fully human. One enhances healing not through a capacity for perfect or enduring empathy but through an authentic commitment to be empathic.[50]

Clinician and client are involved in ongoing, ambiguous internal and interpersonal translating. What is conveyed takes place in but also through words. They are apart from, yet a part of, one another. All of what unfolds is yet to be known and understood more fully. What is said is in part true but will be redescribed. They are sinful.

It is remarkable, given this, that healing of any kind can take place. These difficulties cannot be surmounted, bracketed, or transcended. Rather, they should be acknowledged and embraced. In fact, it is precisely through the mature *acceptance* of these pervasive limitations that healing may unfold.

Most persons do not need or require extraordinary empathy. They experience being understood, having another be present with and to them, not through some remarkable gift or talent but through reasonable human care, what Heinz Hartmann termed *average expectable environment*. The empathic presence through which healing unfolds is good enough: usually approximate and fluctuating, not continual.

Healing is not caused by a clinician's extrahuman power, which leads a client to feel perfectly understood. Rather, it is occasioned by experiencing the fluctuating, approximate presence of a sinful but well-intentioned human being who mediates God's love and forgiveness by faithfully companioning and collaboratively translating what unfolds in fluctuating and approximate ways.

> We have seen . . . how easy it is to project meaning onto meaninglessness . . . there is growing evidence, from a number of directions, that there is more randomness in the world than we would like to imagine, that the scrambled surface is not always deceptive, and that the complete account of a happening may sometimes never be discovered.
>
> To begin to admit that for some events there is no explanation and that the surface of the world is frequently devoid of meaning is to come face to face with a terrifying possibility.[51]

Healing is not caused by the clinician's extraordinary ability to understand another, although a basic capacity is necessary. Healing is not caused by the clinician's discerning and articulating meaning, because the world is frequently devoid of meaning. Healing is occasioned when a suffering person experiences the clinician's commitment, acceptance, hope, as those virtues are present in who and how they are—in their pastoral clinical attitude.

5

The Triad of
Clinical Activities

 earning how to provide professional clinical care is
not unlike going to a foreign land. The territory is
at times familiar, at other times unrecognizable. One looks for "landmarks" but cannot know ahead of time what will count for such landmarks.
Some phenomena and experiences are utterly new.

When more or less familiar with the territory, our existing lexicon is
suitable to describing our experience. At other times, we do not have
words or categories to grasp or express all we are coming-to-know; we need
a new language. A strange, idiosyncratic blend of colloquial terms and technical jargon is developed.

Clinicians usually recognize early in their training that the professional
language they are learning is not shared by all colleagues. Indeed, it
seems as if everyone acquires a different tongue. Even more, it seems as
if everyone has gone to a different territory, identified different landmarks, and experienced different phenomena.

Some respond to this pluralism by withdrawing into their own clinical world, cherishing the illusion that *their* final vocabulary is *the* final
vocabulary. These true believers have found "the way" and are content
to fit everything into their faith system. Others, in contrast, believe that
all forms of clinical care share certain basic features, despite the considerable differences in language and technique.[1]

This chapter tends toward the second approach. I am, in one sense,
more-lumper-than-splitter: lumpers "seek connections between apparently
different things" while splitters "hunt out distinctions and differences."[2]
All clinicians, regardless of perspective, make common core judgments:
diagnosing, setting goals, and establishing a course of intervention.

Diagnosing is judging what is happening and how one's capacities match the needs of the person or persons seeking help. *Setting goals* is speculating about some future terminus, the objective that orients our actions. *Planning a course of intervention* is formulating the ways we move from where we are to where we hope to arrive.

For example, a man reports suffering chronic, debilitating anxiety. He feels agitated, cannot rest, and fears something catastrophic will occur. He wants the clinician to do something. One's questions, observations, and recommendations express a particular clinical perspective. One's focus could include underlying physiological causes, patterns of behavior or unsound cognitive beliefs, disruptions in primary relationships, existential or spiritual problems in his experience and relationship to God, and underlying wishes or motives that remain outside his awareness but find disguised expression in his anxiety. Each of these represents a way of framing phenomena and guiding interventions in particular ways.

Nonetheless, all clinicians, regardless of perspective, make a common series of judgments: What is happening? Where do we go from here? How do we get there? The prospective client has himself made those judgments: I'm anxious. I don't want to be anxious. I want you to do something so that I no longer am anxious.

In this book, diagnosis is regarded as an ongoing process of making judgments about the current state of affairs. Defining goals is an ongoing process of making judgments about the end state of affairs. Correspondingly, planning the course of intervention is itself subject to ongoing revising, as the movement from a changing beginning toward a changing end.

The intrinsic relationship among these three judgments is a matter of practical reason: All understanding is shaped by practical concerns.[3] Knowledge is sought for purposes of *action*—intentional, purposeful behaviors. What one knows informs actions; intended action informs what one seeks to know. Diagnosing, goal setting, and planning a course of intervention can be distinguished but not separated: Each judgment informs and is informed by the others. A biomedically oriented clinician, for example, will frame a request for help in terms of the triad of pathology (diagnosis), health (goal), and cure (process of healing), mutually informing elements of a consistent and coherent perspective.

Unfortunately, not all perspectives are consistent and coherent. In fact, consistency and coherence may be more the exception than the rule: Most clinicians follow the standard but mistaken practice of isolating the theory and practice of diagnosis from the theory and practice of ongoing clinical care. Indeed, framing clinical care as a triad of activities is intended to challenge this commonly accepted understanding. Drawing from discussions in previous chapters, this triad of clinical activities must be a consistent and coherent expression of one's clinical attitude, itself an expression of underlying root metaphors and foundational narratives.

DIAGNOSIS

The English word *diagnosis* derives through Latin from the Greek *diagnosis*, whose oldest form is *diagignoskein*, comprised of *dia* ("two" or "apart") and *gignoskein* ("to know or perceive"). It has been translated "to distinguish," "to differentiate,"[4] "to discern," "grasping things as they really are, so as to do the right thing,"[5] and "to know apart." To know something apart is to lift it out of context, to highlight it. In a comparative process, something is now figure as compared to ground, foreground as compared to background. When speaking with a person who reports feeling sad and overwhelmed, for example, these experiences are understood apart from yet in the context of the person's overall presentation.

Knowing apart is a natural human procedure. The term *sad* might be contrasted with dejected, sorrowful, and unhappy or the term *overwhelmed* with helpless, powerless, and overpowered. In addition, knowing is innately contextualizing and organizing: fitting the data regarding sad and overwhelmed into a context that preexists those data's appearances.

As an ongoing activity, one diagnoses at any and every moment. When a person says in an initial conversation, "I'm feeling very troubled and I don't know if you can help me," a clinician naturally speculates, What does the term *very troubled* mean to this person? Why might she not expect help? Despite this expectation, what prompts her seeking help? In contrast, when a client one has been seeing for a considerable period of time opens a session with the comment, "I was thinking that maybe we should consider talking about stopping our work together," one wonders, What contributes to this idea emerging now? What happened last session? What does he anticipate that is threatening?

Rather than regarding diagnosis as a specific act or series of procedures restricted to the outset of clinical care, diagnosis—the identification of the current state of the self and the suffering of the client—takes place all the time.[6] One does not seek to know anything in abstraction; knowledge is sought in order to act. "Every act of understanding involves interpretation, and all interpretation involves application."[7] "Concern with application is there from the beginning," as Don Browning notes. "Gadamer says it more directly: 'application is neither a subsequent nor a merely occasional part of the phenomena of understanding, but co-determines it as a whole from the beginning.' "[8]

Revisioning diagnosis as an ongoing procedure integrally related to other clinical activities has significant implications. A diagnostic orientation, such as *The Diagnostic and Statistical Manual, Fourth Edition* (DSM IV), or Paul Pruyser's "diagnostic variables for pastoral assessment"[9] cannot be used as if it were an independent clinical perspective. Procedures of knowing apart need to fit prospective goals as well as intended course of action.

Diagnostic Variables

Most discussions of diagnosis focus expressly on diagnostic variables, on systems of classification. The concepts and categories of a diagnostic system are often employed as if they correspond ontologically to entities that exist in time and space.[10] Diagnostic concepts and categories, however, are conventions that have the status of hypotheses. Theodore Millon notes that "no classification in psychopathology today 'carves nature at its joints,' that is, is an inevitable representation of the 'real world.' Rather, our classifications are, at best, interim tools for advancing knowledge and facilitating clinical goals."[11] Our interim tools are subject to confirmation, disconfirmation, modification. Aaron Lazare notes that every clinician approaches every interview in light of "partial formulations based on his [or her] previous experience," which become "hypotheses to be tested." "Each new observation can now be considered in terms of its relevance to a limited number of hypotheses under consideration, instead of being one of thousands of possible facts."[12] Millon's comments are again helpful, and deserve to be quoted at length:

> Because the number of ways we can observe, describe, and organize the natural world is infinite, the terms and concepts we create to represent those activities are often confusing and obscure. For example, different words are used to describe the same behavior, and the same word is used for different behaviors. Some terms are narrow in focus, others are broad, and some are difficult to define. Because of the diversity of events to which we can attend, or the lack of precision in the language we employ, different processes are confused and similar events get scattered hodgepodge across

a scientific landscape; as a consequence, communication gets bogged down in terminological obscurities and semantic controversies.

One of the goals of formalizing the phenomena comprising a scientific subject is to avoid this morass of confusion. Not all phenomena related to the subject need be attended to at once. Certain elements may be selected from the vast range of possibilities because they seem relevant to the solution of a specific question. And to create a degree of reliability or consistency among those interested in a subject, its elements are defined as precisely as possible and classified according to their core similarities and differences.[13]

Diagnosing is acting according to particular procedures that are selected precisely because they are relevant to the solution of a particular question. Certain data are selected to solve a particular question. Specific diagnostic variables enhance the likelihood of gathering data through which that question can be answered. The diagnostic variables employed, like the overall clinical activities, reflect an underlying clinical attitude; all express underlying metaphors.

Root Metaphors

Imagine sitting in the room with a person who is present because he is suffering. One observes how he is dressed and how he sits, speaks, and gestures, whether and when he keeps eye contact, and how psychologically articulate he is in describing his suffering. As the conversation unfolds, a series of choices and decisions are made, some consciously, most beyond awareness. One experiences something as something else, recognizes it because one is prepared to see and hear something *as* something.[14] Certain features among the multitude of data are ignored because they do not fit the approach. Procedures differ depending on one's role: attend to him in his crisis, enable him to find appropriate support and help from other professionals or from family and friends, or help him make some major changes in himself and his life. A tacit map guides action, according to which one evaluates how normal his suffering is, what he might expect to do, and how long any process of care and healing might take. For example, do we want to change his patterns of behavior, identify unconscious motives, or modify an erroneous belief system? Operationalized in our diagnostic variables and underlying our attitude are formative root metaphors that capture our vision of person and of care.[15]

Consider the illustration further. Imagine, again, sitting in the room with this suffering man. How is he envisioned? How is the clinical enterprise conceived? Is this person, say, a seed that will grow, and care a process of organic unfolding in which the caretaker is a cultivator-farmer? Is he a pilgrim, and care a journey to some destination with the therapist as a guide? Is he in the throes of labor with the clinician as a midwife in the birthing process? Is he or does he have a story with the clinician as an editor or a coauthor who provides care by assisting in the identifying, telling, and transforming of the story? Is he the host of some disease and the clinician a skillful surgeon whose task is to excise the pathology? Is he a helpless child needing the clinician as a parent-manager to teach him more mature ways of thinking and behaving?

Each of these metaphors both represents and guides an overall theory and practice of clinical care and, in particular, our diagnostic acts and procedures. The cultivator-farmer, the guide, the midwife, the editor, the surgeon, and the parent-manager each wants to know different phenomena for different motives and purposes. Each wants to understand and know in order to act in a particular way. Again, what is known apart is chosen in conjunction with what one intends to do.[16]

Revisioning Diagnosis

Diagnosis needs to be revisioned. In contrast to traditional views, it is not a procedure that is initiated and completed at the outset of care, according to an isolated set of criteria and commitments. It must be understood in an expanded context involving a question, metaphors, a clinical attitude, and variables.

A particular vision of pastoral diagnosis will be examined in conjunction with this question: How can we collaboratively discern and respond to features of another's self and her suffering while authentically representing our pastoral identity and context as we employ the resources of our confessional traditions and those of the human and behavioral sciences in a consistent and coherent manner?

Casting the basic question in this manner intentionally departs from other pastoral as well as nonpastoral approaches to diagnosis.[17] Diagnosis is not a procedure done by and for the clinician. It is not done independently of the client. It does not take place solely at the beginning of care. It does not focus on a particular dimension (such as "mental disorder," "religious phenomena," "faith development," an "implicit creed," or "lived theology"), in terms of the resources of a particular disciplinary framework (such as *DSM IV-R*, psychoanalytic concepts, Piagetian theory, or theological symbols and concepts). Rather, pastoral diagnosis is an ongoing collaborative process of clinician and client companioning the self of the client as she emerges in and through unfolding experience, through an interdisciplinary theological approach—inclusive of confessional and human and behavioral science resources.

In this perspective, as in most approaches to pastoral diagnosis, the clinician engages the client in part through religious and theological concepts and categories. Whether focusing on a psychological analysis of religious phenomena or a diagnosis of faith development, using expressly theological constructs to interpret (all) clinical material, or discerning an implicit creed or an implicit lived theology,[18] most theorists of pastoral diagnosis have proposed that what makes pastoral diagnosis pastoral is the focus on so-called religious phenomena in conjunction with theological concepts.

The approach presented is authentically pastoral in an additional, equally important sense. The care in which the pastoral clinician engages is ministry. That ministry follows from and is an expression of his pastoral-faith identity. Both care-as-ministry and identity are formed and interpreted through theological reflection. Every dimension of the identity, practice, and theory is inherently pastoral-theological.

PASTORAL DIAGNOSING

Many pastoral clinicians regard pastoral diagnosis[19] as an oxymoron with its two terms mixing like oil and water. *Pastoral* implies care of the person; *diagnosis*, in contrast, implies treatment of the disease. Clinicians intent on preserving an uncontaminated vision of pastoral care pride themselves in avoiding diagnosis, maintaining the illusion that if they do not use the term, they are not engaged in the procedures. As a consequence, they do not critically reflect upon and evaluate their actual diagnostic commitments and judgments.

Pastoral clinicians at the other end of the spectrum understand that a sound theory and practice of diagnosis is central to clinical care. In conjunction with this, they may have embraced *DSM IV-R* as a kind of clinical scripture. Usually, these diagnostically sensitive clinicians pursue one of two directions. On the one hand, they diagnose according to this medical perspective and provide ongoing care from a practical theological perspective, while remaining unaware of their fundamentally inconsistent commitments.[20] They become a *doppelgänger*, "a person who inhabits two parallel universes."[21] On the other hand, they may disregard entirely the authentically pastoral contributions of their confessional theological traditions; their practice and theory of care in general, as well as of diagnosis in particular, are secular. In either case, pastoral diagnosis is a misnomer.

Another group of pastoral clinicians understands pastoral diagnosis as theological diagnosis. These practitioners regard religious and theological language not as professional jargon but as a "grammar" appropriate to the everyday life of every person.[22] They operationalize faith, theology, and spirituality and interpret clinical data through and in relation to theological symbols and scriptural stories.[23] Earlier[24] as well as more recent contributions[25] restrict attention, for the most part, to the use of scriptural metaphors and theological constructs, as if including any connections to or conversation with secular concepts and approaches would jeopardize the validity or diminish the significance of their efforts. At the same time, however, using only theological resources is not without its hazards. First and foremost, a pastoral clinician cannot capture all of human experience through only one universe of discourse. Second, a pastoral clinician cannot identify precisely the varieties of suffering through language that tends to characterize human experience in broad strokes and rather abstract terms. Third, a pastoral clinician cannot afford to be isolated from colleagues in the helping professions and from their respective resources and contributions. Pastoral diagnosis is in this approach singularly yet narrowly theological.

Although there are merits as well as liabilities to these respective approaches, none reflects a vision that integrates pastoral-theological and social and human science resources in an authentic, consistent, and coherent manner and that recognizes that the practice and theory of diagnosis are integral to and must be consistent with one's overall perspective of pastoral clinical care. With these concerns in mind, a newly emerging approach is the most promising for our field.

Several contemporary authors characterize pastoral clinical care as an expressly interdisciplinary enterprise that is interpreted through concepts and resources of confessional *and* secular traditions.[26] Every aspect of the theory and practice of pastoral clinical care, including pastoral diagnosis, is interpreted in an interdisciplinary manner. Interestingly, however, except for a comparatively few perspectives,[27] the vast majority of discussions of pastoral diagnosis typically exclude any reference to nonconfessional contributions. The majority of existing literature on pastoral diagnosis, then, is inconsistent with contemporary approaches to pastoral care, counseling, and psychotherapy. This inconsistency not only reflects but also contributes to pastoral clinicians' inclination to continue to isolate pastoral diagnosis from pastoral clinical care.

Pastoral clinicians need a vision of pastoral diagnosis that is consistent with and integral to an interdisciplinary understanding of pastoral clinical care; that encourages and requires incorporating the full range of resources at our disposal in authentic, consistent, and coherent ways; and that is increasingly more valid and reliable.[28] Developing such an integrated vision departs dramatically from the peculiar but standard way most have been trained to characterize diagnosis—as a separate procedure initiated and completed at the outset of care, interpreted through a theory of diagnosis that is independent of a theory of care.

Diagnostic variables. This section examines the client's presentation in terms of the dual focus of self and suffering and the three domains of content, affect, and action. These "close-to-experience"[29] or "experience-near"[30] terms do not confound the territory by introducing abstract concepts and will therefore be more readily compatible with the constructs and categories of the wide variety of pastoral clinical approaches that integrate diverse psychological and confessional resources in differing ways.

The basic dual focus of self and suffering. Regardless of orientation, most clinicians typically focus their attention on a particular constellation or cluster of data, the area of pain, and dysfunction. Whether interpreted in terms of psychic processes, behavioral patterns, cognitive beliefs, or family myths, most clinicians attend to what is wrong or broken, variously labeled "chief complaint," "presenting problem," or "psychopathology." Under the influence of medical practice, we are geared toward identifying a single specific cluster of data, toward developing a picture with the pathology at the center.

Proceeding this way, one grasps the other's pain and dysfunction in breadth and depth, in part by differentiating its essence from a range of alternatives. Often this concerted attention to pathology is achieved at the expense of attention to the person who seeks help. The client may experience a sense of being missed, as if she is an appendage to her pain. The most attention she might receive is being asked to describe her experience of suffering. Then again, she is regarded only through the lens of her illness.

In contrast, one may want to construct and continually modify a picture that is less like a circle than an ellipse, with two foci: Who is this person or, more technically, who is the self of the person? What is the suffering of this person?[31] The mutually informing features of self and suffering are related in a complementary manner, as context and foreground. Understanding a person involves identifying particular expressions and qualities of that person, in and through her suffering. Understanding a person's suffering presupposes identifying the person who suffers in that particular way.[32]

Consider this illustration. A man who recently lost a friend reports feelings of sadness, hopelessness, and despair. One's first concern is less the sadness (recast as a mood disorder) than conveying one's intention to understand as fully as possible who he is and how he hurts.

Functioning as a psychologist-theologian-ethicist in conversation with a psychologist-theologian-ethicist involves listening, interpreting, and translating the client's report of his experience into a variety of language games as well as engaging the client in light of one's various understandings. As a psychologist, one may identify character structure, strengths, recurrent conflicts, deficits, and symptomatology. As a theologian, one may identify how the other may be denying God's presence, action, and participation in unfolding events and replacing God in mistakenly presuming the wisdom, authority, and responsibility to act independently of God. As an ethicist, one may seek to discern the client's and one's own sense of responsibility.

Three central domains: content, affect, action. The pastoral clinician who focuses on the dual features of self and suffering may differentiate among three related domains: content, affect, and action.[33] *Content* refers to the cognitive, ideational dimension of a person's experience, articulated and conveyed verbally. *Affect*, in contrast, is an area of emotions and feelings, usually experienced in bodily sensations, described only gradually and usually only approximately in words. *Action* refers to what is enacted and expressed in and through particular behaviors and patterns of behavior.

1. CONTENT. The most obvious manner of gathering data and formulating a picture or working model of the self and suffering of the other is by way of the content of the person's report.[34] The other's thoughts, ideas, and memories enable understanding what is currently wrong and constructing a picture or model of who that other is. Many open the process of information gathering by focusing on the other's suffering and asking simply, What hurts? or, more elaborately, Can you tell me a little about what is happening that brings you to meet with me?

One should be equally intentional in gathering data about the other's self. Bear in mind the rather simple question, What feature of the person's presentation seems to capture and represent symbolically something fundamental or pivotal about the other's self? Imagine, for example, that after an initial meeting, one consults with a colleague. During the course of the consultation, one wants to orient the colleague's attention to a particular quality or feature of the person's presentation that somehow seems to be quintessential or prototypical. For example, one might recall that the client's shoulders were remarkably rounded, her posture sagging, as if to convey that she's carrying too heavy a burden; or one might recall that she wears her hair in such a way that one can never really see her face, as if not wanting to be seen; or one could identify an image of her sitting on the edge of her chair and infer needing to hear a word of comfort.

Gathering data involves constructing an organized model of the self. "The whole direction of the therapist's effort is toward elaboration of the full context of meaning in which the whole range of data that he has gathered about the patient falls into a consistent, coherent, and intelligible pattern."[35] Norman Holland suggests a helpful way of thinking about that "consistent, coherent, and intelligible pattern," that "working model" of the other:

> One way of wording that characteristic direction or pattern . . . is to formulate a human identity as a theme with variations. That is, if we imagine a human life as a dialectic between sameness and difference, we can think of the sameness, the continuity of personal style, as a theme; we can think of the changes as variations on that theme. I can understand another person as living out changes and variations on a persistent core just as a musician might play out an infinity of variations on a single melody, as a mathematician might generate a myriad of functions from a single variable, or as a linguist might transform one kernel sentence into hundreds of different utterances.[36]

Alongside formulating a picture of the self, one needs to construct a picture of the other's suffering. What does he mean by *sadness?* What does he experience that he describes that way? This tactic serves several purposes as it conveys several messages. First, it encourages the person to specify, as carefully as possible, what he is experiencing. Second, it heightens the client's awareness that words do not correspond to universally shared emotional states but are terms in his personal lexicon available to describe some experience. Furthermore, the client will realize that these terms conceal and obfuscate as well as disclose.

Appreciating some of the quality of someone's sadness requires understanding its history and course. When inquiring, How long have you been feeling this sadness? we enlist the client to elucidate features of his diagnosis. Is it something that just began? Is it lifelong? What was taking place when the suffering began? Understanding what *sad* and *empty* and *depressed* have come to mean involves identifying three features of the origins of these feelings: the context, the precipitants of the suffering, and the precipitants of the request for help. What was happening at the time when you first experienced feeling sad? What in particular precipitated, provoked, or caused your sadness? What in particular precipitated or prompted your seeking help?

As a psychoanalytically informed clinician, one presumes that much of what a person experiences reflects continuing the past in the present—unconsciously repeating particular patterns of expectation or unconsciously reenacting patterns of relationship. If the present experience is, in part, a repetition of the past, the precipitants both of the experience of suffering and of the request for help are themselves repetitions. One might inquire, What, in particular, contributed to what had been a more or less balanced self to become more injured, more out of balance? (The nature of that event again informs us about how the self is made and what past history has been like.) What, in particular, contributed to what had been an injured self to have the need—and the hope—of restored balance? The nature of this moment, of this event, gives us clues about past experiences of seeking care and thus about the way in which the self is built.

Discerning what precipitated a person's seeking help contributes to identifying what made that help not only necessary but also possible. Informing us about how they have experienced help in the past alerts one that the client likely approaches with the expectation that the clinician will respond in a similar manner. Precise exploration is needed: What did you hope, expect, or anticipate that I might do, or how I might be, that would make a difference? One may formulate hypotheses not only about how the client has gotten help in the past but also about the nature and makeup of the self who engages others in particular ways. For example, the client might respond, "I thought by just getting these things out with a sounding board that I'd feel some relief." Talking or catharsis helps. She also reveals, however, that care is a rather impersonal or depersonalized process between someone who gets relief from getting things out and someone who is just a sounding board. How different the impression would be of a client who responded, "I know there are ways in which I've gotten depressed and felt lost when I've lost someone who feels like a part of me, and I've found it helpful for someone to help me identify why I am stuck in this pattern." This response reveals someone who is able to connect this experience with similar experiences, to experience a pattern, wherein another will help her discern something she is unable to know alone.

One may also presume that a person's decision to meet with a particular clinician involves some kind of repetition. One may explore past experiences and current expectations with such questions as, How did you come to the decision to see me in particular? What do you know of me, of what I do, that contributed to your seeking me out? The person might respond, "I've heard that you're a warm and sensitive person, someone 'pastoral,' and I felt safer with that than with someone who might challenge me or hurt me." This individual has learned that he needs to be protected from the prospect of being confronted and injured by someone. Were he to have said, "I would rather come to a pastoral counselor than a secular therapist, because I trust that God will be present in our work," one learns that God is a part of the other's experience. The client also implies that God is not present in work with nonpastoral caregivers and possibly that there is a special, even magical way in which being pastoral invokes God's presence.

Because assessments of the person's current state are intimately connected to formulating goals of care, one should explore what the person hopes and intends to accomplish through prospective work by asking such questions as, What objectives do you have for our work? What do you hope to achieve or attain? What do you anticipate you will experience that will serve as a clue or signal that you have attained what we have worked for and are ready to begin preparation to end our work together? The person might respond, "I just want to feel better about myself." An inability to specify what that might mean reveals how his interior life may be rather colorless; one would want to assess to what degree that expressed a trait or state, was characterological or situational, chronic or acute.

While enlisting the person to collaborate in diagnosing and in formulating goals, one also explores how the other envisions moving from where she is to some desired place. "How might we work together in a way that you anticipate will help?"[37] The response about getting things out with a sounding board indicates an implicit plan. One may inquire if she has found that to be helpful in the past.

Each of these series of questions inevitably leads clinician and client to move readily across time and space, examining in the here-and-now in conjunction with past experience. Through that, one can formulate a history of the suffering in the context of a history of the self. One way of proceeding would be to ask the person to provide an overview of her life, beginning with earliest memories and moving through time to include memories that come to mind that are important to her and her story. The client could be asked to include some understanding of her family, the relationships among family members, and how one can understand who she is by how she fits (and does not fit) within that family context. Throughout, one may note themes and variations that emerge and listen for the client's own working model of self.

Implicit in the questioning are hidden communications about the clinician's attitude and method of care. Although not verbalized directly, one may convey some of the following messages:

> We need to take care in identifying as fully as possible who you are and what you are experiencing. While I might have some basic knowledge about persons, and about clinical care, I am ignorant of who you are and need your help to help you. Together we will judge what is wrong, consider the goals of our work, and plan a course of intervention. It is important that we identify how what I understand you to imply—what I infer—plays an important part in our making sense of what is happening and what to do: What is beyond the obvious, what might be hidden, is very relevant. I respect your way of experiencing and describing things and will honor what you want to do and how you envision doing that, but I want to proceed carefully and sensitively, so that we work collaboratively enough, even though you might experience me not only as an ally but also as an adversary.

In a collaborative process, the clinician is not an objective data gatherer who in her wisdom and expertise magically arrives at a masterful private assessment that empowers her to act in some way with or on the client. Rather, the clinician should be presenting to the client what she is identifying and how that is being put together. The client could hear how he was heard and could correct the hypothesizing. As he contributes to re-shaping the clinician's picture, he is also implicitly, if not explicitly, challenging and enhancing his own picture of himself and his suffering. Ultimately the questions, Why? Why now? From when? To where? are relevant to every moment of every session. They contribute to what and how we know apart.

2. AFFECT. Another central domain of every person's self and suffering is the affect she experiences. *Affect* refers to the feeling tone, the emotional flavor of a person's self-presentation and self-report. A person might remark quite directly, "I feel sad and overwhelmed." She might convey sadness in her posture, her facial expression, her tone of voice, her movements. She might betray sadness by provoking in the clinician a sense of sadness while simultaneously conveying little directly about how she feels in her words and actions.

Regardless of how it is communicated, attending to and understanding affect are a central project of effective clinical care: Every thought and every action of every person are not only influenced but also motivated by affect.[38] We engage in behaviors, establish relationships, and pursue activities that are likely to enhance our experiencing positive feelings and minimizing negative feelings. Most important, we experience, perceive, and apprehend in a manner that enables us to enhance positive feelings and minimize negative feelings. We deny, repress, select out of awareness painful memories, or the pain of some memories. We select out of awareness features of current experience that might evoke pain. We select out of awareness features of the future that might precipitate pain, frequently by protecting ourselves from anticipated dangers by limiting our actions and relationships.

Affect motivates all thinking and action. "Sometimes thoughtful therapists are dismayed when patients candidly acknowledge that insight is not their primary goal in psychotherapy; they just want to feel better. Actually, such comments are closer to the affectual wishes that bring people to seek the help of a therapist."[39] Our concern, then, is to be able to appreciate and grasp her affect. One way to accomplish this task is by encouraging and enabling the person to describe her feelings more and more accurately.

Describing feelings accurately is inherently difficult, for a variety of reasons. Affect is a dimension of human experience that is present from birth and that becomes patterned in quality, shape, and meaning from an early age. Our affective experience is, as research reveals, initially a genetically encoded reflex phenomenon.[40] In a manner similar to other reflex actions, such as the knee jerk or blinking, this response does not involve any reflective evaluation of what precipitated its occurrence: It "just happens." Often it seems that, even as adults, we feel something and only subsequently identify what stimulated our response and why we responded that way. Our earliest and most enduring experiences of affective states, then, are of patterned, reflexive, preverbal moods that happen to us.

Daniel Stern has found it helpful and necessary to discriminate between two fundamentally different kinds of affective experience: category affects and vitality affects. He suggests that we usually understand affective experience in terms of discrete categories, such as "happiness, sadness, fear, anger, disgust, surprise, interest, and perhaps shame, and their combinations." We also typically attend to two different dimensions: activation and hedonic tone. By *activation,* we mean the intensity or urgency of the feeling; by *hedonic,* the degree to which the feeling quality is pleasurable or unpleasurable.[41]

Vitality affects, according to Stern, may occur independently of or in conjunction with categorical affects:

> The expressiveness of vitality affects can be likened to that of a puppet show. The puppets have little or no capacity to express categories of affect by way of facial signals, and their repertoire of conventionalized gestural or postural affect signals is usually impoverished. It is from the way they move in general that we infer the different vitality affects from the activation contours they trace. Most often, the characters of different puppets are largely defined in terms of particular vitality affects; one may be lethargic, with drooping limbs and hanging head, another forceful, and still another jaunty.[42]

Affects confront us in patterned, reflexive ways and are embedded in our experience and memory in a preverbal way. Gradually, of course, we acquire the capacity to communicate in words, to become verbal, and have by this time a preverbal history and storehouse of affective experience and patterns. But language is a double-edged sword: "It drives a wedge between two simultaneous forms of interpersonal experience: as it is lived and as it is verbally represented."[43] Interpersonal experience has a history, before it becomes verbally represented. "There is a stretch of time in which rich experiential knowledge 'in there' is accumulated, which somehow will later get assembled (although not totally) with a verbal code, language."[44] As these comments indicate, we lead "two lives . . . original life as nonverbal experience and a life that is a verbalized version of that experience."[45]

As Stern explains, there are many ways in which language is not adequate to the task of communicating about lived experience. "Points of slippage" occur, one of which is in the realm of internal states, because "affect as a form of personal knowledge is very hard to put into words and communicate."[46] What is true of "original global experience" is thus true of affective states:

> Several different relationships can exist between nonverbal global experience and that part of it that has been transformed into words. At times, the piece that language separates out is quintessential and captures the whole experience beautifully. Language is generally thought to function in this "ideal" way, but in fact it rarely does, and we will have the least to say about this. At other times the language version and the globally experienced version do not coexist well. The global experience may be fractured or simply poorly represented, in which case it wanders off to lead a misnamed and poorly understood existence. And finally, some global experiences . . . do not permit language sufficient entry to separate out a piece for linguistic transformation. Such experiences then simply continue underground, nonverbalized, to lead an unnamed (and, to that extent only, unknown) but nonetheless very real existence.[47]

Through language we may be able to describe accurately qualities of certain internal states. We may be able to describe only poorly, or not at all, qualities of other internal states: Certain felt experiences remain at the limit of or beyond description.

As we acquire the capacity to be verbal and to describe internal states, our experience of affect undergoes developmental, maturational shifts to what Michael Basch calls *feeling* and subsequently *emotion*. Affect becomes feeling "when the involuntary basic affective reaction begins to be related to a concept of the self." "Emotion, a further step in affective maturation, results when feeling states are joined with experience to give personal meaning to complex concepts such as love, hate, and happiness."[48]

One way of understanding this evolution of affect-feeling-emotion is in the gradual acquisition of a way of identifying and making certain states of experience meaningful, through which they are owned as part of, expressions of, a self. By doing so, the self attains a sense of connection and possibly of mastery. Typically, the process of identifying and making meaningful involves, or essentially amounts to, the process of putting experience into words. But this procedure of putting experience into words is, as we have seen, a hazardous one.

Prior to language, all of one's behaviors have equal status as far as "ownership" is concerned. With the advent of language, some behaviors now have a privileged status with regard to one having to own them. The many messages in many channels are being fragmented by language into a hierarchy of accountability-deniability.[49]

Some affect-feeling-emotion is known and owned, and some is unknown and disowned. Thus, our effort to discern and identify the affect-feeling-emotion of any other person, of any client, is as central to our healing enterprise as it is magnificently difficult. Affects are at the heart of motivation for all thinking and acting. Affects are, at the same time, extraordinarily difficult to capture, express, and modify, although that is at the center of our work.

One should presume considerable slippage between vocabulary and felt experience, and in the area of affect and feelings such slippage is most acute. Thus, at all times one should seek to be present to and with another in their unnameable affect, appreciating how feeling states can be understood and shared apart from words. At other times one might modify this slippage by helping the person develop a more extensive "personal vocabulary of affect." Roth notes,

> It has been my observation that for most people, the most significant change in psychotherapy—the product of insight as contrasted with the process of insight—is the suppression and repression of the moment-to-moment insights of treatment and their replacement by an altered, condensed, sustained affective state. This affective state is the crystallization of the personality changes achieved through the therapeutic process. It is reflected in an altered, basic characterological mood, dispositions to mood and affect, and new capacities to acknowledge, bear, and experience affective states.[50]

A person would be helped to achieve "an altered, basic characterological mood, dispositions to mood and affect, and new capacities to acknowledge, bear, and experience affective states" by experiencing the collaborative presence of the clinician, at times in the experience of unnamed sharing and intuitive understanding and at other times in identifying and describing painful emotional states that led the person to seek and continue to need help.

3 ACTION. *Action* refers to the ways in which persons disclose features of self and suffering through patterns of behavior. Action involves the process of the engagement and the pattern of the clinical relationship.

The Process of the Engagement. Compare the following scenarios, keeping in mind the question, What does this reveal about self and suffering? A woman contacts a clinician through an emergency service late at night and asks to be called as soon as possible. She reports having got this clinician's name from an acquaintance several weeks ago and had not wanted to call until she absolutely had to. She says she feels desperate and alone. When she meets the clinician the following evening, she is agitated and launches into what is happening. She speaks at a frantic pace, with little eye contact, as if gathering steam. She leaves little space for questions, comments, or observations. She appears exhausted by the end of the initial meeting and uncertain about what to do. After meeting several times for purposes of evaluation, they agree to meet weekly. As work proceeds, she reveals a ritualized style: Each hour is filled with ideas that seem to have some apparent connection to her but seem tangential to the clinician. Each meeting has a frantic pace, as if filling up the time, making sure everything that needs to be said is said, and getting everything out.

Others also approach this clinician. A man appears at the clinician's office without an appointment and sits in the waiting room for several hours while a series of clients enter and depart. He returns the following day, says nothing until asked, and then reveals that he did not want to be alone, wanted to find out what therapy was all about, and did not know how to get in. An initial appointment is then made for the following day. He arrives twenty minutes late and says that an emergency came up suddenly at home. He says he does not know what to say or where to begin and repeatedly looks at the clinician for direction. After meeting with him to assess the nature and history of his suffering, the clinician agrees to meet. The man begins each hour in silence, after several minutes remarking, "I really don't know what to say." Although he seeks encouragement and follows suggestions, he contributes little of his own initiative.

Consider another of this clinician's contacts. A man calls during working hours, asking if it would be possible to meet. He says he is sad and overwhelmed and wonders if it would be possible to have home visits. He says that being seen going to a clinician would make him feel uncomfortable. With some firm encouragement, he reluctantly agrees to meet in the office in a few days. Although he appears forthright at the outset, he rarely responds directly to any of the clinician's initial questions, instead choosing to report things that he hopes will aid in understanding. A couple of times he remarks, "I think you'd really get to know and understand me if you would see me in my home." Nevertheless, the clinician and he agree to work together in the office. Soon the clinician becomes aware that these meetings have a pattern. The man begins each hour remarking about the weather and describes what he is wearing that keeps him protected from the elements. He then asks how the clinician is and whether the fluctuations in weather have been bothersome. He goes on, slowly, almost painstakingly, to talk about what would be seen were the visit to occur in his home. He deflects any observations about how his tone of voice sounds so sad, about how important it is for him to be understood through his home.

The process of the time together reveals a lot about the self and the suffering of each individual client. In the first scenario, the woman can come only when things are beyond her ability to manage, and then she uses the time frantically and desperately to get things out. It makes us wonder about why she withheld care for herself for so long, as if she did not deserve it. Can she ask for help only in emergencies? Is she afraid that no one will respond to her unless she presents in an emergency? Is she aware that her presumptuousness in calling so late and dumping so much on the clinician alienates the caretaker from being as present as he might be?

In the second scenario, the man is lost and forlorn, presenting like a child who does not know where to go or how to get there. How has he survived this long? Who was his deceased spouse, who had enabled him to survive? What is lacking in his childhood that leads him to require another to supply direction?

In the third scenario, the man needs protection. He senses an inability to communicate who he is and what he is needing, as if he will be unable to help the clinician to understand him. Even though he wants to be seen, he has to protect himself and hide from inquiries and observations about how he is experiencing his loss.

As these scenarios illustrate, persons reveal much about who they are and how they hurt by the very process of contact and ongoing work. The data discerned from the process can be used to amplify and enhance the pictures and hypotheses one is formulating, while taking into account the content and affect presented. Content, affect, and process are not categories that exist independently of one another. Rather, each of these dimensions or domains is mutually informing entrances into the self and the suffering of the self, which together contribute to constructing an accurate and useful understanding with and for the client.

Relationship. A person conveys essential aspects about her self and suffering through a second area of "action," in the relationship that is formed between that person and the clinician. The various literatures on care, counseling, and psychotherapy abound with discussions of the helping relationship. The following account focuses on one aspect of the clinical relationship as it is characterized in psychoanalytic theorizing, particularly in the psychoanalytic psychology of the self.

Psychoanalytically oriented theorists differentiate among various co-existing dimensions of a clinical relationship: the real relationship, the classical transference, the narcissistic transference, and the working alliance. In this context, psychoanalytically informed care centers around the identification and working through of the transference. Like all psychoanalytic concepts, however, transference has been described and defined in innumerable ways. Consider the following view: *Transference* refers to the clinician's interpretation of certain features of the client's perception, understanding, and experience of the clinician that the clinician regards to be distorted, biased, inappropriate, or having to do more with the client than with the clinician and having more to do with the reexperience/reenactment of patterns of perception, experience, and relationship with past significant figures, of which the client is not fully aware.

A clinician's hypothesizing may take different formulations: In a more classical approach, the clinician might attend to ways in which she is experienced and related to as if she were a person or were in part reminiscent of a person from the client's past. In theoretical terms, the clinician is experienced through the object representations of a past person or persons. In an object relations approach, the focus shifts to the experience and reenactment of a pattern of relating: How are the relationship and the respective roles enacted in the pattern of a past relationship? The internalized object relations (rather than the singular object representation per se) provide the schema through which to understand the reenactment of the past in the present. In a self psychological perspective, the clinician maintains a consistent focus on the ongoing experience of the self of the client and observes ways in which that client experiences the other, or the relationship.[51]

Formulating this description of transference takes into account a number of important issues. First, because a clinician is a participant-observer (i.e., is part of the field of observation), she never attains an ultimately objective understanding of anything that occurs. All her interpretations, including interpreting certain phenomena as transference, have the status of hypotheses. They require verification, are subject to disconfirmation or falsification, and require ongoing collaborative exploration. Second, the hypotheses about transference represent the totality of neither the clinical relationship nor the client's experience of the clinician and the relationship: Transference refers to certain limited dimensions or qualities. Third, by familiarity with the clinician's own personality by means of her own therapy experiences and by becoming increasingly familiar with how she is experienced as a clinician, the clinician develops a sense of a *baseline*. In conjunction with this norm, the clinician at times hypothesizes that certain features of the client's experience are distorted. Fourth, the judgment that certain perceptions or experiences have more to do with the client than with the clinician is always an assessment of relative proportions. Fifth, the hypothesis about a reexperience of past figures refers to the genetic and adaptive points of view: One makes sense of the present in terms of the past. To put it differently, one assumes that the client has learned to experience people in a certain way and that it is appropriate and beneficial to explore the nature, problems, and limitations of that learning. Finally, the claim, "of which the client is less than fully aware," refers to the topographic point of view: the client is not aware that what he is experiencing says as much if not more about himself than about what is out there. One presumes that the client is unaware because awareness causes unpleasure or pain: He does not entirely want to be or become aware of what he has kept from consciousness. This, then, assumes both the dynamic and economic points of view: The client wishes to reveal and conceal.

Like all major concepts in psychoanalytic theory and practice, transference has been understood in a variety of ways. Heinz Kohut and Philip Seitz have drawn from Freud's *The Interpretation of Dreams* to develop a metapsychological understanding. Transference as a metapsychological concept refers to an internal, intrapsychic process wherein unconscious, repressed, primary process materials are amalgamated with conscious, secondary process contents.[52] Approaching transference as a metapsychological concept has several important implications. First, transference is understood to refer to intrapsychic processes that occur within a person's mind. As a consequence, all of what unfolds and is enacted between the participants is interpreted intrapsychically from the point of view of the internal world of the client.[53] Thus, for example, a client experiences the clinician as cold and distant, in some ways reminiscent of his father. The clinician is a new object in the current interpersonal world that is experienced as the old object in the past interpersonal world.[54] Yet this experience represents an interpersonalized expression of intrapsychic processes: What is happening within his mind is being engaged in a repetitive pattern, now precipitated and enacted interpersonally. The interpersonalized experience is significant in the ways in which it reveals how his intrapsychic world is constructed.

In addition to focusing attention on intrapsychic processes, understanding transference as a metapsychological concept also enables us to appreciate that transference is an ever-present psychic activity. Freud noted this when he spoke of transference as "a universal phenomenon of the human mind."[55] One need not await dramatic, fully formed expressions of the transference but be sensitive to transference reactions, moment to moment. They are more or less ever present.[56]

Thinking about transference as a metapsychological concept referring to a particular kind of ever-present intrapsychic process offers a third implication. A self's ongoing experience is usually "like Janus, two-faced, with one face turned to the past, the other to the present."[57] In theoretical terms, transference is an amalgamation of unconscious and conscious, primary process and secondary process, past and present.[58] By definition, then, it involves what is real and current as well as what is inaccurate and past. Experience is a compound phenomenon, a compromise formation, elements from past blended with elements from the present, features that are reasonable and plausible joined with dimensions that are unconscious and irrational.[59]

Inherent in this understanding is the recognition of transference as a blend of conscious and unconscious. Transference expresses what can be known, what is acceptable to consciousness in conjunction with what has been relegated to unconsciousness, because it is unacceptable and in part painful. Transference expresses revealing-concealing. There is inherent "resistance to the awareness of the transference" as well as "resistance to the working through of the transference."[60]

Kohut's writings have added considerably to our capacity to recognize certain phenomena as expressions of transference. He proposes approaching the client as a self that seeks restoration of equilibrium, cohesiveness, and self-esteem through including another in the self as self-object, as a part or extension of the self of the client. Observing the relationship involves identifying the function or functions the clinician is providing for the client that the client is unable to provide on her own behalf. In other words, the clinician is able to recognize the structural deficits in the client's self, what was not internalized. One then infers something about the nature and quality of the selves with whom the client had relationships that failed to afford the opportunity to build a self that included those psychic functions.

For example, a woman who has recently lost an important person is hopeless and despairing. The clinician feels drained through the process of the interview, exhausted by the conversation. Usually after the fact, the clinician becomes aware of having to provide something—energy, vitality—that the client lacks. As the work progresses, she indicates that this is not the first time she has lost someone dear to her. In remembering past losses, she posits the idea that these losses were justified because something was wrong with her: She did not deserve to be happy and was supposed to suffer. Periodically the clinician feels almost compelled to contradict her self-accusations and try to make her feel better. The clinician unconsciously and uncharacteristically extends the time of the initial consultation, as if to provide some attention, even affection.

In attending to the transference and through that to the unique dimensions of the relationship that convey features of the client's self, one assumes a fundamental connection among different expressions of self and suffering: across content, affect, process, and relationship. Most especially, one expects statements about suffering will be enacted in the relationship. To extend the example, in what ways will the client enact the fear of losing the clinician and the shame of not feeling deserving of the clinician's attention or warmth?

Diagnosis and care are significantly enhanced when how the client enacts suffering is taken into account. In fact, Kohut argues that "the crucial diagnostic criterion is to be based not on the evaluation of the presenting symptomatology or even of the life history, but on the nature of the spontaneously developing transference."[61] This argument brings into dramatic focus how both clinician and client can understand most fully and deeply who the client is and what she is suffering when they can observe relevant data firsthand, in the room, in the relationship.

FORMULATING GOALS

The elements of the triad of clinical activities are interpenetrating. Formulating goals is not only informed by but is informing of diagnosing. This section examines an element—goals—that has been implied throughout and only occasionally discussed directly. This element is distinguishable but not separable from the other elements.

Although using the term *goal* to signify the end state of the process to which the clinician and client orient movement, goals need constantly to be reevaluated: Where we are going is a function of where we are. A person initiating a clinical relationship and process has a particular self-understanding and way of making sense of what is wrong, what hurts. For example, a man who states simply, "I'm anxious—I want you to do something so that I'm no longer anxious," has a pointed but imprecise goal because he lacks clarity regarding his current state.

As he continues conversations, however, he appreciates more fully that his anxiety is a chronic condition that emerges periodically. He traces its origins to his childhood in a dysfunctional family. He recovers memories of having been abused and withdrawing into his room when his father returned home from an alcoholic binge. He recalls turning to an imaginary playmate and even praying in his distress that someone would take his feelings away so that he could relax. As he more fully appreciates who he is and how he is suffering, his ability to redescribe what he is seeking is enhanced. He realizes that the most he could have hoped for, until this time, was for someone to do something to or for him so that he would feel better. He now recognizes connections between his past life and his present experience. He senses that his anxiety is not totally uncaused. He feels empowered, liberated by the ability to identify what precipitates experiences of danger; he can actively choose to avoid some situations and modify others. This context describes the goal of clinical care as developing more satisfying relationships with friends. At the same time, he fails to understand why he has been living such an isolated existence.

As he pursues conversations further, he becomes more directly aware of an element of the clinical relationship that had been present from the beginning, but much more manageable and therefore irrelevant. He is convinced that the clinician will hurt him, does not have his interests in mind, and does not want him to succeed. He considers terminating, noting that he has already achieved maybe as much as he can.

Client and clinician explore the connections between the man's experience with the clinician, others, and his father. He recognizes a grid brought to the work, a way of making sense of the clinician. He becomes confused: The clinician does not react in a degrading or abusive manner, even when regarded and treated as if she were a degrading, abusive man. In fact, she seems supportive and concerned.

Coincidentally, his appreciation of his self and his suffering has deepened, as has his understanding of the goal of our work. He becomes increasingly more convinced that the clinician will not sabotage his growth. As he feels more hopeful about his future, in conjunction with reporting that his acquaintances are becoming truer friends, he talks about stopping when he feels sufficiently convinced that these developing friendships will provide the sustenance and care he has sought all along and that he no longer has to find it primarily with the clinician.

As his understanding of himself and his suffering has changed, he is less concerned with the simple thought of doing something to or for him so that he won't feel anxious and he is no longer intent on seeking people to do things with. Rather, he is reoriented in his relations with himself and with others. In a way, he is a different self, with different suffering, seeking different goals.

Persons reveal who they are through the expression of the goals they are seeking. They disclose "This is who I can become" and "This is who I want to become." In a sense, they designate what is possible as well as what is optimal or ideal. As the preceding scenario illustrates, these indices are mutually informing and reciprocally related. Every clinical process, then, can be thought about in terms of monitoring the changes in the client's understanding of the actual (this is who I am), the possible (this is who I can be), and the ideal (this is who I want/ought to be). In addition, every clinical process can be thought of as monitoring the changes in the client's understanding of the relationships between the judgments of what is actual, possible, and ideal.[62]

The clinical relationship and process are imbued through and through with normative judgments. What are the criteria of the possible and of the ideal? From what sources or authorities do these criteria emerge? Who makes the judgments about these criteria? How does one adjudicate the competition and conflict between the client's understanding and the clinician's?

Reflecting on the general direction as well as the particular form a person's goals take exposes the unusually explicit overlap between descriptive and normative judgments. Who a person might become (what is possible) is assessed in conjunction with who a person should become (what is obligational, what is responsible). When we ask, Toward what *telos* should we move? In what direction should we orient? the responses require theological and ethical as well as psychological interpretation.

Frequently, the general direction and the specific form can be represented in images of particular idealized figures or metaphors. One desires to emulate Jesus or a disciple or some famous historical figure. In contrast, goals can be characterized through metaphors such as wholeness or holiness, balance or harmony. Further, a vision of the virtuous person or central principles, such as being able to fulfill the two great commandments, can express a goal.

Theological and ethical literatures as well as psychological writings abound with images of human fulfillment. Interpretations of salvation, perfection, sanctification, faith, holiness, and spirituality, as well as discussions of ethics and responsibility, character and virtue, provide relevant input. Not insignificantly, implicit normative visions in the positive cultures of some contemporary psychologies can also be discerned.[63]

In much the same way that no person functions exclusively in one identity—as psychologist or as theologian—our perspectives through which we make sense of ourselves and others bear the influence of many literatures. This diversity necessitates critical reflection on the implicit as well as explicit directions and goals of theory and practice, as well as consideration of the ways they are informed by an authentic understanding of the Christian tradition and are the consequences of a consistent and coherent conversation among the Christian tradition, cultural information, and personal experience.

Some are convinced of the efficacy of an eductive approach and are client-centered not only in process but also in direction and goals. The client knows what is best. Others realize that every person subtly and not so subtly imposes her subjectivity. Still others believe that the clinician has the ability, the authority, and the responsibility to designate possible and ideal goals for the client.[64]

Collaboratively formulating goals is an interdisciplinary task. Psychologically, it involves developing the capacity to be empathic with selves—with other selves, as well as with one's self. Ethically, healing involves developing the capacity to engage others as an end in themselves, as a Thou, to act expressing agape. Theologically, it involves developing the capacity to mediate the love, acceptance, and forgiveness that were first given to us. Medically, it involves developing the capacity to deal with pathology, which may mean the cessation of pathology or the appropriate acceptance of pathology.

Healing as a process of enhancing well-being involves developing the capacity to deal with suffering, which may require seeking reasonable and appropriate ways of ending suffering, whenever possible. It may also mean seeking reasonable ways of accepting suffering, whenever necessary or inevitable.

Discriminating between goals that are reasonable for clinical intervention and life goals is crucial.[65] A person seeking help may articulate objectives that are more akin to ultimate goals for his lifetime. Given that pastoral clinical care is of limited duration, the goals of care must be concrete and reasonably attainable.

Although the point may be self-evident, healing is not a singular process, taking place in a singular dimension, to be interpreted along the lines of one variable. Healing is not identical for every self. Some persons are content-oriented, wanting to develop new ideas, put things in a new perspective, and gain some mastery and control by virtue of knowing. Others are more concerned to change their mood, to diminish the intensity and depth of anxiety and/or depression. They may achieve such by developing ways of describing felt experience more accurately. Others are particularly intent on acting in new and different ways.

For some, change may involve identifying and transforming root metaphors embedded in foundational narratives. For others, change may revolve around functioning differently as psychologists, theologians, and ethicists, in part because they have been engaged—and can engage themselves and others—in conversation in light of these various identities. Given that the self is intersecting-overlapping and that a self is in relationships and *is* relationships, healing the self is healing relationships.

ESTABLISHING A COURSE OF INTERVENTION

Developing a plan is essentially identifying the linkage between current state and end-state. The limitations of personality, expertise, time, energy, and other resources influence to what degree the respective parties are willing and able to formulate and revise their approaches. It is crucial that the plan of care genuinely connects the diagnosis with the goals and that judgments about each accurately fit the needs and capacities of the client, the abilities of the clinician, and the collaborative relationship.[66]

Consider again the different scenarios presented earlier. One woman contacts us late at night, through our emergency service. Although she has had our number for several weeks, she has waited until she had to call, seemingly unaware of how her choice of time had any impact on us. She feels quite desperate and alone, and we meet at the earliest possible time. Hours are filled with her frantic narration, with little interaction. What appears most important to her is simply getting things out.

In some ways, the dominant features of this woman's presentation of her self and her suffering emerge in action, in the process of engagement in the relationship. The affect of feeling desperate and alone, as amplified by the content of her narrations, primarily serves to deepen our grasp of some of what she requires. She appears unable to indicate anything about reasonable goals for one's work, other than getting things out. Caught inside this need, she is unable to articulate clearly any of what that might mean.

She needs the other to provide a presence, a willingness simply to listen and see. Others fail to fill this need for her, and she cannot provide it for herself. This deficit in her self reveals failures in her past experience, particularly in childhood, where she might have internalized a capacity to listen and hear herself and a capacity to enlist others to do that well with her.

Being present as she gets things out will contribute to her stabilizing, calming down, and feeling less desperate and alone. Questions remain about her ability and willingness to examine how she got into such desperate straits as well as how she has frequently sought help for crises. A clinician could agree to meet to provide what she is aware of needing, while also observing her longing not only to survive but also to recover and heal in a manner that would leave her less prone to recurrence.

A plan of treatment involves attending to her experience as she becomes potentially more aware of deeper problems and deeper requests than she is yet able to express. She is unavailable for any kind of intervention beyond providing understanding. Exploratory questions about how she might find support and comfort in some of her friends, family, neighborhood, and church community are simply deflected. Subsequent to her regaining her balance, a new goal and plan would be formulated. In a sense, then, the plan of care is to support her in the manner she requests yet to attend to preconscious material in the hope of establishing a clearer series of goals and a revised plan.

Another person seems like a lost child who does not know where to go or how to get there. He appears in the waiting room and watches a series of clients enter and leave. Aside from making a physical appearance, he takes no initiative to request an appointment. In initial meetings, he discloses little except to convey how lost he feels since his friend's death.

Negotiating a delicate balance is required. He needs to be found, to have someone guide him out of this isolated territory. He needs the conversation time structured and clear guidance in managing his daily routine. (Too readily providing what is missing has liabilities, however.) One might observe that he appears to need another person to figure out where he is and lead him to another place. He must collaborate in formulating goals and a plan. One should be particularly attentive to his still, small voice, presuming that by helping him hear himself he will gradually speak more articulately and forcefully.

A third person presents a peculiar request: to be seen in his home. Given how uncomfortable he feels about being seen asking for help, he considers his request legitimate. Much of his conversation feels tangential, yet heavily symbolic, as when he talks about needing to be protected from the elements. He conveys the sense that he is so vulnerable that he could easily be hurt more. The plan of care is initiated from the outset; the clinician is firm with him about meeting in the office. Concerned to have him come out from the safety and isolation of his home, his clinician appreciates yet challenges his fear.

6

The Two Questions

Theory of Change [handwritten annotation]

wo questions central to pastoral clinical care have been addressed: What is pastoral psychotherapy? and How does pastoral psychotherapy heal? That is, what is it that we do? And how does it work? Addressing these questions and the questions behind them has suggested the structure of this book.

Answers to the two questions assume an interpretation of basic clinical activities that others may not share. Before addressing these questions, we need to consider the prior question, What are our basic clinical activities? The triad of clinical activities was presented as an expression of— a way of operationalizing—something integral to the ongoing process and relationship: the clinician's attitude. That attitude was regarded as an expression of underlying judgments and commitments that a clinician has made about persons, about who we are to be and become: a theological anthropology. Finally, formulating a theological anthropology presupposes a particular vision of doing theology.

Certain basic assumptions inform the discussion. First, there are, to adapt William James's phrase, varieties of suffering experience and varieties of healing experience.[1] Formulating an interpretation of healing that does not take this diversity seriously is a wrong-headed enterprise.[2] Thus every client, every clinician, and every clinical relationship are unique.[3]

Second, each person functions according to her own experience and understanding of healing, what we might call an operative theory of change. Glimpses of another's theory are available through exploring the other's diagnosis, goals, and plan of care.

Third, healing is not something that simply happens or is done to or for another. Rather, it is a collaborative activity in which the pastoral clinician participates with the other, in ways reflecting their respective theories of change, and in which collaborating provides the occasion for healing. Participating with another presupposes an immediate felt sense of the other's understanding of healing.

ANSWERING THE TWO QUESTIONS

What Is Pastoral Psychotherapy?

Pastoral psychotherapy is a kind of conversation, a kind of theologizing in which the participants are understood to have multiple identities, experiencing and interpreting in interdisciplinary ways. In this conversation, the pastoral clinician faithfully companions and collaboratively translates with the client—by focusing on the self and suffering of the client by way of the content of the client's report, instead of the affect the client experiences or conveys and the actions the client makes, as they collaboratively diagnose, set goals, and plan a course of care. More particularly, pastoral psychotherapy is a relationship and process in which persons practice being on-the-boundaries, tolerate ambiguities, and articulate and respond to ongoing questions with the hope of future understanding.

How Does Pastoral Psychotherapy Heal?

Pastoral psychotherapy provides the occasion for healing by the client's experiencing being faithfully companioned while collaboratively translating, and through that process acquiring an attitude, a style of relating-knowing and experiencing-reflecting.[4] In the midst of experiencing a sense of presence and safety, the client gains a deepened appreciation of being on-the-boundaries, an openness to the unexpected, an enhanced expectation of coming-to-understand, and, in the context of identifying and disconfirming patterns, living into and through new patterns of more flexible commerce and connection within her self and between her self and others.[5]

OWNING A THEORY OF HEALING

Each person functions according to his own experience and understanding of healing, what might be termed an operative *theory of change*. To connect personal experience with this term, consider an example that has a clinical feel to it. Think about an experience of being unexpectedly anxious. Your heart is racing. You are beginning to perspire. You feel agitated. Your body is starting to shake. Your stomach is turning over almost violently. Images are running through your mind. You cannot focus or concentrate. You feel confused, even frightened. At a point you feel almost helpless to do anything but suffer uncontrollably. What do you do? How does your response express an underlying perspective?

Each person responds differently. For example, one might ask, What's going on? When did this start? What was happening when I first started to feel this way? Asking sets in motion a learned adaptive response, a plan of self-care.

Several things are implied. First, one presumes an ability to make sense of what is initially irrational, and that making sense or understanding will help. Second, one anticipates, in shifting from being helpless and passive to being active, that a person can transcend experience, gain perspective, and respond intentionally. Finally, one implies that there are psychological solutions to the physical-mental event of anxiety.

Consider another response. In the midst of anxiety, one might say forcefully, even angrily: Get hold of yourself. There's absolutely no reason to be frightened. You're not in any danger. It's in your head. You're strong. You'll be okay. In addition to this pep talk, spoken from strength and imputing strength, one might get involved in a physical activity. Not being able to flee from internal danger, one meets unknown power with power: doing something physical.

This approach implies a prospective pattern of change. Support, encouragement, and challenge may be integral to change. Mind and body are interrelated. Exercise is important: symbolically for illustrating a sense of power, vitality, and strength; physiologically for contributing to changes in mood.

Consider a third approach. While anxious, one might imaginatively absent oneself from the situation. One envisions a safe, comfortable place. One conjures feeling relaxed and peaceful. One breathes deeply, slowly, taking in the nourishing oxygen, as a psychological exercise or a spiritual technique. One experiences meditative mastery or a receptiveness to divine healing presence.

Consider a fourth approach. One responds to anxiety by locating a prized object: a particular place, a picture or symbol, praying. One might call or meet with a friend. Having another present, whether imaginatively and symbolically or physically, is comforting and soothing. Talking may be less important than not being alone. Healing in this perspective presupposes a kind of relationship or at least presence. It may involve the literal, bodily presence of another person or the mediated presence of a person or spirit through something symbolic.

Additional options are available. Some seek a way of avoiding and distracting. Others want a plan of mastery, a kind of systematic desensitization. Still others pursue a magic potion or medication that would alleviate the symptom. Each of these patterns of response reveals a vision of the self and, within that context, a vision of healing.

The variety of working options illustrates that every person who seeks help not only suffers but also has ways of coping with and adapting to suffering that are only in part successful. Their solution to the problem is the problem. Most persons are not fully aware that they have applied solutions from the past to problems in the present or that they are enacting an underlying theory of change. As a result, few people are able to articulate what will help and why it will help. In this regard, care involves intentional and explicit conversation about the participants' differing understandings of healing.

By articulating as carefully and fully as possible one's theory of change, one's operative commitments can be identified, evaluated, and modified. Further, one appreciates the process of discerning an implicit theory of change. Because one's personal understanding of healing and theory of change are forged in one's personal history of suffering, identifying a theory involves reexperiencing that suffering. As a result, one will actively avoid identifying one's theory.

Identifying One's Theory of Change

Think of an event in which change happened. Try to tell the story of that change, describing in some detail, in an experience-near way, what took place. Pay attention to some of the following questions and concerns: (1) Who or what changed? (For example, was it one's self, behavior, feelings, beliefs, needs, relationship?) (2) To what does the term *change* or *changed* refer? How would one differentiate change with respect to growth, development, maturation, transformation, conversion, progression, healing, or cure? (3) What, in particular, precipitated, caused, or enhanced the change? What are the salient features, the necessary elements, contributing to change? Conversely, what elements inhibit or preclude change?

What metaphor is embedded in the narrative of change? Is it a puzzle to be solved, someone being birthed, an athlete to be coached, a student to be taught, a child to be parented, an infant to be held, a stranger to be befriended, a slave to be freed, a tumor to be excised, a garden to be cultivated, an apparatus to be balanced, a programme to be realized?[6]

Spelling Out Features of a Theory of Change

A clinical vignette: A young woman, referred by her pastor, calls for an appointment. She has never been in counseling or therapy. Although reluctant to say much about the nature of her concern, she indicates that she is feeling nervous a lot. Saying that much seems to heighten her nervousness.

She appears for the first meeting wearing a suit. She speaks in a reserved, at times gruff voice. She extends her hand but seems to feel awkward in doing so. She looks directly at the clinician only initially. When entering the office, she gives the impression of being scared: Her eyes look as if she is frightened; she scans the environment and sits down nervously. It seems as if she cannot decide whether to look at the clinician or in another direction; neither conveys safety.

The clinician begins the conversation, recalling the phone conversation and her words, "feeling nervous a lot." She seems momentarily pleased that someone has listened and continues, "I feel really nervous being here and don't know if this is going to work." The clinician acknowledges that often people feel uncomfortable when coming in for the first time to talk to a stranger and that she might become more relaxed as the conversation continues. The clinician asks her to say a little more about feeling nervous. She hesitatingly proceeds.

The nervousness she describes as having to do with her performance at work and with revealing herself more and more to her few friends is conveyed not only in her words but also in her affect and presence. The clinician appreciates how difficult speaking must be for her. While aware of silently admiring her courage, the clinician feels summoned to protect her, as if she were unsafe. The clinician senses that some of what she anticipates needing protection from is the clinician.

Three Terms of Clinical Participation

Three terms—*self, suffering,* and *healing*—guide and inform clinical participation.

SELF

Self means several things:

(1) Self is complex, interdimensional, experiencing and translating across a variety of domains—physical, mental, social, and spiritual—engaging across a variety of domains of relatedness, through multiple identities. The woman's nervousness, for example, is at once a physical-mental-social-spiritual event.

One needs to explore *how* she experiences nervousness. As preeminently physical? In a particular place in her body? Having deeper symbolic meaning? As part of a pattern, related to past events or to ways in which her mother or father dealt with performance or exposure? Characterized as something social and interpersonal? Precipitated by certain kinds of events or particular kinds of people? Does she explicitly connect her suffering to larger issues, like fears about who she is, what she is supposed to do with her life, why she was born in the first place? Might she talk about what God expects from her, or how could God not only allow but also cause such suffering?

(2) A self is in relationships or *is* relationships, intersecting and overlapping other people and fulfilling psychic functions on behalf of one another. The heightened nervousness that led the woman to call might be the result of the experience of a breakdown in her relationship(s), by definition in her self. To put it technically, her nervousness is in some measure a consequence of disruption in her selfobject relationships. What happened between her and someone else? Who are the people in her life, her selfobject milieu? How do her descriptions convey the quality of relationship?[7]

She reports feeling threatened and peculiarly unsafe when alone with a boss who reminds her of her father. When she tried to tell one of her few friends about it, the friend failed to understand and acted as if her concerns were all her imagination. Feeling alone, the woman sought to be with someone strong who might protect her. She expects that no one could really understand her difficulty and that none of her friends truly knows or understands her. She wishes she could trust people more but feels the problems are due mainly to something they lack.

(3) A self lives on-the-boundaries between being and becoming, past and future, knowing and not knowing, being separate and being connected, being righteous and being sinful, where the kingdom of God is already/not yet.[8] The spatial image of having one foot grounded and

the other exploring; one in the known, another in the yet to be known; one in the past, another in the future represents the precariousness of existence.

This woman's suffering indicates directly and tragically how the world is unsafe. She is unable to protect herself from dangers without and within. Why, for example, does this man who reminds her of her father make her feel uncannily that something happened that she cannot remember fully? Why is she unable to sleep soundly? Why do certain strange images intrude unexpectedly, violating her consciousness? Why are particular dangers construed as a battle between forces of good and evil?

(4.) A self is God's, made in God's image, revealing God's ongoing presence and action. One surmises that her God may have various undesirable traits, as one who has failed to protect and make the world safe, and as one who is present only in limited and possibly punitive ways. One can appreciate her desire and need to be on a faith journey.

(5.) A self experiences, observes, and understands herself and others in subjective and partial ways. One listens to ways in which she has made sense as well as ways in which she questions her understanding. For example, when she confronts the clinician about knowing that the clinician does not fully believe her story and she assumes that the clinician has a different sense of God, implications can be explored. Was she experiencing the clinician to be like so many others who not only did not understand but also were convinced that their understanding was right? Was she expressing a hope that the clinician did have a different understanding and vision of a safer world of trustworthy people and a loving God? She recognizes that at times she will become aware of something emerging in herself by initially discovering it in others.

SUFFERING

Approaching another in terms of *suffering* means several things. Suffering bears a family resemblance to illness, sickness, pain, complaint, disease, and sin.[9] Suffering involves a first-person description of what is wrong or what hurts, a felt sense of what is awry.

Assuming that a person immersed in a satisfactory selfobject milieu experiences basic equilibrium, a sense of esteem, and a feeling of well-being, one infers that suffering expresses a disruption in the milieu, that is, the self. Her seeking help indicates a fear of that disruption continuing or devolving further toward the reexperience of a primitive agony, as well as a hope of restoring the previous balance or promoting growth and change in unknown ways.

While she has a sense of what her feeling nervous is all about and has some expectations about what will help, she is also aware, however indirectly and dimly, that her experience of suffering is a limit experience. She is finite. She does not fully know what is wrong; she cannot heal herself. An additional, deeper threat revealed through her suffering deepens her suffering: The insufficiency experienced in the particular condition of her nervousness discloses her insufficiency in general. Suffering discloses that one is always in the territory of the big questions. Suffering is a limit situation that exposes the depth of our insufficiency; in deepening our suffering, it paradoxically reveals the arena in which healing must take place and thus enhances the possibility of that deeper healing.

HEALING

Approaching her in terms of healing also orients one's presence and response.

1. Healing has to do with wholeness. Suffering is in part physical, but pastoral clinical care is not oriented toward cure. Suffering is in part spiritual, yet pastoral clinical care is not exclusively focused on the care of souls. Healing involves gaining contact, making connections, and restoring relationships with others and oneself ↙ w/ God .

Every event has a surplus of meaning, in part because it is experienced across so many dimensions—in terms of images, voices, memories, feelings, sensations, and words—in mind and body. Ernest Rossi's comments about state-dependent learning are especially instructive.[10] Persons experience events and register (or encode) the memory of these events in the context of particular states. These states involve mental and physical dimensions.

Someone who is relaxed is recording the memory of what is happening in a nonanxious state. Were she suddenly and unexpectedly informed of an emergency call, her autonomic nervous system would be activated; she would become hyperalert, ready for fight or flight. Her experiencing is being encoded in a different, now aroused, state. As the temporary emergency is solved and her state becomes more relaxed, what and how she registers again shift.

Think about the woman who reported being nervous. She not only metaphorized but also did so in the context of particular states. The word *nervous* triggers a certain reaction. When she speaks about being alone, she enters a different state. As she describes her experiencing, she is translating not only images but also a spectrum of events that are state-dependent.

Because we register or encode experience in the context of a specific state, we have access to particular experiences only when we are in the state in which it was registered. Likewise, each particular state offers access to a range of memories that were registered in that state. State-dependent learning means two things. First, we will not have full access, when we are relaxed, to what we were experiencing in an aroused state. Second, in an aroused state, we have access to other experiences that were encoded when we had previously been in that state. Rossi offers a good illustration. A person who has had alcohol registers memory in a state different from when he is entirely sober. Full access to these memories is not available except when he is in that alcohol-altered state.

In a simple sense, then, we register experiences across a variety of states that are not continuous with one another: We have boundaries between state-dependent memories. We do not have ready access to the range of our experience, to the fullness of our memories, to the continuity of our self-experience. In addition, we experience unexpected, at times unwelcome access to memories when we have reentered a previously experienced state.

What does this mean for healing? To return to the clinical illustration, one assumes that certain experiences remain inaccessible. Better said, one assumes that much of her self remains unknown, inaccessible, discontinuous within the self because borders exist between different states. These boundaries are in place in part because she does not want to reexperience particular states. In contrast, one of the goals of care is to enable her to become more connected with herself, that is, to establish commerce across the internal boundaries and borders. Given that selves overlap, commerce across internal borders is at the same time commerce across interpersonal borders.

2. *Healing* defined positively is not simply or primarily the absence of something, such as suffering, but the presence of something or a moving toward that presence. Thus, one can differentiate healing-from disease and healing-to well-being, soundness, wholeness.

Although alleviating the woman's experience of nervousness is a worthy goal, changes in her suffering will also involve changes in her self. She might, for example, learn to enable some of her friends to understand her more fully and to care for her more deeply. She might feel more knowable, acceptable, lovable. She might approach others not as people from whom she has to protect herself, but as people worthy of her care and concern who need her comfort and understanding. In the midst of this change of outlook, she would likely undergo some changes in her sense of God, less as the impotent protector or vengeful intruder than as the gracious creator or healing redeemer.

3. Healing has to do with holiness. This quality of life we seek to enhance has to do with moral and religious relationships, with God and neighbor. Healing has to do with coming to engage one another in more loving and just ways.

4. Healing is ultimately a gift from God. Although assuming responsibility for the suffering we experience, we should work actively to heal ourselves and one another. The effort to promote self-healing, however, unwittingly diminishes awareness of God's participation: We assume that if our faith has made us well, it is because of our work of faith.

Many aspire to this kind of self-healing and regard their perspective as deeply spiritual or religious. This self-healing is ultimately distracting from and competitive with the healing discussed here. Healing emerges through grace; the faith through which we interpret self and suffering in a new way is itself a gift of grace.[11]

Enhancing the occasion for healing involves relating to another in a manner in which she cannot relate to her self. Help and growth are contingent upon others: Something must come from outside, beyond the self.

Viewing the interdimensional self as having multiple identities disposes us to engage the person in a manner that helps her speak more articulately about her experience psychologically, theologically, and ethically. For example, she may recognize that certain feelings are precipitated by particular events and that, knowing such triggers, she will not as easily be caught unaware. She may recognize that some of the danger may be more imaginary than real, more relevant to the past than to the current moment. She might learn to choose among a variety of responses or antidotes that mitigate her suffering passively. One may listen with her to how she describes how her nervousness emerges at times when she fears being unable to be who she is supposed to be and do what she is supposed to do. This tension between ambitions and ideals, or between ego and superego, can involve exploring what for her is right and wrong, virtuous and evil, and how she can understand and transform her sense of moral agency.[12]

The clinician's own struggle to live on-the-boundary of knowing–not knowing, being–becoming plays an integral part in her praxis. All clinicians selectively attend, excluding as well as reducing the data to fit a picture according to which one can proceed.[13] All clinicians collapse mystery into meaning and reduce mystery to problem.[14] Several things should be eminently clear: No one has a blueprint for all people, learned through experience but generalizable to all; and no one is outside or above the unfolding process and relationship—objective, neutral, unfazed. Rather, each one is in it, going through something for the first time. Each is human, fallible, on-the-boundaries.

What, finally, is integral to enhancing healing? Healing is occasioned by the client's experiencing and acquiring features of the clinician's attitude, method, and presence. In a safe atmosphere, the client gains a deepened appreciation of limits, courage to face an open future, and develops more enhancing relationships within her self and between her self and others' selves. In brief, she acquires a capacity to mediate holy regard through faithfully companioning and collaboratively translating with and for herself and others.[15]

That this woman is suffering indicates that something is awry in her style of experiencing-reflecting, of knowing-relating to herself and others, including God.[16] She is asked to describe her suffering in detail, the objectives she has, and the prospective path she envisions taking to reach those objectives. Taking for granted that content, affect, and action are interrelated domains of self-expression, she conveys as well as betrays features of her self and suffering. She communicates an essential element of her self and suffering in how she engages the clinician.

By alternately attending to her suffering in particular and to her self in general, from the inside and from the outside, the clinician models an attitude. The clinician immerses herself in the immediate experience, experiences along with, and steps back to observe how that fits with respective working models of her self.

This shifting or oscillating between suffering and self, experiencing and observing, inside and outside—between figure and ground—has important implications. It enables grasping something as deeply as possible on its own account and grasping something in conjunction with or as an avenue to something else. In a practical clinical sense, it is working on acute symptomatology as well as character.

In a collaborative enterprise of internal and interpersonal translating, both try to make sense of what is happening within her and between them.[17] She becomes progressively clearer about her suffering and her self, clarifying her own maturing awareness in conjunction with assimilating some of the clinician's impressions. These changes are evidenced in her thinking differently about herself, feeling different, and relating to the clinician in a changing way.

The clinician assumes that the client will be influenced by words, actions, and self.[18] In particular, the clinician should be particularly sensitive to what the client has caught. The clinician is not and cannot be entirely conscious of her clinical attitude. The clinician operates according to an attitude that differs, to some degree, from what she consciously identified and will be appropriated in different ways by different clients.

ESSENTIAL FEATURES OF A THEORY OF CHANGE

A Sense of Presence and Safety

Experiencing the clinician to be more or less present to her in her unfolding experience in general, as well as in her nervousness in particular, she became alert to an underlying attitude.[19] To describe it from her point of view, she might say:

> You're with me—I'm not entirely alone. I'm at times anxious about not being able to describe what I'm experiencing, but I feel your presence. I feel safe to go exploring, revealing more to me and you, knowing that you'll help me make sense of it. You stay with me whether I'm nervous, angry at you, scared that you will hurt or leave me. You're somehow my ally, even advocate, even though I also experience you as my adversary and worse. You at times hear and see me in ways that I know are true, though I couldn't have said it that way. In other words, you seem to help me experience what's happening more deeply and fully, as well as observe or reflect upon everything. Because you accept what I say, no, accept who I am, without running away, or criticizing me, I feel you accept me in ways that I can't accept myself. That makes me wonder if maybe I'm not a good judge of me, and that maybe I am accept-able, love-able. You hang in there with me, even when I'm most frightened, or despairing, and when I can be re-

markably eloquent about how I should be justifiably hopeless. You have faith for me, and in me. I've made you into someone other than who you are: I tend to expect that you'll hurt me, or allow something to happen, or that you're withholding something from me. But you haven't fulfilled my expectations. In fact, you've helped me realize that I brought patterns of expectation to you. And, in identifying what some of them are, I realize with your help how I learned that, and how it is usually inaccurate to many people with whom I live and work.[20]

This suffering person experiences danger in a variety of ways. She hurts and is unable to help herself. She does not really know what is wrong or who she is. She has not been able to relate to and enlist others in a way that heals. This suffering discloses a deeper suffering of insufficiency, finitude, absolute dependence. She must feel safe to be and become, to retrieve the past and enter the future, to go through a triumph of hope over experience.

A clinician conveys safety by being willing to be on-the-boundaries with her, as both come to know, come to reexperience primitive agonies. Responding consistently to all of what she experiences, across various states and memories, encourages her to be consistently present to herself. By remaining present with and to her in her danger, the clinician communicates that her nervousness and fear can be held, contained, managed. It is as if one says through action, "Go to the heart of danger and there you will find safety."[21]

One might elaborate upon the experience of presence and safety in terms of holy regard[22] and attunement.[23] Respect is conveyed in a variety of ways. While she realizes that a clinician cannot do other than listen and make sense as an outsider, even one who is curious, suspicious, playing the doubting game, she has the ongoing felt sense that her evolving understanding has been regarded as real and plausible. The significance and meaningfulness of her ideas are futher affirmed by the clinician wanting to make fuller sense of what she implies and says in passing. Collaborating and comparing notes about what she says, as well as about respective working models, reveal the clinician's healthy regard for both perspectives. Two contributions to her acquiring a holy regard of her self can be identified: She may internalize the clinician's regard of her; and, in observing the clinician's self-regard, she may internalize what it is like for a self to experience her self in that way.[24] As the word *attunement* suggests, she experiences a basic good-enough resonance regarding ideas that are implied, affect that has yet to be described, in being present to and with her.[25]

A Deepened Appreciation of Being-on-the-Boundaries

Everyone has various experiences of or indirectly senses never fully understanding all that is happening. One experiences freedom and an open future yet feels destined, as if the future were limited or closed. One may describe the boundary situation in various ways: Persons are nature and spirit; finite yet self-transcending; created in God's image, yet fallen; conscious, yet unconscious; connected, yet isolated; seeing, but through a glass darkly.

Pastoral clinical care reaffirms that we are always on-the-boundaries. We are on the road to perfection but never really get there. The kingdom of God is already but not yet. We try to know fully who we are, as if the unconscious were a container whose contents could be made entirely conscious, but realize that we are always coming-to-know, are always unconscious as well as conscious.

Boundaries emerge within oneself: One seems not only to act but to be different with various persons. With some, one is safe, relaxed, confident; with another, threatened, wary, vigilant; and with still another, playful, humorous, adventuresome. Not unlike multiple or split personalities or multiple selves, one experiences living or functioning from various internal locations or places.

Internal boundaries can be experienced in a different sense. One becomes aware that something from the past is playing itself out in the present, as if past and present are ambiguously enmeshed. Certain memories, habits, and behaviors that are unavailable to consciousness are retained in one's body: One is separated from oneself. One may feel driven or compelled, wanting to know the source and motives, yet indirectly aware of not wanting to know.

Finally, there are boundaries between selves. One has a mask, or persona, needing to save face. The boundary may be signaled in the experience of a protective barrier insulating one from the other.

Some clinicians try to analyze the therapeutic process in ways that reveal an imposed boundary; they try to discern whether what was unfolding came from the client or from the clinician. They mistakenly isolate the participants and carve the flow of experience and relationship into different parts. They thereby try to manage the ambiguity of the process; they confuse intimacy and attendant anxiety by keeping the client and themselves at an imaginary distance from one another.

By practicing with the client—living through on that boundary where both are on the boundaries—the client challenges early wishes, undergoes what Donald Winnicott and Paul Ricoeur refer to as *disillusionment*.[26] To be human means always exploring, knowing and not knowing, living on convictions while critically seeking their transformation.[27]

In the midst of this threatening ambiguity, we harbor fantasies of a utopian resolution: a place to be reached, a goal attained. We deny the ever-present territory of the big questions and our inability to answer them once and for all. The clinical relationship and process do not aim for or bring about the resolution of these inevitable ambiguities. Rather, they bring to the fore that these are the conditions of being human, to which we have to reconcile ourselves.[28] There will always be more to retrieve from memory. There will always be other states and dimensions of self, with which one can attain fuller commerce and connection. There will always be something new that has the capacity to provoke us to change.

An Openness to the Unexpected

In the midst of ambiguously living on the boundaries, one denies the territory of the big questions by presuming that one has sufficiently answered them. One fits everything into schemata and paradigms.

Accepting life's ambiguity contributes to becoming open to the unexpected. One is more willing to be confronted with something truly new. One becomes aware of foreclosing recognition of the unexpected by recognizing unconscious patterns of perception and engagement that one unwittingly repeats.

An Enhanced Expectation of Coming-to-Understand

Heinz Kohut has written about the curative role of empathy as involving principally understanding and, from the client's point of view, the experience of being understood.[29] Focusing on the experience of understanding—or, more properly, of being understood— accentuates the content of what the client comes to know, if not the importance of understanding meaning, perspective, ideas. More crucial is the ongoing experience of being understood, such that the client has the sense: I can be understood; another can grasp with me what has been difficult to describe. What may be pivotal is not simply the experience of being understood, per se, but the lived experience that disposes one to expect and trust that she will come to be understood and understand that which is yet-to-be-known. The content of what is understood is potentially less important than the repeated, practiced experience of coming to be understood, such that this serves as an experiential preparedness and expectation to be understood anew. In promoting the triumph of hope over experience, we build upon an integral dimension: expectant trust, what some call the placebo effect.[30]

Living New Patterns of Commerce and Connection[31]

The client on-the-boundaries is not fully aware of her self, her suffering, and her understanding of healing. An important feature of each of these elements are the wishes, needs, and expectations she brings, which again are for the most part unknown.

Some of those unspoken, unidentified needs and expectations will be intuitively fulfilled. In a certain sense, she will feel in familiar territory and, in that measure, experience a basic sense of comfort. In addition, however, certain needs will be met only accidentally and haphazardly; she will experience a range of less than positive emotions. Furthermore, certain negative expectations will be constellated, in which her fears that she will not be helped, that she will be hurt, emerge more fully.

In this context, one has the occasion for her to experience the unexpected in several ways. She may consciously expect the clinician neither to respond in ways that do not help nor discover that her experience of the clinician's failure reveals an underlying pattern of experience and engagement. Thus she unexpectedly discovers patterns of experiencing and relating.

She concurrently experiences herself and the clinician according to old patterns and in terms of newly forming patterns. What is unfolding is an ambiguous blend of past and present, old and new, transference and alliance. She uses the experiences of repetition to recover past memories and own disowned thoughts and feelings. To the degree to which that happens along with and in the midst of something new, she can more clearly differentiate past from present, who she was from who she is becoming.

At the same time, in her safety she will gradually identify that she lives on the boundaries: what and where those boundaries are, why they are there. In conjunction with this, she will be moving across a variety of boundaries, from past to present, memory to memory, state to state. As she does so, her experience and understanding of her self will change in a pivotal way. She will develop an underlying sense of the continuity and coherence of her self. Rather than being a different self in each state, or a past and a present, an unconscious and a conscious, she will know from experience that she is the self inclusive of these different states, memories, and experiences. In other words, in the process of developing commerce across boundaries, a more solid supraordinate self emerges.

In the clinical relationship, the client experiences her self, the other, and the relationship, in ways that no longer primarily repeat the past but are truly new and unexpected. In that regard, client and clinician are practicing together, exploring and experimenting—living through. With this client in particular, she is, from the very beginning of contact, practicing performing and revealing her nervousness, as she anticipates being wounded. She is, however, exploring such questions as, What's the nervousness about? What will unfold?

Companioning sets in motion two mutually informing processes. She is in a position to resume growth and explore, change, mature.[32] In addition, she is in a position to take in—*internalize*—features of the clinician's and others' styles of experiencing and observing, knowing and relating. In other words, some of her healing involves internalizing functions:

1. The intention to observe her self and her experience carefully

2. A capacity to observe, through such questions as Why? Why now?

3. Willingness, openness, and acceptance in such exploration

4. Faith and courage, in the midst of uncertainty, anxiety, pain

She gradually acquires a style of knowing and relating to her self and her suffering; she internalizes aspects of the clinician's attitude.

Practicing on-the-boundaries, living through in that ambiguous process of repeating the past while creating something new, she is becoming a different self, engaging in a different way. What she practices with the clinician, she practices in an ongoing way with others—not after termination, but along the way. She experiences safety on the boundaries, related to what Tillich called the courage to be. Moving across those various boundaries, she becomes.

HOW, CONCRETELY, MIGHT CHANGE/HEALING SHOW ITSELF?

Every client, every clinician, and every clinical relationship is more or less unique. That is, we are different from one another, not only as clients but as clinicians; each of us is different with and in each of our respective clinical relationships.[33] Change unfolds in diverse ways. Although various goals of clinical care are products of that care, some goals evolve not at the end of the clinical relationship but all along the way: Healing is taking place in the process itself.

Practicing with another in the territory of the big questions while being on-the-boundary is the locus of healing that may be most pivotal. Clinical care as a corrective emotional experience promotes acquiring a new style of knowing and relating, one that is collaborative, tentative, evolving, open to the new. This corrective emotional experience, at its heart the transformation of an attitude, may be enhanced in a variety of ways.

SIGNS OF HEALING

Healing may manifest itself in a variety of ways. The healing of the self is the healing of the self's relationships—or the self as relationships. As a psychologist, one listens for another's increased capacity to be empathic with herself and with other selves.[34] This involves developing flexible commerce across different dimensions and states, across various self-object relationships, domains of intersubjective relatedness, and domains of experience.[35] The person acquires the capacity to execute psychic functions more fully on her own behalf. In regard to content, she may have recovered memories, formulated new ideas, constructed modified representations of herself and others, reframed her past and future. In regard to affect, she may have developed a deeper appreciation of living on-the-boundary, where there is an inevitable slippage between language and felt experience. She may have developed a more nuanced vocabulary of affect, a diminution of the intensity and ubiquity of her experience of suffering. In regard to action, she is likely repeating less, remembering and living through newly acquired patterns of perception, expectation, relationship.

As a theologian, one understands healing to involve the developing capacity to experience and mediate the love, acceptance, and forgiveness that was first given us. In other words, one will be more fully able to fulfill the two great commandments: Loving God with all one's heart, soul, strength, and mind, and loving the neighbor as oneself. I view this less as a move toward perfection and more, as Tillich says, as a struggle with accepting acceptance. "Salvation as God's unconditional gift is not the goal of life but its presupposition."[36] Ethically, healing involves developing the capacity to engage others as ends in themselves, as a Thou, to act expressing agape.[37]

In a most basic sense, the other will be modifying underlying root metaphors and narratives. She will be a different psychologist-theologian-ethicist, having a different attitude, method, and presence.[38]

POSTSCRIPT

I have raised more questions than I have answered, some of them big questions. I have illustrated the ambiguities of being on-the-boundaries. I have sought to engender an attitude of tolerating that ambiguity in the hope and expectation of future understanding. And I have sought to engender that attitude through faithful companioning.

Notes

Preface

1. See, for example, Paul Tillich, *On the Boundary: An Autobiographical Sketch* (New York: Scribner, 1966).
2. See, for example, William James, *Essays on Radical Empiricism* and *A Pluralistic Universe* (New York: E. P. Dutton, 1971; originally published 1912, 1909).
3. Herman Nunberg, cited in Peter B. Neubauer, "The Role of Insight in Psychoanalysis," in *Psychoanalytic Explorations of Technique: Discourse on the Theory of Therapy*, edited by Harold P. Blum (New York: International Universities Press, 1980), 29.
4. Jerry M. Lewis, "Marital Therapy and Individual Change: Implications for a Theory of Cure," in *Cures by Psychotherapy: What Effects Change?* edited by J. Martin Myers (New York: Praeger, 1984), 1.

1. The Context of Pastoral Clinical Care

1. Richard D. Chessick, *How Psychotherapy Heals: The Process of Intensive Psychotherapy* (New York: Science House, 1969), 2–3.
2. See, for example, Conrad W. Weiser, *Healers—Harmed and Harmful* (Minneapolis: Fortress Press, 1994) for a discussion of inappropriate motivations that lead approximately 25 percent of persons into ministry.
3. Paul Tillich, *Biblical Religion and the Search for Ultimate Reality* (Chicago: University of Chicago Press, 1955), 11.
4. Peter L. Berger and Hansfried Kellner, *Sociology Reinterpreted: An Essay on Method and Vocation* (Garden City, N.Y.: Anchor Press/Doubleday, 1981), 66.
5. For example, they may formally diagnose features of their clients' suffering according to *The Diagnostic and Statistical Manual of Mental Disorders*, 4th ed. (Washington, D.C.: American Psychiatric Association, 1994) and actually provide care according to an essentially pastoral-theological perspective. Of course, codes from the classification system are needed by most copayment plans for reimbursement, but I am pointing to a practice beyond this fiduciary need.
6. Two essays on theological anthropology are recommended: Theodore Runyon, "Kingdom, Creation, and Covenant: The Human Condition in Biblical and Theological Perspective," 12–27; and Robert S. Bilheimer, "The Human Condition in Biblical Perspective," 28–42, both in *Changing Views of the Human Condition*, edited by Paul Pruyser (Macon, Ga.: Mercer University Press, 1987).
7. N. R. Hanson, *Perception and Discovery* (San Francisco: Freeman, Cooper, and Co., 1969), 149-70.

8. Paul Tillich, "Seeing and Hearing," in *The New Being* (New York: Charles Scribner's Sons, 1955), 129.

9. David Tracy, *Plurality and Ambiguity: Hermeneutics, Religion, Hope* (San Francisco: Harper & Row, 1987), 18. For understanding psychoanalysis as a radical questioning of the self, see Stanley Leavy, *In the Image of God* (New Haven: Yale University Press, 1988), 104.

2. Theologizing

1. Already in 1975, Gordon Kaufman (*An Essay on Theological Method* [Missoula, Mont.: Scholars Press, 1975], ix) noted the chaotic contemporary theological scene. He reaffirmed this judgment more recently ("Critical Theology as a University Discipline," in *Theology and the University: Essays in Honor of John B. Cobb, Jr.*, edited by David Ray Griffin and Joseph C. Hough [Albany: State University of New York Press, 1991], 37). Edward Farley (*Ecclesial Reflection: An Anatomy of Theological Method* [Philadelphia: Fortress Press, 1982], 200 n. 7) traces one aspect of the ambiguity to the Reformation's habitus of human being versus the Thomistic view of theology as a science. David Kelsey (*The Uses of Scripture in Recent Theology* [Philadelphia: Fortress Press, 1975], 134-35) has noted how theologians make arguments that belong to many different fields of argument.

Proposals for organizing the varieties of theological enterprises include Don S. Browning, *A Fundamental Practical Theology: Descriptive and Strategic Proposals* (Minneapolis: Fortress Press, 1991); Edward Farley, *Theologia: The Fragmentation and Unity of Theological Education* (Philadelphia: Fortress Press, 1983) and *The Fragility of Knowledge: Theological Education in the Church and the University* (Philadelphia: Fortress Press, 1988); Robert Neville, *A Theology Primer* (Albany: State University of New York Press, 1991); David Tracy, *The Analogical Imagination: Christian Theology and the Culture of Pluralism* (New York: Crossroad, 1981).

2. Westerners often take for granted that reality is understood as component parts that can be put together. For a helpful discussion of Descartes's "disastrously influential" ideas, see Robert Neville, *Recovery of the Measure: Interpretation and the Philosophy of Nature* (Albany: State University of New York Press, 1989), esp. chap. 2. See also Paul Tillich's discussion of the importance of approaching reality in terms of dimensions rather than levels (*Systematic Theology*, 3 vols. [Chicago: University of Chicago Press, 1951–1963], 3:14–15) and the two ways of approaching God: overcoming estrangement (awareness is given in the question) or meeting a stranger (attempting to bridge a seemingly insurmountable gap; 1:206).

3. Numerous nuances and distinctions need to be glossed over as these concepts are examined.

4. The story is standard fare in Gilkey's course on Paul Tillich's theology. The story is not meant to suggest that theology has any intrinsic relation to substance use or abuse. On the face of it, this association seems unfortunate; it is neither acci-

dental nor incidental. Indeed, this association is quite integral to the narrative of the situation and to theologizing itself.

5. A more traditional, kerygmatic theology (as proclamation of and reflection on the gospel) shall be expressed in the following chapters.

6. To use a well-known Tillichian phrase, reason becomes separated from its depth.

7. See, for example, Thomas Groome, "Theology on Our Feet: A Revisionist Pedagogy for Healing the Gap between Academia and Ecclesia," in *Formation and Reflection: The Promise of Practical Theology,* edited by Lewis Mudge and James Poling (Philadelphia: Fortress Press, 1987), 57; Edward Farley, *Theologia,* 135; and Edward Farley, "Interpreting Situations: An Inquiry into the Nature of Practical Theology," in *Formation and Reflection,* 10.

8. Approaching all persons as theologians raises an interesting question: What distinguishes a professional or specialist? The differences are several. Nonspecialists do not presume the self-conscious identity of lay theologian. They inevitably reflect upon their religious or faith experience but usually only in passing or when an accident or crisis requires. They may not do so self-consciously or with any particular kind of language or reflection. As a consequence, they readily disown that certain questions and issues are theirs, acting as if reflecting on human finitude and failings—and other matters—is the province of a particular group of professionals.

Professional theologians, like all human beings, reflect upon faith and religious experience when provoked by crisis—by the experience of limits. In addition, however, they do so in a sustained, ongoing way, as a vocational project.

9. Coining such awkward terms is not without precedent. Late in his career, Charles Pierce "adopted the term 'pragmaticism'—a name 'ugly enough to keep it from kidnappers' in order to distinguish his doctrine from other versions of pragmatism." (Richard Bernstein, *Praxis and Action: Contemporary Philosophies of Human Activity* [Philadelphia: University of Pennsylvania Press, 1971], 166). Although it is admittedly cumbersome to speak about theologizing rather than theology, about faithing rather than faith, traditional ways of capturing this area of experience in terms of nouns (*religion, theology, faith*) and adjectives (*religious, theological, faithful*) tend to deny to our awareness that these are active enterprises. Rather than focusing on one's theology, as if it were primarily an object to be examined, independently of its author, I would recommend examining one's theologizing, how one goes about that enterprise in this particular domain of human experience. See Roy Schafer's reflections on action language in psychoanalysis (*A New Language for Psychoanalysis* [New Haven: Yale University Press, 1976]), where he discusses some of the liabilities of speaking in nouns and adjectives and some of the benefits of thinking and speaking in terms of verbs and adverbs. I am guided in approaching theology as an activity, theologizing, because of discussions of psychoanalytic theory and practice.

10. Nicholas Lobkowicz, *Theory and Practice: History of a Concept from Aristotle to*

Marx (Notre Dame, Ind.: University of Notre Dame Press, 1967), 3; Dennis P. Mc-Cann and Charles R. Strain, *Polity and Praxis: A Program for American Practical Theology* (Minneapolis: Winston Press, 1985).

11. Bernstein, *Praxis and Action.*

12. Lobkowicz, *Theory and Practice,* 3–5; see also Thomas Groome, *Christian Religious Education: Sharing Our Story and Vision* (San Francisco: Harper & Row, 1980), 153.

13. Groome, *Christian Religious Education,* 154. Nicholas Lobkowicz ("Theory and Practice," in *Marxism, Communism, and Western Society,* edited by C. D. Kernig [New York: Herder & Herder, 1973] 8:163) notes the difference between Aristotle's and Plato's ideas and later views: "Both the two contexts referred to [Aristotelian and Platonic] have but little to do with the opposition between theory and practice as we understand it today. Within the first, it is not theory and practice— in the modern sense—that are contraposed, but two kinds of practice, while within the second it is two kinds of theory. In neither context is there any reflection on the relation between theory and practice in the sense of knowing versus acting."

14. See, in particular, Lobkowicz, *Theory and Practice;* Lobkowicz, "Theory and Practice"; Bernstein, *Praxis and Action.* See also Groome, *Christian Religious Education.*

15. Stephen Toulmin, "The Recovery of Practical Philosophy," *American Scholar* 57 (Summer 1988):348-49.

16. Ibid., 341.

17. Ibid., 349.

18. Richard Bernstein, *Beyond Objectivism and Relativism: Science, Hermeneutics, and Praxis* (Philadelpha: University of Pennsylvania Press, 1985), 38. See also Langdon Gilkey, *Reaping the Whirlwind: A Christian Interpretation of History* (New York: Seabury Press, 1976), 369, n. 4; and Matthew Lamb, *Solidarity with Victims: Toward a Theology of Social Transformation* (New York: Crossroad, 1982), 65–88.

19. Browning, *Fundamental Practical Theology,* characterizes this interplay of "dialectical movements from traditions of theory-laden practice to theory and back to new theory-laden practices" in terms of a "practice-theory-practice" model (39, 40).

20. David Tracy's (*Blessed Rage for Order: The New Pluralism in Theology* [New York: Seabury Press, 1975]) definition of *praxis* illustrates this interpenetration of understanding, interpretation, and application: "In short, the aim of all thought is *praxis.* Such *praxis,* of course, is not to be identified with practice. Rather *praxis* is correctly understood as the critical relationship between theory and practice whereby each is dialectically influenced and transformed by the other. The principal tool for such analysis is a dialectical method whereby one negates present actualizations of theory and practice in order to project future theoretical and practical possibilities" (243).

21. Quentin Hand, "Pastoral Counseling as Theological Practice," *The Journal of Pastoral Care* 32 (1978):101.

22. Groome, "Theology on Our Feet," 57.

23. Charles Gerkin, *Widening the Horizons: Pastoral Responses to a Fragmented Society* (Philadelphia: Westminster Press, 1986), 60. Thomas Ogletree, "Dimensions of Practical Theology: Meaning, Action, Self," in *Practical Theology*, ed. with an Introduction by Don S. Browning (San Francisco: Harper & Row, 1983), 85, puts it well: "The origin of theology is practical; it arises out of prior worldly involvements. Its end is likewise practical; it plunges us once more into the sea of experience." Martin Marty (*Health and Medicine in the Lutheran Tradition* [New York: Crossroad, 1983], 59) gets at another feature: "The meaning of the cross does not disclose itself in contemplative thought but only in suffering experience. The real theologian makes discoveries not in the study or classroom but in the sickroom."

24. See pp. 21–24. The anecdote could be misread to suggest that theology and religion were not only distinguishable but separable states and that religion was somehow more meaningful. Religion and theology, like thinking-doing-being, experience-reflection, are always of a part.

25. See, for example, Hans Kung and David Tracy, eds., *Paradigm Change in Theology: A Symposium for the Future*, trans. Margaret Kohl (New York: Crossroad), 1989.

26. See, for example, Tracy, *Blessed Rage for Order;* Tracy, *Analogical Imagination;* Don S. Browning, *Religious Ethics and Pastoral Care* (Philadelphia: Fortress Press, 1983); Browning, *Religious Thought and the Modern Psychologies* (Philadelphia: Fortress Press, 1987).

27. See Bibliography, s.v. Disciplines as Hermeneutical or Interpretive.

28. Charles Gerkin, *The Living Human Document: Re-Visioning Pastoral Counseling in a Hermeneutical Mode* (Nashville: Abingdon Press, 1984), esp. 200, n. 1.

29. See, for example, Tracy, *Analogical Imagination.*

30. See Bibliography, s.v. Conversation as Metaphor. Richard Rorty, *Philosophy and the Mirror of Nature* (Oxford: Basil Blackwell, 1980), 389–90, proposes that the most apt metaphor for philosophy is conversation: "If we see knowing not as an essence, to be described by scientists or philosophers, but rather as a right, by current standards, to believe, then we are well on the way to seeing *conversation* as the ultimate context within which knowledge is to be understood. Our focus shifts from the relation between human beings and the objects of their inquiry to the relation between alternative standards of justification, and from there to the actual changes in those standards which make up intellectual history." This he considers recasting ("Solidarity or Objectivity," 26) as "the continual reweaving of a web of beliefs." He suggests ("The Contingency of Language" in *Contingency, Irony, and Solidarity* [Cambridge: Cambridge University Press, 1989], 9) "a picture of intellectual and moral progress as a history of increasingly useful metaphors rather than of increasing understanding of how things really are."

31. Theologizing as conversation is, by definition, apologetic. Theology is "an-

swering theology," answering "the questions implied in the situation." Tillich, *Systematic Theology*, 3 vols. (Chicago: University of Chicago Press, 1951–1963), 1:6.

32. Nowhere is this more apparent than in this chapter, where my choice of subjects and representative texts expresses my own background and exposure. See writings in the psychology of knowledge, such as Robert D. Stolorow and George E. Atwood, *Faces in a Cloud: Subjectivity in Personality Theory* (New York: Jason Aronson, 1979); and *Affect, Cognition, and Personality*, edited by S. Tomkins and C. Izard (New York: Springer, 1965), esp. 72–97.

33. As Karl Mannheim put it: "Strictly speaking, it is incorrect to say that the single individual thinks. Rather, it is more correct to insist that he participates in thinking further what other men have thought before him." Karl Mannheim, *Ideology and Utopia: An Introduction to the Sociology of Knowledge*, trans. L. Wirth & E. Shils (New York: Harcourt, Brace and World, Inc., 1936).

34. *The Vocation of the Theologian*, edited by Theodore W. Jennings, Jr. (Philadelphia: Fortress Press, 1985) including Geoffrey Wainwright, "Theology as Churchly Reflection," 9–24; Rosemary Radford Ruether, "Theology as Critique of and Emancipation from Sexism," 25–36; José Míguez-Bonino, "Theology as Critical Reflection and Liberating Praxis," 37–48; Theodore W. Jennings, Jr., "Theology as the Construction of Doctrine," 67–86; Langdon Gilkey, "Theology as the Interpretation of Faith for Church and World," 87–103; John B. Cobb, Jr., "Theology as Thoughtful Response to the Divine Call," 104–19; James H. Cone, "Theology as the Expression of God's Liberating Activity for the Poor," 120–34.

35. Robert Neville (*The Tao and the Daimon: Segments of a Religious Inquiry* [Albany: State University of New York Press, 1982], 13) concurs: "There is no one method to theological inquiry; rather, there are many methods. The appropriateness of a particular method or combination of methods rests on historical factors."

36. See James W. McClendon, Jr., *Biography as Theology: How Life Stories Can Remake Today's Theology* (Nashville: Abingdon Press, 1974).

37. "The movement in conversation is questioning itself. Neither my present opinions on the question nor the text's [or the other's] original response to that question, but the question itself, must control every conversation. . . . It is a willingness to follow the question wherever it may go" (David Tracy, *Plurality and Ambiguity: Hermeneutics, Religion, Hope* [San Franscisco: Harper & Row, 1987), 18).

38. If theologizing is a fundamentally human activity, its necessary plural forms are not restricted to the varieties of "Christian theology." Shirley Guthrie's brief definition highlights this point: "Theology in general is disciplined reflection about God as the ultimate origin, meaning, and goal of the world and human life. . . . Christian theology is a form of theology that seeks to understand the world and human life in light of faith in the creative, reconciling, and renewing purposes of God revealed in the history of ancient Israel and in Jesus, as that history is interpreted in the Bible and further interpreted in the past and present thought of the Christian church." Shirley Guthrie, "Christian Theology," in *Dictionary of Pas-*

toral Care and Counseling, Rodney Hunter, General Editor (Nashville: Abingdon Press, 1990), 1266.

The claim that Christian theology is a particular "form or expression" of a "universal category" of theology is itself a particular theological claim. Many argue that the Christian faith is unique, founded upon a unique revelation. For them, Christianity and Christian theology cannot be regarded as one among several religions or "faiths," because it is not a particular species in any genus. It is one of a kind. Others consider that Christian faith and Christian theology share certain features or qualities with other "faiths" and "theologies." In engaging in interfaith dialogue, they move from the particular to the universal. Others still—and I count myself among them—affirm the uniqueness of the Christian faith and Christian theology, and choose to move from the universal to the particular.

39. Rorty, "The Contingency of Language." Compare Anne Carr's discussion of "revisioning Christian categories" (*Transforming Grace: Christian Tradition and Women's Experience* [San Francisco: Harper & Row, 1988]) and Robert Neville's "reconstituting" or "reconstructing" the categories (*Theology Primer,* xxiv).

40. Tillich ("The Conception of Man in Existential Philosophy," *Journal of Religion* 19 [1939]:203–4) writes, "The theological approach to man is, so to speak, transmethodological. It is in and beyond the methods at the same time. . . . Theology has no method of its own, but it has a point of view for all methods and in all realms." See also Julie T. Klein, *Interdisciplinarity: History, Theory, and Practice* (Detroit: Wayne State University Press, 1990); Ellen Messer-Davidow, David R. Shumway, and David J. Sylan, *Knowledges: Historical and Critical Studies in Disciplinarity* (Charlottesville: University Press of Virginia, 1993).

41. David Tracy modified this inherently interdisciplinary approach in his "revised method of correlation." See, for example, Tillich, *Systematic Theology,* and Tracy, *Blessed Rage for Order.* James N. Poling and Donald F. Miller, *Foundations for a Practical Theology of Ministry* (Nashville: Abingdon Press, 1985), 29–61, provide a useful discussion of various styles of integrating disciplinary resources.

42. See Bibliography, s.v. Metaphor's Functions and Narrative's Functions.

43. George Lakoff and Mark Johnson, *Metaphors We Live By* (Chicago: University of Chicago Press, 1980), 5. See also Julian Jaynes, *The Origin of Consciousness in the Breakdown of the Bicameral Mind* (Boston: Houghton Mifflin, 1977), 48–66.

Albert Mehrabian, (*An Analysis of Personality Theories* [Englewood Cliffs, N.J.: Prentice-Hall, 1968]) writes: "A metaphor or analogy . . . typically determines the kind of theory (i.e., categories, assumptions, and hypotheses) which underlies observation and description. . . . [A] metaphor serves to generate a theory and the theory in turn serves as a guide in observation; however, since the type of metaphor used determines the kind of theory which is generated, it follows that the metaphor which is selected indirectly influences the kinds of observations which are initially made in an unfamiliar area" (5). The progress in theorizing, beyond the stage in which a metaphor is selected for the study of a specified class of prob-

lems, consists of the translation of the categories of the metaphor into concepts
of the theory which includes the explicit statement of criteria for the measurement
of the concepts. If the criteria for classification of phenomena into categories are
found sufficiently reliable and valid, then the theorist proceeds to test some of the
propositional statements, derived from the metaphor, which relate the categories to each other. In actual experimentation, such propositional statements are
frequently referred to as either basic assumptions of a theory, or hypotheses to be
tested (p. 14). In Mehrabian's analysis, metaphors capture assumptions that underlie goals and interests that guide observation, description, attention, and selection of phenomena.

44. Lakoff and Johnson, *Metaphors We Live By*, 3.

45. Ibid., 19–20.

46. Sallie McFague, *Metaphorical Theology: Models of God in Religious Language*
(Philadelphia: Fortress Press, 1982), 56.

47. Stephen Pepper, "The Root Metaphor Theory of Metaphysics," in *Essays on
Metaphor*, edited by Warren Shibles (Whitewater, Wisconsin: The Language
Press, 1972), 15–26.

48. Pepper himself discussed four "relatively adequate world theories": two
"analytical" perspectives—formism and mechanism—and two "synthetic" perspectives— contextualism and organicism. Formism has as its root metaphor "sim-
ilarity," "the simple common-sense perception of similar things." The root
metaphor of mechanism is a machine. Pepper suggested that the commonsense
point of origin of contextualism is what he refers to as "the historic event." The
root metaphor of organicism is the organism.

49. Andrew Ortony, "Metaphor: A Multidimensional Problem," in *Metaphor
and Thought*, edited by Andrew Ortony (Cambridge: Cambridge University Press,
1979), 1. Ortony provides a helpful philosophic context for Pepper's comments
and for those who will subsequently extend his thinking. These ideas reflect
what Ortony calls a "constructivist" perspective. In this approach, knowledge involves "going beyond the information given" by way of "mental construction."
"The constructivist approach seems to entail an important role for metaphors in
both language and thought, but it also tends to break down the distinction between
the metaphorical and the literal. Since, for the constructivist, meaning has to be
constructed rather than merely 'read off,' the meaning of non-literal uses of language does not constitute a special problem. The use of language is an essentially
creative activity, as is its comprehension" (2). This constructivist perspective can
be exemplified in the thinking of another influential twentieth century philosopher, Karl Popper. Don R. Swanson, "Afterthoughts on Metaphor: Toward a Psychology of Metaphor," in *On Metaphor*, edited by Sheldon Sacks. (Chicago: University of Chicago Press, 1979), 161. Swanson describes Popper's view as claiming that "we gain knowledge of the world by trial-and-error elimination. Theories
are conjectures or hypotheses, and experience is the testing of hypotheses. Con-

frontations with the real world lead us to eliminate erroneous theories; we then reshape our conjectures and try again. The better theories emerge as the survivors in a process of natural selection. We approach, but never attain, a true model of objective reality by endless cycles of conjectures and refutations." All our knowing, then, may be an endless process of hypothesis testing. We understand and experience one thing in terms of another, constructively going beyond the information given. We reshape our conjectures. This is the movement of living and acting in and according to metaphor.

50. Tracy, "Metaphor and Religion: The Test Case of Christian Texts," in *On Metaphor,* 89. Tracy continues: "In a particular religion, root metaphors form a cluster or network in which certain sustained metaphors both organize subsidiary metaphors and diffuse new ones. These networks describe the enigma and promise of the human situation and prescribe certain remedies for that situation."

Sallie McFague (*Metaphorical Theology,* 18) describes Christian religious thinking—Christian theology—as metaphorical: "If metaphor is the way by which we understand as well as enlarge our world and change it—that is, if the only way we have of dealing with the unfamiliar and new is in terms of the familiar and the old, thinking of 'this' as 'that' although we know the new thing is both like and unlike the old—if all this is the case, then it is no surprise that Jesus taught in parables or that many see him as a parable of God. A metaphorical theology, then, starts with the parables of Jesus and with Jesus as a parable of God."

51. Browning, *Religious Ethics and Pastoral Care,* 57, 58.

52. Just here it is most helpful to recognize that metaphor becomes a natural bridge across theories. Whereas McFague and Mehrabian argue that metaphors underlie their respective enterprises of theology and personality theory, Browning (*Religious Thought and the Modern Psychologies*) goes one step further to claim that the critical conversation between theological and social scientific resources should involve the deep metaphors of the respective partners.

53. Stanley Hauerwas and L. Gregory Jones (*Why Narrative? Readings in Narrative Theology* [Grand Rapids: Eerdmans, 1989]) have noted that narrative is used in a variety of ways such that "proponents of one or more of these uses of narrative are not necessarily proponents of all of them. Indeed some of the uses conflict with each other. . . . Moreover, proponents of a version of one or more of the uses of narrative may not accept a different version of that use" (2).

54. Cited in James Hillman, "The Fiction of Case History: A Round," in *Religion as Story,* edited by James B. Wiggins (New York: Harper & Row, Publishers, 1975), 127.

55. Hauerwas and Jones, *Why Narrative?,* 4.

56. T. R. Sarbin, "The Narrative as a Root Metaphor for Psychology," in *Narrative Psychology: The Storied Nature of Human Conduct,* edited by T. R. Sarbin (New York: Praeger, 1986).

57. Roy Schafer, "Narratives of the Self," in *Psychoanalysis: Toward the Second Century*, edited by Arnold M. Cooper, Otto F. Kernberg, and Ethel Spector Person (New Haven: Yale University Press, 1989), 162–63. Schafer builds upon Lakoff and Johnson's analysis of metaphor and metaphoric entailment. He writes, "Metaphor entailment is exemplified by the basic spatial metaphor, 'good is up.' This metaphor entails that, among other attributes, intelligence, good taste, and wealth are up, while stupidity, vulgarity, and poverty are down. For example, very intelligent is 'highly' intelligent. These are entailments insofar as consistency and coherence of discourse are the goals, which they usually are. These few remarks on metaphor and entailment suggest that metaphor says the same as story line. Again, however, story line seems to be the more inclusive term of the two. As I noted earlier, metaphor may establish a story line, and what is called *'unpacking a metaphor'* is in certain respects much like laying out the kind of story that is entailed by the metaphor" (162-63).

Julian Jaynes has a helpful way of illustrating how these associations are extensive and naturally generative. In every linking—say, for example, conversation is musical—each of the terms generates lines of associations that are constantly interactive. Thus, conversation may lead to associations like dialogue, discourse, words, friendship, inquiry, support, while musical may lead to associations like melodic, harmonic, rhythmic, . . . In using this metaphor, I am not simply extending two independent lines of associations, I am generating mutually interactive associations, harmonic and words, inquiry and tempo, . . . See his *The Origin of Consciousness*.

58. Sarbin, "The Narrative as a Root Metaphor," 8.

59. Frederick Wyatt, "The Narrative in Psychoanalysis: Psychoanalytic Notes in Storytelling, Listening, and Interpreting," in *Narrative Psychology: The Storied Nature of Human Conduct*, edited by T. R. Sarbin (New York: Praeger, 1986), 193–210. Roy Schafer, for example, discusses in *The Analytic Attitude* (New York: Basic Books, 1983) psychoanalytic theories "as" narratives: "psychoanalysis is an interpretive discipline whose practitioners aim to develop a particular kind of systematic account of human action. . . . Psychoanalytic theorists of different persuasions have employed different principles or codes—one might say different narrative structures—to develop their ways of doing analysis and telling about it . . . these structures provide primary narratives that establish what is to count as data. Once installed as leading narrative structures, they are taken as certain in order to develop coherent accounts of lives and technical practices" (212).

60. Alisdair MacIntyre, "The Virtues, the Unity of a Human Life, and the Concept of a Tradition," in *Why Narrative?* edited by Hauerwas and Jones, 101.

61. Stephen Crites, "Myth, Story, History," in *Parable, Myth and Language*, edited by Tony Stoneburner (Cambridge: Church Society for College Work, 1968). Cited in McFague, *Metaphorical Theology*, 139.

62. MacIntyre, "The Virtues," 103.

63. Hillman, "The Fiction of Case History," 129.
64. Gerkin, *Living Human Document*, 26.
65. Ibid., 20.
66. Theologizing is not restricted to the ongoing explicit use of traditional theological language: Traditional theological language is not at all sufficient and may, in a broader more flexible sense, be unnecessary. As Paul Holmer says (*The Grammar of Faith* [New York: Harper & Row, 1978], 28): "For theology is not a more meaningful kind of prose than is, say, everyday speech or the words of the Bible. . . . Just as the meaning of a piece of logic is not another piece of prose about logic but the achievement of logical acuity and accuracy of thought and inference, so the meaning of Jesus' life and death is not a theory of the atonement or an elaborate Christology. We are fooled into this, perhaps lulled into it, by the demand for meaning."
67. See, for example, Poling and Miller's discussion of those who do theology from a "critical scientific approach," in *Foundations for a Practical Theology of Ministry*. Some of these theologians may use traditional theological language only rarely.
68. See Lakoff and Johnson, *Metaphors We Live By*.
69. For example, as a Lutheran I might assume the man has some duplicity in his illness: As a sinner, he bears some responsibility for his despondency. As a psychoanalytically oriented clinician, I also take for granted that there are secondary gains to his depression: He has unconscious motives, and responsibility, for continuing to suffer. At the same time, my attention to his unconscious motives and to the impact of experiences in childhood may compete with our attention to his relationship with God and God's participation in his healing. Once I take seriously that my praxis is interdisciplinary, I have to examine and critically evaluate the consistency and coherence of that perspective.
70. Tillich, *Systematic Theology*, 1:12, 14.
71. Geoffrey Wainwright makes an important point: "To be doing theology, it is not enough to be addressing 'God-shaped questions,' or, in Brian Hebblethwaite's more sophisticated phrase, to reckon with the possibility of 'an ultimate horizon of meaning.' Philosophy is an honorable name for that way of looking at things. You can even call it the philosophy of religion. But *theology* presupposes that there are 'God-shaped answers.' " "Theology as Churchly Reflection," 15.
72. Holmer, *The Grammar of Faith*, 28.
73. Tracy, *Blessed Rage for Order*, 105.
74. Ibid., 93.
75. Letty Russell, "A Feminist Looks at Black Theology," in *Black Theology II: Essays on the Formation and Outreach of Contemporary Black Theology*, edited by Calvin E. Bruce and William R. Jones (Lewisburg, Pa.: Bucknell University Press, 1978), 259.
76. I take this idea from Tillich. See the discussion of Winnicott's contribution to theologizing about person in chapter 3. In many ways, using the metaphor "ter-

ritory of the big questions" has a deep affinity with some of Winnicott's thinking. He suggests the spatial metaphor of an "area of experiencing," argues that this is "the place where we live," and further observes that we are characteristically unaware of the nature of the territory and that we "live" there all the time.

77. I do not think it incidental that Gilkey's story focuses on persons who are drinking. One of the tragic truths of human existence is that many of us faithfully avoid the big questions, in part because we have such difficulty grasping and articulating them, much less responding to them. Even more regrettably, many of us feel unable to deal with this helplessness and anxiety without the aid of something that will dull our senses.

We human beings do not want to be aware that we can never finally avoid the territory of being and having the big questions. Interestingly, however, one of the ways of attempting to avoid that territory is by denying to awareness that we are in that territory. One way we accomplish that is by maintaining the illusion that theologizing presupposes and requires a special context, status, language game, or sacred setting. We neither want to recognize nor admit that theologizing is something we are all doing.

78. Tillich, *Systematic Theology*, 1:12.

79. H. Richard Niebuhr, *The Responsible Self: An Essay in Christian Moral Responsibility* (San Francisco: Harper & Row, 1963), 126.

80. James D. Whitehead, "The Practical Play of Theology," in *Formation and Reflection: The Promise of Practical Theology*, edited by Lewis S. Mudge and James N. Poling (Philadelphia: Fortress Press, 1987), 36, 39.

81. Gerkin, *Living Human Document*, 47.

82. Russell, "A Feminist Looks at Black Theology," 252.

83. No one experiences or reflects, practices or theorizes except in particular ways. Kaufman writes ("Critical Theology," 42): "The critical theology I am envisioning here is not a kind of generic theological reflection, unencumbered by any specific loyalties or faith-commitments. It is important to recognize that critical work of this sort can be carried on effectively only by persons who are well aware of what commitment to a specific way of life means, and what it may cost—that is, who know from within what a faith-commitment is and what it demands of individuals and communities."

84. Gordon Kaufman, "Theology as a Public Vocation," in *The Vocation of the Theologian*. Edited and with an Introduction by Theodore W. Jennings, Jr. (Philadelphia: Fortress Press, 1985), 55.

85. Kaufman, "Critical Theology," 38. He continues, "As envisioned here, critical theology would be a discipline that attempts (1) to uncover and explore the major faith-complexes that provide orientation within modern culture (and within the university itself), developing appropriate concepts and theoretical frameworks for articulating these studies sharply and clearly; (2) to develop criteria for comparing and assessing these faith-orientations, so that it would become

possible to make critical judgments with respect to them; and (3) to make constructive proposals for transformations and improvements in these orientations that seemed appropriate and important" (41).

86. Poling and Miller, *Foundations for a Practical Theology of Ministry*, 32.

87. Browning, *Religious Ethics and Pastoral Care*, 99, 99–119.

88. Ibid., 51. See James D. Whitehead and Evelyn E. Whitehead, *Method in Ministry* (New York: Seabury Press, 1980), 2, 12–19.

Groome (*Christian Religious Education*, 184) states that "critical reflection" is one of the five basic components of "shared Christian praxis," in addition to present action, dialogue, the Story, and the Vision. Through critical reflection, we employ "critical reason to evaluate the present, critical memory to uncover the past in the present, and creative imagination to envision the future in the present" (185).

Poling and Miller (*Foundations for a Practical Theology of Ministry*, 69, 77–82, 91–92) enumerate the following steps in their essential components of practical theology: "description of lived experience; critical awareness of perspectives and interests; correlation of perspectives from culture and the Christian tradition; interpretation of meaning and value; critique of interpretation; guidelines and specific plans for a particular community." See also John Patton, *From Ministry to Theology: Pastoral Action and Reflection* (Nashville: Abingdon Press, 1990).

89. This citation, commonly attributed to St. Ignatius, is usually found in the following form: "Work as if everything depended on you, pray as if everything depended on God." See William Barry, S.J., "Toward a Theology of Discernment," *The Way*, Supplement 64 (Spring 1989): 129–40.

90. Holmer, *The Grammar of Faith*, 25.

3. Theologizing about Person

1. Alan W. Watts (*The Way of Zen* [New York: Vintage Books, 1957], 5) writes: "Thus scientific convention decides whether an eel shall be a fish or a snake, and grammatical convention determines what experiences shall be called objects and what shall be called events or actions."

2. Ibid., 5.

3. Ibid., 9.

4. See Stephen Toulmin, "Self-Knowledge and Knowledge of the Self," in *The Self: Psychological and Philosophical Issues*, edited by Theodore Mischel (Totowa, N.J.: Rowman and Littlefield, 1977), 291–317. See also Edward Farley, *Good and Evil: Interpreting a Human Condition* (Minneapolis: Fortress Press, 1990); Frank Johnson, "The Western Concept of Self," in *Culture and Self: Asian and Western Perspectives*, edited by Anthony Marsella, George De Vos, and Francis Hsu (New York: Tavistock Publications, 1985), 91–137; James Lapsley, "The 'Self,' Its Vicissitudes and Possibilities: An Essay in Theological Anthropology," *Pastoral Psychology* 35 (1986):23–45; Jerome D. Levin, *Theories of the Self* (Washington: Hemisphere

Publishing, 1992); Stephen A. Mitchell, *Relational Concepts in Psychoanalysis: An Integration* (Cambridge, Mass.: Harvard University Press, 1988), and *Hope and Dread in Psychoanalysis* (New York: Basic Books, 1993); Chris R. Schlauch, "The Intersecting-Overlapping Self: Contemporary Psychoanalysis Reconsiders Religion—Again," *Pastoral Psychology* 42 (1993):21-43; Charles Taylor, *Sources of the Self: The Making of Modern Identity* (Cambridge, Mass.: Harvard University Press, 1989).

5. According to Edmund Carpenter, "[the Eskimo] use many words for snow which permit fine distinctions, not simply because they are much concerned with snow but because snow takes its form from the actions in which it participates. . . . Different kinds of snow are brought into existence by the Eskimo as they experience their environment and speak; words do not label things already there. Words are like the knife of the carver. They free the idea, the thing, from the general formlessness of the outside" (*Eskimo Realities* [New York: Holt, Rinehart and Winston, 1973], 43, cited in John R. Carnes, *Axiomatics and Dogmatics* [New York: Oxford University Press, 1982], 12.)

6. See Bibliography, s.v. Metaphor's Functions.

7. See Bibliography, s.v. Narrative's Functions.

8. George Lakoff and Mark Johnson, *Metaphors We Live By* (Chicago: University of Chicago Press, 1980), 3.

9. Sallie McFague, *Metaphorical Theology: Models of God in Religious Language* (Philadelphia: Fortress Press, 1982), 56.

10. James Olney, *Metaphors of Self: The Meaning of Autobiography* (Princeton: Princeton University Press, 1972), 31.

11. Lakoff and Johnson, *Metaphors We Live By*, 5.

12. My use of *mirror* points to a kind of correspondence between the comparative structure of metaphor and the comparative structure and movement of human knowing. In the end, however, this is but another metaphor.

13. M. H. Abrams, *The Mirror and the Lamp* (London: Oxford University Press, 1953), 31-32, cited in McFague, *Metaphorical Theology*, 43.

14. Elizabeth Sewell, *The Human Metaphor* (Notre Dame, Ind.: University of Notre Dame Press, 1964), 15.

15. N. R. Hanson, *Perception and Discovery* (San Francisco: Freeman, Cooper, and Company, 1969).

16. J. Carnes, *Axiomatics and Dogmatics* (New York: Oxford University Press, 1982), 12.

17. Stephen Crites, "The Narrative Quality of Experience." *Journal of the American Academy of Religion* 39 (September 1971): 297.

18. Stephen Crites, "Angels We Have Heard," in *Religion as Story*, edited by J. B. Wiggins (New York: Harper & Row, Publishers, 1975), 30-31.

19. Ibid., 31-32.

20. The term *slippage* is taken from Daniel Stern's *The Interpersonal World of the Infant* (New York: Basic Books, 1985).

21. Ernest Lawrence Rossi (*The Psychobiology of Mind-Body Healing: New Concepts of Therapeutic Hypnosis* [New York: W. W. Norton, 1986], 20, 23) presents a lucid discussion of "information transduction," which is, from another angle, a re-description of "internal translation." Rossi writes, "Transduction refers to the conversion or transformation of energy or information from one form to another . . . all biological life [is] a system of information transduction." He continues, "virtually all modern approaches to mind-body communication attempt to facilitate the process of converting words, images, sensations, ideas, beliefs, and expectations into the healing, physiological processes in the body."

22. Sigmund Freud suggests this notion of "internal translation" when he writes about psychic processes involving two different languages: "the dream thoughts and the dream content are presented to us like two versions of the same subject-matter in two different languages," Sigmund Freud, *Interpretation of Dreams* in *The Standard Edition of the Complete Psychological Works of Sigmund Freud*, edited and translated by James Strachey (London: Hogarth Press, 1962) 4:277.

23. The term *primitive agonies* is D. W. Winnicott's. Donald W. Winnicott, "Fear of Breakdown." In *D. W. Winnicott: Psycho-Analytic Explorations*. Edited by Clare Winnicott, Ray Shepherd, Madeleine Davis (Cambridge, Mass.: Harvard University Press, 1989, 89.

24. My illustration of a theological perspective is intentionally comparatively brief and should be understood in light of the more expanded discussion presented in the previous chapter.

25. The reader is probably aware of how the discussion has shifted into a considerably different "language game," one that carves meaning out of felt experience in a considerably different way.

26. Heinz Kohut, *The Restoration of the Self* (New York: International Universities Press, 1977), 306.

27. Heinz Kohut, "Introspection, Empathy, and Psychoanalysis," in *The Search for the Self: Selected Writings of Heinz Kohut—1950–1978*, edited and with an introduction by Paul H. Ornstein (New York: International Universities Press, 1978), 209.

28. I have intentionally used the qualifier potentially different. In some relationships, the self understood via introspection and empathy may be for the most part identical to the self understood colloquially.

29. The words *distorted* and *inappropriate* are meant to be descriptive, not pejorative. *Distortive* refers to "inaccurate"; *inappropriate* refers to "not appropriate to the current person and moment."

30. This discussion is drawn directly from Heinz Kohut and Philip Seitz's analysis in "Concepts and Theories of Psychoanalysis," in *Search for the Self*, 348.

31. Kohut, *The Restoration of the Self*, 310–311.

32. Heinz Kohut, "The Psychoanalyst in the Community of Scholars," in *Search for the Self*, 705.

33. See Kohut and Seitz, "Concepts and Theories of Psychoanalysis," in *Search for the Self,* 1:337–374.

34. Kohut, *The Restoration of the Self,* 177.

35. Kohut referred to these narcissistic transferences as "archaic interpersonal" relationships. From the outside, relationships are regarded as "interpersonal." When regarded from the inside, these same relationships always have some aspect that is "intrapsychic": The self of another is in some ways a part of one's self.

36. This is one of the many ways in which self psychology and discussions of narrative converge: selves are overlapping, of a part; we are each in and of one another's story.

37. I will restrict my attention to that aspect of Winnicott's theorizing in and through which he outlines an alternative model of person, focusing on his formative essay, "Transitional Objects and Transitional Phenomena," in *Playing and Reality* (New York: Basic Books, 1986), originally published in 1953.

38. Winnicott, "Transitional Objects and Transitional Phenomena," 2.

39. Ibid., 10.

40. Ibid., 12.

41. Ibid., 13.

42. The term *"illusionistic world"* is Paul Pruyser's. My understanding of Winnicott's thinking is deeply influenced by Pruyser's discussion in *The Play of the Imagination: Toward a Psychoanalysis of Culture* (New York: International Universities Press, 1983).

43. I should note that in referring to the image(s) of God as transitional objects, I am not proposing that God is a transitional object. I am suggesting that certain images that our clients (or we) have of God may function in a manner psychically parallel to the way in which other transitional objects function. In other words, I am not reducing God to a psychic phenomenon, only noting the fact that we experience God through processes and structures that can be interpreted psychologically.

44. See Robert Michels's excellent article, "The Scientific and Clinical Functions of Psychoanalytic Theory," in *The Future of Psychoanalysis: Essays in Honor of Heinz Kohut,* edited by Arnold Goldberg (New York: International Universities Press), 125–135. His comments on a clinical theory functioning as the clinician's transitional object are on page 131.

45. Don Browning, *Religious Thought and the Modern Psychologies: A Critical Conversation in the Theology of Culture* (Philadelphia: Fortress Press, 1987), 5. For another example of how this concept of cultures is worked out, see James Davison Hunder, *Culture Wars: The Struggle to Define America* (New York: Basic Books, 1991).

46. See Sigmund Freud, "Obsessive Acts and Religious Practices," edited and translated by J. Strachey, *The Standard Edition of the Complete Psychological Works of Sigmund Freud* (London: Hogarth Press, 1907) 9:115–28; "Totem and Taboo," in *The Standard Edition,* 1913, 13:1–161; "The Future of an Illusion," in *The*

Standard Edition, 1927, 21:1–56; "Civilization and Its Discontents," in *The Standard Edition*, 1930, 21:57–146; "Moses and Monotheism," in *The Standard Edition*, 1939, 23:1–138.

47. Richard Bernstein, *Beyond Objectivism and Relativism: Science, Hermeneutics, and Praxis* (Philadelphia: University of Pennsylvania Press, 1985), 8, 9.

48. Stephen Toulmin, "Self Psychology as a 'Postmodern' Science," *Psychoanalytic Inquiry* 6 (1986):466.

49. Bernstein, *Beyond Objectivism and Relativism*, 9.

50. Ibid., 18.

51. Winnicott, "The Place Where We Live," in *Playing and Reality*, 104.

52. Pruyser, *The Play of the Imagination*, 68.

53 The terms are Paul Pruyser's, taken from *The Play of the Imagination*.

54. See Adam Phillips, *Winnicott* (Cambridge, Mass.: Harvard University Press, 1988).

55. Recent psychoanalytic theorizing provides a series of concepts through which to interpret the experience of such "presence": selfobject (Kohut), transitional object (Winnicott), transformational object (Bollas), alternative object (Bollas), primary process maternal presence (Horton), evoked companion (Stern), imaginary companion (Nagera), and narcissistic guardian (Benson and Pryor). See, for example, Sheldon Bach, "Notes on Some Imaginary Companions," *Psychoanalytic Study of the Child*, 26 (1971):159–71; Ronald M. Benson and David B. Pryor, "'When Friends Fall Out': Developmental Interference with the Function of Some Imaginary Companions," *Journal of the American Psychoanalytic Association*, 21 No. 3 (1973):457–73; Ronald M. Benson, "Narcissistic Guardians: Developmental Aspects of Transitional Objects, Imaginary Companions, and Career Fantasies," *Adolescent Psychiatry* 8 (1980):253–64; Christopher Bollas, *Forces of Destiny: Psychoanalysis and Human Idiom* (London: Free Association Books, 1989); Christopher Bollas, "The Transformational Object." In *The British School of Psychoanalysis: The Independent Tradition*, edited by Gregorio Kohon (New Haven: Yale University Press, 1986), 83–100; Paul C. Horton, *Solace: The Missing Dimension in Psychiatry* (Chicago: University of Chicago Press, 1981); Heinz Kohut, *The Analysis of the Self: A Systematic Approach to the Psychoanalytic Treatment of Narcissistic Personality Disorders* (Madison, Conn.: International Universities Press, 1971); Humberto Nagera, "The Imaginary Companion: Its Significance for Ego Development and Conflict Solution," *Psychoanalytic Study of the Child* 24 (1969):165–96; Daniel N. Stern, *The Interpersonal World of the Infant: A View from Psychoanalysis and Development Psychology* (New York: Basic Books, 1985).

56. The reference is, of course, Reinhold Niebuhr's, to sin as "inevitable but not necessary." See his *Nature and Destiny of Man*, vol. 1 (New York: Scribner's, 1941).

57. The notion of resistance is drawn from Merton Gill, who, in his discussions of transference, speaks about resistance to the awareness of transference and resistance to the working through of transference. Merton Gill, *Analysis of Transference*,

vol. 1 (New York: International Universities Press, 1982). The distinction between the fact and the act of sin is Tillich's. See *Systematic Theology: Existence and the Christ* (Chicago: University of Chicago Press, 1957), 2:55–58.

58. Tillich, *Systematic Theology*, 2:60. One of the ways in which the structure of finitude becomes the structure of destruction is illustrated in one's presuming that selves are independent, to be known by being "objective" and "neutral." Kohut's and Winnicott's writings challenge this. Understanding and knowledge of persons are less about seeking "objectivity" in detachment than about appreciating "subjectivity" from within the experiential context of one another. One cannot fully bracket preunderstandings, as if that were contaminating the neutral knowledge of the object, but use one's understanding of subjectivity as an entrance into appreciating the experience of others. One is part of the tapestry to be interpreted. As Kohut (*How Does Analysis Cure?* edited by Arnold Goldberg [Chicago: University of Chicago Press, 1984], 36) explains, "in principle, the observing agency is always a part of what is being observed, that again, in principle, there is no objective reality." See also Roy Schafer, *The Analytic Attitude* (New York: Basic Books, 1983), 184, 188.

Richard Palmer (*Hermeneutics: Interpretation Theory in Schleiermacher, Dilthey, Heidegger, and Gadamer* [Evanston, Ill.: Northwestern University Press, 1969], 23) discusses this from a hermeneutic angle, noting the importance of method: "Method and object cannot be separated: method has already delimited what we shall see. It has told us what the object is as object. For this reason, all method is already interpretation; it is, however, only one interpretation, and the object seen with a different method will be a different object." See also George Atwood and Robert Stolorow, *Faces in a Cloud* (New York: Aronson, 1979), 65, for the relevance of Winnicott's thinking.

4. The Pastoral Clinical Attitude

1. See Bibliography, s.v. Attitude.

2. Icek Ajzen, in "Attitude Structure and Behavior," puts it this way: "It is generally acknowledged that attitude is a latent variable or hypothetical construct. Being inaccessible to direct observation, it must be inferred from . . . responses. . . ." In *Attitude, Structure, and Function*, edited by Anthony R. Pratkanis, Steven J. Breckler, and Anthony G. Greenwald (Hillsdale, N.J.: Lawrence Erlbaum Associates, 1989), 242.

3. See Michael J. Lambert, *The Effects of Psychotherapy* (Edinburgh: Eden Press, 1979), 1:9–49.

4. Steven J. Breckler and Elizabeth C. Wiggins ("On Defining Attitude and Attitude Theory: Once More with Feeling," in *Attitude, Structure, and Function*, edited by Pratkanis, Breckler, and Greenwald, 418–19), write, "Attitudes are said to serve four basic functions. . . . First, attitudes guide behavior toward valued goals and

away from aversive events (the adaptive or utilitarian function). Second, attitudes help to manage and simplify information processing tasks (the knowledge or economy function). Third, attitudes allow people to communicate information about their personality and values (the expressive or self-realizing function). And fourth, attitudes protect people from unacceptable or threatening thoughts, urges, and impulses (the ego-defensive function)." Again, it is important to note that they are referring to attitudes, although clearly these ideas are also relevant to an attitude-in-general.

5. See George L. Engel's discussions of reduction and exclusion in "The Need for a New Medical Model: A Challenge for Biomedicine," in *Concepts of Health and Disease: Interdisciplinary Perspectives,* edited by Arthur Caplan, H. Tristram Engelhardt, and James McCartney (Reading, Mass.: Addison-Wesley, 1981), 589–607; and Engel, "A Clinical Application of the Biopsychosocial Model," *American Journal of Psychiatry* 137 (1980): 535–44.

6. David Shapiro, *Psychotherapy of Neurotic Character* (New York: Basic Books, 1989), ix.

7. Hans Loewald, "On the Mode of Therapeutic Action of Psychoanalytic Psychotherapy," in *How Does Treatment Help? On the Modes of Therapeutic Action of Psychoanalytic Psychotherapy,* edited by Arnold Rothstein (Madison, Conn.: International Universities Press, 1988), 55.

8. Roy Schafer, *The Analytic Attitude* (New York: Basic Books, 1983).

9. Heinz Kohut, "Extending Empathic Understanding, Sharing an Attitude," in *The Kohut Seminars on Self Psychology and Psychotherapy with Adolescents and Young Adults,* edited by Miriam Elson (New York: W. W. Norton, 1987), 188.

10. It is important to highlight the phrase "in which she or he has experienced." Although it is important to be self-conscious and self-critical about one's clinical attitude, one should assume that features of that attitude are unconscious, and that the client will experience an attitude different from what we consciously intend. By focusing on the attitude the client internalizes, we can learn to identify features of our attitude that are unconscious.

11. Schafer, *Analytic Attitude,* 3, 4.

12. Many authors, in various contexts, have considered the importance of regard. Self-understanding is a function of how one has been understood. Sartre has a well-known discussion of the regard of the other, in which in the experience of being object/objectified we lose our self. By comparison, Kohut has an interesting comment about how the mother (or primary caretaker) relates to the infant as if it were a self; the infant experienced-as-a-self experiences itself as a self. Dewey's analysis of the self as in part made up of the others' regard of us is also relevant. Probably the best-known analogy to my proposal of holy regard is Rogers' "unconditional positive regard." Both Thomas Oden, *Kerygma and Counseling* (Philadelphia: Westminster Press, 1966), and Don Browning, *Atonement and Psychotherapy* (Philadelphia: Westminster Press, 1966), understand unconditional positive re-

gard to be possible and constructive, because it is an expression of God's love for us. I consider holy regard to be of a different order. It is not love per se but a way of experiencing and relating to another as the Christ in her or him, as if that other were Christ: an infinite respect and reverence, a devotion to the well-being of the other, a sense of deep humility of how to care for the other. That is possible precisely because of God's holy regard of us, through others. To speak about holy regard, then, keeps in the forefront our appreciation that I and another are mediating a presence greater and other than both of us, that is present in and through both of us.

13. Recall Søren Kierkegaard's distinction between direct and indirect communication.

14. This image came to me during the process of a rather threatening clinical hour. I imagined being in a plane that was being thrown about by turbulence. There was little I could do but pray, hold on tightly to the arms of the seat, and hope that by my calming presence we could together negotiate our way through this section of the skies to a more or less safe landing. Compare Michael Franz Basch's image of mountain climbers connected by a rope, in *Doing Psychotherapy* (New York: Basic Books, 1980).

15. See Bibliography, s.v. Narrative's Functions, for works by these authors.

16. Kleinman, *The Illness Narratives* (New York: Basic Books, 1988), 3.

17. Daniel Stern, *The Interpersonal World of the Infant* (New York: Basic Books, 1985), 15.

18. Robert Cummings Neville, *Recovery of the Measure: Interpretation and Nature* (Albany: State University of New York Press, 1989), 27.

19. Please note that functioning as psychologist implicitly involves functioning as psychologist of religion and religious phenomena. As a consequence, the pastoral clinician-as-psychologist may utilize a variety of "psychological" perspectives.

20. See Heinz Kohut, "Introspection, Empathy, and Psychoanalysis: An Exploration of the Relationship between Mode of Observation and Theory," in *The Search for the Self*, vol. 1, chap. 12, edited by Paul Ornstein (New York: International Universities Press, 1959/1978).

21. See Schlauch, "Empathy as the Essence of Pastoral Psychotherapy." My use of *polarity* follows Paul Tillich, who describes how "each pole is limited as well sustained by the other one" (*Systematic Theology*, 3 vols. [Chicago: University of Chicago Press, 1951], 1:198).

22. Compare the following discussion with Roy Schafer's interpretation of "the guiding vision of psychoanalysis." He writes, "For my descriptive and expository purposes I shall be adapting and applying certain terms that have found favor with certain literary critics and philosophers. These terms—comic, romantic, tragic, ironic—refer to certain general visions or imaginative modes of comprehending the form and content of human situations and the changes they undergo" ("The

Psychoanalytic Vision of Reality," in *A New Language for Psychoanalysis* [New Haven: Yale University Press, 1976], 25).

23. For more technical, and precise, analyses of the intricacies of engagement, see especially Daniel Stern's discussion of "domains of relatedness," in *Interpersonal World of the Infant*, 26–34 and part 2, 37–182, and Stanley Greenspan, *The Development of the Ego: Implications for Personality Theory, Psychopathology, and the Psychotherapeutic Process* (Madison, Conn.: International Universities Press, 1989), 131–83.

24. Arnold Goldberg, *The Prisonhouse of Psychoanalysis* (Hillsdale, N.J.: The Analytic Press, 1990), 158.

25. Edgar Levenson, "Show and Tell: The Recursive Order of Transference," in *How Does Treatment Help? On the Modes of Therapeutic Action of Psychoanalytic Psychotherapy*, edited by Arnold Rothstein (Madison, Conn.: International Universities Press, 1988) , 135.

26. Henri J. M. Nouwen, *Out of Solitude: Three Meditations on the Christian Life* (Notre Dame, Ind.: Ave Maria Press, 1974), 33–34.

27. Arnold Goldberg, *The Prisonhouse of Psychoanalysis*, 113.

28. Ibid., 116.

29. This needs, of course, to be qualified. The capacity for such internal conversation is a developmental psychological achievement. Some persons may have little, if any, awareness or experience of themselves as subjects-agents. See, for example, Julian Jaynes's fine characterization of the interior experience of a person who lacks this ability to be subject and object, I and me, in *The Origin of Consciousness in the Breakdown of the Bicameral Mind* (Boston: Houghton Mifflin, 1977). See Mary Field Belenky, Blythe McVicker Clinchy, Nancy Rule Goldberger, and Jill Mattuck Tarule's analysis of different "ways of knowing," especially their chapter on "silence," in *Women's Ways of Knowing: The Development of Self, Voice, and Mind* (New York: Basic Books, 1986), 23–34.

30. Among the many discussions of internal-external and the liabilities of these terms, I recommend Roy Schafer's *Aspects of Internalization* (New York: International Universities Press, 1968); his revised views challenging his earlier approach, in "Internalization: Process or Fantasy," in *A New Language for Psychoanalysis*, 155–178; Arnold Goldberg, "Self Psychology and Alternative Perspectives on Internalization," in *Reflections on Self Psychology*, edited by Joseph D. Lichtenberg and Samuel Kaplan (Hillsdale, N.J.: The Analytic Press, 1983), 297–312.

31. Heinz Kohut uses this term to contrast with "introspection."

32. Martin Buber, *I and Thou*, Second Edition. (New York: Charles Scribner's Sons, 1958).

33. Michael Polanyi, *The Logic of Liberty: Reflections and Rejoinders* (Chicago: University of Chicago Press, 1951), 22. Recent scholarship in psychology and philosophy continues to entertain this problem, under a variety of themes. Is psychology art or science? Should a clinician pursue narrative truth or historical truth? Should we

approach the person in terms of a logic of forces or an interpretation of meanings? Some contemporary scholarship has challenged the sharp contrast Dilthey drew, arguing that these activities interpenetrate. Clinical theory and practice properly involve understanding motives, reasons, and meanings, as well as explaining causes and forces.

34. Steven Kepnes, "Bridging the Gap between Understanding and Explanation Approaches to the Study of Religion," *Journal for the Scientific Study of Religion* 25 (1986):508.

35. Recent literature has observed a shift away from a subject-object model toward models variously regarded as subject-subject, relational, intersubjective. See, for example, Edward Farley, *Good and Evil: Interpreting a Human Condition* (Minneapolis: Augsburg Fortress, 1990); Stephen A. Mitchell, *Relational Concepts in Psychoanalysis: An Integration* (Cambridge: Harvard University Press, 1988); Stephen A. Mitchell, *Hope and Dread in Psychoanalysis* (New York: Basic Books, 1993); Danah Zohar, *The Quantum Self: Human Nature and Consciousness Defined by the New Physics* (New York: Quill, 1990).

36. See Ellyn Kaschak, *Engendered Lives: A New Psychology of Women's Experience* (New York: Basic Books, 1992); Miriam Greenspan, *A New Approach to Women and Therapy* (New York: McGraw-Hill, 1983), 161–231; Judith V. Jordan, Alexandra G. Kaplan, Jean Baker Miller, Irene P. Stiver, and Janet L. Surrey, *Women's Growth in Connection: Writings from the Stone Center* (New York: Guilford Press, 1991). Hazel Markus and Daphna Oyserman, "Gender and Thought: The Role of the Self-Concept," in *Gender and Thought: Psychological Perspectives*, edited by Mary Crawford and Margaret Gentry (New York: Springer-Verlag, 1989), 100–27.

37. Mary Belenky et al., *Women's Ways of Knowing*, 102.

38. This polarity of separate-connected arises in self psychologists' capturing the relationship between self and selfobject in two dramatically different ways. On the one hand, we may say that the self includes, if you will, the selfobject: The selfobject, or, more properly, the functions of the other as selfobject, are experienced as part of or as extensions of the self. In that sense, the self is of a part, connected with, the selfobject. On the other hand, we may say that the self has a selfobject. In this sense, we are thinking about the self in its more colloquial meaning, from the outside, where self is separate (if only physically) from selfobject. Indeed, the term *selfobject* is itself a conflation of these two vantage points, noting how the selfobject is of the self (*self*object) and other than the self (self*object*).

39. Clyde Kluckhohn and Henry A. Murray, "Personality Formation: The Determinants," in *Personality: In Nature, Society, and Culture*, edited by Clyde Kluckhohn and Henry A. Murray (New York: Knopf, 1961), 53, cited in Norman Holland, *The I* (New Haven: Yale University Press, 1985), 130.

40. Because this capacity is itself a developmental achievement, I have used the qualifier "potentially."

41. Gabriel Marcel, *The Mystery of Being. I. Reflection and Mystery*, translated by G. S. Fraser (London: Harvill Press, 1950), 211.

42. D. W. Augsberger, *Pastoral Counseling across Cultures* (Philadelphia: Westminster Press, 1986).

43. Peter Elbow, *Writing without Teachers* (London: Oxford University Press, 1973), 148, 149.

Richard Bernstein's discussion (*The New Constellation: The Ethical-Political Horizons of Modernity-Postmodernity* [Cambridge, Mass.: MIT Press, 1992]) of two contrasting styles of argumentation—the adversarial and the dialogical—elucidates the stance of doubting and believing. The former Bernstein traces from the analytical movement in which "the other is viewed as an opponent, and the aim is to locate specifically what is wrong in the opponent's position." This style sifts the details and examines every vague claim, locating the issues of disagreement. But Bernstein contrasts it with the dialogical encounter in which the other is assumed to have something to say, a conversational partner. "This requires imagination, sensitivity and perfecting hermeneutical skills. There is a play, a to-and-fro movement in dialogical encounters, a seeking for a common ground in which we can understand our differences." He concludes: "An engaged fallibilistic pluralism that is true to what is best in the pragmatic tradition requires a delicate balance between these different styles of argumentation and encounter" (337-38).

44. Paul Ricoeur, *Freud and Philosophy* (New Haven: Yale University Press, 1970).

45. Some philosophers and theologians have spoken to this polarity of doubting and believing, although in different terms. I would like to examine briefly the contemporary American philosopher Richard Rorty's recent discussions of several interrelated pairs of terms—ironist-metaphysician, solidarity-objectivity, pragmatist-realist—as a means of enhancing our appreciation of this dynamic.

Richard Rorty (*Contingency, Irony, and Solidarity* [Cambridge: Cambridge University Press, 1989], 73) suggests that all human beings have what he calls a final vocabulary: a set of words they employ to justify their actions, their beliefs, and their lives. They are the words in which we tell, sometimes prospectively and sometimes retrospectively, the story of our lives. He contrasts ways in which the ironist and the metaphysician approach their final vocabularies. The ironist assumes a plurality of final vocabularies, has radical and continuing doubts regarding the status of his own, knowing that it cannot be closer to reality. The metaphysician, in contrast, operates according to common sense, assuming "that the presence of a term in his own final vocabulary ensures that it refers to something which *has* a real essence." The metaphysician regards scientific revolutions as "insights into the intrinsic nature of nature," whereas the ironist regards them as "metaphoric redescriptions of nature" (16).

Rorty ("Solidarity or Objectivity?" in *Objectivity, Relativism, and Truth: Philosophical Papers*, vol. 1 [Cambridge: Cambridge University Press, 1991], 21) extends these ideas through his analysis of solidarity and objectivity, and pragmatists and realists. Some individuals, seeking solidarity, give sense to their lives "by telling the story of their contribution to a community." Others, desiring objectivity, "describe themselves as standing in immediate relation to a nonhuman reality." Realists "wish to ground solidarity in objectivity. . . . [They] have to construe truth as correspondence to reality." Pragmatists "wish to reduce objectivity to solidarity. . . . [They] view truth as . . . what is good for *us* to believe" (22).

Metaphysician-realists pursue objective truth; ironic pragmatists seek workable or functional understanding. For the former, inquiry is "the application of criteria to cases"; for the latter, it is "the continual reweaving of a web of beliefs" (26).

Interestingly, Paul Tillich addresses some of these themes in his philosophical theology. Tillich characterizes faith as a polarity of doubt and belief. Nothing that we know is certain; everything always contains an element of ambiguity. At the heart of these issues is his discussion of the Protestant principle. According to Tillich ("The Protestant Principle and the Proletarian Situation," in *The Protestant Era*, translated and edited by James Luther Adams [London: Nisbet and Company, 1951]), all ideas, beliefs, doctrines, and faiths are subject to the dual threats of demonization and profanization. In the former, we elevate the conditional to the status of unconditional; in the latter, conversely, we lower the unconditional to the status of conditioned. In this context, he formulates the Protestant principle as "the divine and human protest against any absolute claim made for relative reality" (163), "a permanent criterion of everything temporal" (viii). This principle challenges us to be constantly aware that everything temporal is conditioned, finite, ambiguous, relative. Nothing about how, what, and why we understand and know as we do is final. To use Rorty's terms, we must be ironists, for whom no final vocabulary is absolutely final.

Tillich acknowledges that the Protestant principle is not and cannot be the sufficient "theological expression of the true relation between the unconditional and the conditioned," precisely because a thoroughly and consistently self-critical principle inevitably arrives at the point where "the protest has endangered its own basis" (xix). In other words (Paul Tillich, *Systematic Theology* [Chicago: University of Chicago Press, 1963]), we cannot live out of a thoroughly doubting stance. "The Protestant principle is not enough; it needs the 'Catholic substance,' the concrete embodiment of the Spiritual Presence" (3:245). That is, we must be rooted and stand somewhere, assume and believe something.

The polarity of doubting-believing, particularly when understood to be relevant not only to our understanding and knowing the other but also to ourselves, reflects how we inevitably must believe and at the same time question what we believe. We must be rooted somewhere yet recognize the provisional character of what, how, and why we understand as we do, that is, self-critically doubt our observations and interpretations. We function as metaphysicians, presuming the efficacy of our final vocabulary. We function in terms of the Catholic presence, in relation to the God of theological theism. We presume we are realists in pursuit of objectivity, of the really real, the Truth. At the same time, we must function as ironists, anticipating the redescription of our final vocabulary, as it is subject to the Protestant principle, as we seek the God beyond the God of theological theism. In claiming some sense of resonance across Elbow's, Rorty's, and Tillich's ideas, I am not suggesting a simple parallelism. I am, however, proposing that Rorty's and Tillich's pairs of terms be regarded as polarities that have some underlying affinity with the issue of doubting and believing. To use a metaphor, they circulate in a shared territory.

46. See Tillich, *Systematic Theology: Existence and the Christ* (Chicago: University of Chicago Press, 1957), 2:55–56: "Sin is a universal fact before it becomes an individual act, or more precisely, sin as an individual act actualizes the universal fact of estrangement."

47. The term *something* is unfortunate but is, of course, symbolic.

48. Martin Buber captured this when he stated that behind every I-Thou relationship is the Eternal Thou.

49. It should be apparent that the pastoral clinician not only regards herself to be mediating a gift; she regards the other as potentially mediating a gift. In this regard, God's presence can be revealed in myriad ways—through each person, through their relationship. In a truly collaborative relationship, both participants bring something to the other and are open to being changed through their relationship. Pastoral clinical care is not done by the pastoral clinician, to or for the client, but is care that evolves with the client, through the relationship.

50. Donald Spence (*The Freudian Metaphor: Toward Paradigm Change in Psychoanalysis* [New York: W. W. Norton, 1987]) challenges theorists who idealize empathy: "It has become fashionable nowadays to speak of empathy as another kind of instrument, equally as precise as Freud's calculus, a psychological X-ray which allows us to read the inside of someone else's mind. . . . [S]uch a notion is a dangerous oversimplification which obscures the fact that empathy is often confused with unwitting projection. . . . You will notice that empathy, [is] seen as a kind of immaculate perception" (44–45). Later in his discussion, he explains, "A rather similar concept [to empathy] was identified by Ruskin in his work on painters in the nineteenth century. . . . Ruskin was keenly sensitive to the mischief produced when we use our feelings to make decisions about the object of interest, and called the phenomenon the pathetic fallacy. . . . If empathy is an act of sympathetic projection onto the object, it may help us at times to understand and anticipate certain behaviors in certain contexts, but it is clearly an act of selection and identification and is certainly not an impartial instrument. Because it is personal and partial, it can easily become pathetic, and I think Ruskin's description can be applied to many case histories in which the author's reactions to the material are mistakenly confused with the patient's meanings" (62–63).

I suggest that we bear in mind Spence's connection of empathy with the pathetic fallacy, but for a reason other than he intends. The first step in empathy is projection: One seeks imaginatively to infer what it might be like to be experiencing what the client is reporting. One puts one's self in the other's place, in the other's shoes. In addition, however, one attempts to qualify this imaginative perception, asking not what might I be experiencing were I to say what you've said, but what you might be experiencing in saying that. Of course, Spence's rejoinder—one with which I agree—is that even that imaginative act is highly projective; it cannot be otherwise.

The problem rests with how we understand elevating—or as Kohut put it, idealizing—empathy. Spence is mistaken if he concludes that self psychological theorists are proposing that healing takes place because a clinician has a remarkable power to bracket his subjectivity and immerse himself in the inner experience of another in an objectively accurate, constant manner—beyond projection, so to speak. The spirit of those theorists and of the attitude I am characterizing is dramatically different.

51. Spence, *The Freudian Metaphor*, 203–4.

5. The Triad of Clinical Activities

1. Although his comments specifically address pluralism in philosophy, I consider Richard Bernstein's discussion equally applicable to clinical perspectives. He writes, "There are two extremes that must be avoided. On the one hand, the provincialism that is so fashionable among 'true believers' of different philosophic orientations can blind us to a serious, sympathetic understanding of other philosophers who are working in different idioms. The vehement polemics of the proponents of different positions are among the least illuminating, informative, and lasting aspects of philosophic inquiry. The idea that there is *the* correct method of philosophizing is a myth and a delusion. On the other hand, it is false to think that all significant philosophic positions are equally correct, that once we genuinely understand what a philosopher is saying and why he [or she] is saying it, then all sharp disagreements disappear. Frequently, different philosophic orientations have more in common than is first apparent, but they also have sharp differences in emphasis, style, and doctrine that cannot be wished away" (*Praxis and Action: Contemporary Philosophies of Human Activity* [Philadelphia: University of Pennsylvania Press, 1971], 4).

2. These comments are drawn from Richard D. Chessick's discussion of W. Bromberg's *The Nature of Psychotherapy* (New York: Grune & Stratton, 1962), cited in *How Psychotherapy Heals: The Process of Intensive Psychotherapy* (New York: Science House, 1969), 17.

3. I am drawing heavily from Don Browning's analysis of Gadamer in *A Fundamental Practical Theology* (Minneapolis: Fortress Press, 1991). See also the discussion of "praxis" in chap. 2 in this book.

4. P. Nathan, *Cues, Decisions, and Diagnoses: A Systems-Analytic Approach to the Diagnosis of Psychopathology* (New York: Academic Press, 1967), 16.

5. Paul Pruyser, *The Minister as Diagnostician* (Philadelphia: Westminster Press, 1976), 30.

6. W. W. Meissner writes, "The analyst is continually making a diagnostic assessment of the patient, both in terms of his long-range, overall impression of the status and capacity to function of the patient's personality, and in terms of the short-range, moment-to-moment reading of the patient's level of regression, his state of consciousness, the level of transference interference, the degree of effective alliance, the state of defensive organization, and so on." *What Is Effective in Psychoanalytic Therapy: The Move from Interpretation to Relation* (Northvale, N.J.: Jason Aronson, 1991), 145.

7. Richard J. Bernstein, *Beyond Objectivism and Relativism: Science, Hermeneutics, and Praxis* (Philadelphia: University of Pennsylvania Press, 1985), 38, quoting Gadamer.

8. Browning, *Fundamental Practical Theology*, 39. The citation is from Hans-Georg Gadamer, *Truth and Method* (New York: Crossroad, 1982), 289.

9. Pruyser, *The Minister as Diagnostician*, 61.

10. K. Menninger, M. Mayman, and P. Pruyser, *The Vital Balance: The Life Process in Mental Health and Illness* (New York: Penguin Books, 1963); Norman Holland, *The I* (New Haven: Yale University Press, 1985).

11. Theodore Millon, "On the Nature of Taxonomy in Psychopathology," in *Issues in Diagnostic Research*, edited by C. G. Last and M. Hersen (New York: Plenum Press, 1987), 4. Millon writes, "psychopathologic states and processes may be classified in terms of any of several data levels we may wish to focus on, and any of a variety of attributes we may wish to identify and explain. Beyond this, each data level lends itself to a number of specific concepts and categories, the usefulness of which must be gauged by their ability to help solve the particular problems and purposes for which they were created. . . . "

12. Aaron Lazare, "Hypothesis Testing in the Clinical Interview," in *Outpatient Psychiatry: Diagnosis and Treatment*, edited by A. Lazare (Baltimore: Williams & Wilkins, 1979), 132.

13. Millon, "On the Nature of Taxonomy," 6, emphasis added.

14. N. R. Hanson, *Perception and Discovery* (San Francisco: Freeman, Cooper and Company, 1969); J. Carnes, *Axiomatics and Dogmatics* (New York: Oxford University Press, 1982). "Observation is 'theory-laden.' " The phrase comes from N. R. Hanson, *Perception and Discovery*, 131. I find John Carnes's modification helpful. He writes, "To avoid the intellectualist implications of the word 'theory' . . . , R. M. Hare (in Flew and MacIntyre, 1955) coined the word 'blik' to stand for those nonverifiable, non-falsifiable world-perspectives or world-views which determine for us what is out there and how it shall be known. I will adopt Hare's word because of its 'neutrality' and will sometimes speak of observations and facts being blik-laden, rather than theory-laden, to keep in our minds the fact that observation is guided and shaped by factors other than our intellectual commitments" (*Axiomatics and Dogmatics*, 12).

15. See, for example, works by D. Browning, G. Lakoff and M. Johnson, S. McFague, and A. Mehrabian in Bibliography, s.v. Metaphor's Functions; and Terrence Tilley, *Story Theology* (Wilmington, Del.: Michael Glazier, 1985).

16. See, for example, Paul Pruyser, *The Psychological Examination: A Guide for Clinicians* (New York: International Universities Press, 1979); L. Rice and L. S. Greenberg, editors, *Patterns of Change: Intensive Analysis of Psychotherapy Process* (New York: Guilford Press, 1984).

17. See Bibliography, s.v. Diagnosis.

18. In addition to works cited in Bibliography (s.v. Diagnosis; and by D. Browning, D. Capps, C. Gerkin, and J. Patton, s.v. Disciplines as Hermeneutical or Interpretive), see Donald Capps, *Biblical Approaches to Pastoral Counseling* (Philadelphia: Westminster Press, 1980); J. H. Ellens, "Biblical Themes in Psychological Theory and Practice," in *Christian Counseling and Psychotherapy,* edited by D. G. Benner (Grand Rapids: Baker Book House, 1987), 23–33; Merle R. Jordan, *Taking on the Gods: The Task of the Pastoral Counselor* (Nashville: Abingdon Press, 1986); H. Wahking, "Therapy with Theological Constructs and Tactics," in *Christian Counseling and Psychotherapy,* edited by D. G. Benner (Grand Rapids: Baker Book House, 1987), 15–22; and M. Yeomans, editor, *Clinical Theology* (London: Darton, Longman, and Todd, 1986).

19. In some ways, it is helpful to speak of the process of *diagnosing* rather than the nature of *diagnosis* because the former suggests doing something, whereas the latter can be misused to suggest a static conclusion one has attained.

20. Ken Mitchell, "The Book That Has Most Influenced My Practice of Pastoral Psychotherapy," *The Journal of Pastoral Psychotherapy* 1 (1987):77–82.

21. William Muehl, "Opinion: A Statement of Communication," *Reflections* 85 (Yale Divinity School) (1990):26–27.

22. Paul Holmer, *The Grammar of Faith* (New York: Harper & Row, 1978).

23. See Bibliography, s.v. Operationalizing Approaches.

24. See, for example, E. Draper, *Psychiatry and Pastoral Care* (Englewood Cliffs, N.J.: Prentice-Hall, 1965); R. J. Fairbanks, "Diagnosis in Pastoral Care," *The Journal of Pastoral Care* 6 (1952); Seward Hiltner, *Religion and Health* (New York: Macmillan, 1943); Hiltner, *Pastoral Counseling* (Nashville: Abingdon Press, 1949).

25. See, for example, Seward Hiltner, *Theological Dynamics* (Nashville: Abingdon Press, 1972), and "Toward Autonomous Diagnosis" in *Diagnosis and the Difference It Makes,* edited by Paul W. Pruyser (New York: Jason Aronson, 1976); Paul W. Pruyser, editor, *Diagnosis and the Difference It Makes* (New York: Jason Aronson, 1976); Paul W. Pruyser, *The Minister as Diagnostician* (Philadelphia: Westminster Press, 1976), and "The Diagnostic Process in Pastoral Care" in *Psychiatry, Ministry, and Pastoral Counseling,* edited by A. W. R. Sipe and C. J. Rowe (Collegeville, Minn.: Liturgical Press, 1984); Ralph L. Underwood, "Personal and Professional Integrity in Relation to Pastoral Assessment," *Pastoral Psychology* 31 (1982):109–17; H. S. Gaskill, "The Diagnostic Interview," in *Psychiatry, Ministry, and Pastoral Counseling,*

edited by A. W. R. Sipe and C. J. Rowe (Collegeville, Minn.: Liturgical Press, 1984): 78–102; D. P. Hobson and M. Jacob, "Possibilities and Pitfalls in Pastoral Diagnosis," *Pastoral Psychology* 34 (1985):30–41.

26. See, for example, Don. S. Browning, *Religious Ethics and Pastoral Care* (Philadelphia: Fortress Press, 1983); B. K. Estadt, M. Blanchette, and J. R. Compton, editors, *Pastoral Counseling* (Englewood Cliffs, N.J.: Prentice-Hall, 1983); John Patton, *Pastoral Counseling: A Ministry of the Church* (Nashville: Abingdon Press, 1983); Gerkin, *The Living Human Document: Re-Visioning Pastoral Counseling in a Hermeneutical Mode* (Nashville: Abingdon Press, 1984); Gerkin, "Faith and Praxis," *Pastoral Psychology* 35 (1986):3–15; Merle R. Jordan, *Taking on the Gods: The Task of the Pastoral Counselor* (Nashville: Abingdon Press, 1986); Chris R. Schlauch, "Defining Pastoral Psychotherapy," *The Journal of Pastoral Care* 39 (1985):219–28; ; Schlauch, "Defining Pastoral Psychotherapy II," *The Journal of Pastoral Care* 41 (1987):319–27; Schlauch, "Empathy as the Essence of Pastoral Psychotherapy," *The Journal of Pastoral Care* 44 (1990):3–17; Schlauch, "Expanding the Contexts of Pastoral Care," *The Journal of Pastoral Care* 44 (1990):359–71.

27. See, for example, Browning, *Religious Ethics and Pastoral Care;* Donald Capps, *Pastoral Counseling and Preaching* (Philadelphia: Westminster Press, 1980); Capps, *Biblical Approaches to Pastoral Counseling;* Capps, *Pastoral Care and Hermeneutics* (Philadelphia: Fortress Press, 1984); Carl D. Schneider, "Faith Development and Pastoral Diagnosis," in *Faith Development and Fowler,* edited by C. Dykstra and S. Parks (Birmingham: Religious Education Press, 1986).

28. See, for example, J. P. Feighner and J. Herbstein, "Diagnostic Validity," in *Issues in Diagnostic Research,* edited by C. G. Last and M. Hersen (New York: Plenum Press, 1987), 121–40; W. M. Grove, "The Reliability of Psychiatric Diagnosis," in *Issues in Diagnostic Research;* C. R. Cloninger, "Establishment of Diagnostic Validity in Psychiatric Illness: Robins and Guze's Method Revisited," in *Validity of Psychiatric Diagnosis,* edited by L. N. Robins and J. E. Barrett (New York: Raven Press, 1989), 9–18; B. P. Dohrenwend, "The Problem of Validity in Field Studies of Psychological Disorders," in *Validity of Psychiatric Diagnosis;* and E. Robins and S. B. Guze, "Establishment of Diagnostic Validity in Psychiatric Illness: Its Application to Schizophrenia," in *Validity of Psychiatric Diagnosis.*

29. John Patton, "The New Language of Pastoral Counseling," in *Spiritual Dimensions of Pastoral Care: Witness to the Ministry of Wayne E. Oates,* edited by G. L. Borchert and A. D. Lester (Philadelphia: Westminster Press, 1985), 74.

30. See Heinz Kohut, *The Analysis of the Self* (New York: International Universities Press, 1971); Kohut, *How Does Analysis Cure?* edited by A. Goldberg and P. Stepansky (Chicago: University of Chicago Press, 1984); Arnold Goldberg, *A Fresh Look at Psychoanalysis* (Hillsdale, N.J.: Analytic Press, 1988).

31. In the previous chapter I characterized the basic polarity of the introspective-empathic attitude of the pastoral clinician qua practical theologian of care (psy-

chologist-theologian-ethicist) as self-experience: Who is the self? What is she experiencing? Pastoral diagnosing represents a variation on that theme, qualifying the basic polarity to consider self-suffering: Who is the self? What is the suffering that she is experiencing?

32. Our bifocal attention to the self and the suffering of the person can be enhanced by, but does not focus expressly on his "mental status." A person's mental status is assessed in terms of Judgment, Insight, Mood, Memory, Orientation, Thought processes and content, Speech, Intelligence, General appearance and behavior, and Affect (JIM MOTSIGA; see Draper and Steadman, "Assessment in Pastoral Care," in *Clinical Handbook of Pastoral Counseling*, edited by R. J. Wicks, R. D. Parsons, and D. Capps [New York: Paulist Press, 1984], 127). Data from these various domains contribute to a picture of a person's current state and provide some indications of long-term functioning and capacities.

33. In his essay "The Structure of Individual Attitudes and Attitude Systems," William J. McGuire writes, "The trichotomy of human experience into thought, feeling, and action, although not logically compelling, is so pervasive in Indo-European thought (being found in Hellenic, Zoroastrian, and Hindu philosophy) as to suggest that it corresponds to something basic in our way of conceptualization, perhaps (Sagan, 1977) reflecting the three evolutionary layers of the brain, cerebral cortex, limbic system, and old brain. The trichotomy is reflected in Locke's analyzing knowledge into semeiotika, practica, and physica in his *Essay Concerning Human Understanding* and was explicitly revived as a classification by von Wolff in his 18th-century reprofessionalization and systematization of philosophy, whence it provided the basis of division for Kant's three Critiques of pure reason, judgment, and practical reason.

"This tripartite division has been used pervasively in psychology . . ." (*Attitude, Structure, and Function*, edited by Anthony R. Pratkanis, Steven J. Breckler, and Anthony G. Greenwald (Hillsdale, N.J.: Lawrence Erlbaum Associates, 1989), 40.

34. Ralph Greenson uses the idea of "working model" in his article, "Empathy and Its Vicissitudes," *International Journal of Psychoanalysis* 41 (1960):418–24.

35. Cited in Norman Holland, *Five Readers Reading* (New Haven: Yale University Press, 1975), 255–56.

36. Holland, *The I*, 35.

37. Again, the ways in which a person describes the goals of care and the prospective course of intervention are quite informing of our diagnosing of her current state of her self and suffering.

38. Michael Franz Basch, *Understanding Psychotherapy: The Science Behind the Art* (New York: Basic Books, 1988), 69.

39. Sheldon Roth, *Psychotherapy: The Art of Wooing Nature* (Northvale, N.J.: Jason Aronson, 1987), 274–75.

40. Basch, *Understanding Psychotherapy*, 72.

41. Daniel Stern, *The Interpersonal World of the Infant* (New York: Basic Books, 1985), 54–55.
42. Ibid., 55–56.
43. Ibid., 162.
44. Ibid., 168.
45. Ibid., 174.
46. Ibid., 178.
47. Ibid., 175.
48. Basch, *Understanding Psychotherapy*, 78.
49. Stern, *The Interpersonal World of the Infant*, 180.
50. Roth, *Psychotherapy: The Art of Wooing Nature*, 275.
51. Thus, for example, a classically oriented clinician might observe, "It seems as if I remind you of your father." An object relations clinician, in comparison, could reflect, "There are ways in which our relationship seems similar to the way in which you and your father related to one another." A self psychologically oriented clinician might say, "You describe your experience with me in ways that sound a lot like how you experienced yourself in relation to your father."
52. Heinz Kohut and Philip Seitz, "Concepts and Theories of Psychoanalysis," in *The Search for the Self: Selected Writings of Heinz Kohut: 1950–78,* edited by Paul H. Ornstein (New York: International Universities Press, 1978), 1:337–74.
53. Thus, "clinical transference" is an interpersonal expression and enactment of intrapsychic processes.
54. In some ways, the traditional understanding of "clinical transference" mistakenly lends the clinician to be working "interpersonally" rather than "intrapsychically."
55. Sigmund Freud, *An Autobiographical Study* (New York: W. W. Norton, 1952 [1935]), 80.
56. In this regard, see Merton Gill, *Analysis of Transference,* vol. 1 (New York: International Universities Press, 1982); Gill, *Analysis of Transference,* vol. 2 (New York: International Universities Press, 1982).
57. Herman Nunberg, "Transference and Reality," *International Journal of Psychoanalysis* 32 (1951):5.
58. Heinz Kohut and Philip Seitz, "Concepts and Theories of Psychoanalysis," in *The Search for the Self,* 337–74.
59. Although space does not permit a fuller elaboration, it is important to note how closely this understanding of ubiquitous compound formations is to the nature of metaphor. If metaphor is a compound formation, an amalgamation of known and yet-to-be-known, it bears a striking resemblance to this "universal phenomenon of the human mind," an amalgamation of manifest (conscious) and latent (preconscious, yet-to-be-known). See the discussion of metaphor and the metaphorizing process in chapter 3.

60. Gill, *Analysis of Transference*, vol. 1.

61. Kohut, *Analysis of the Self*, 23.

62. Psychoanalytic theorists have differentiated between intrasystemic and intersystemic modifications in the tripartite structural model of the mind. In the former, one can speak about, for example, modification within the superego; in the latter, in modifications between superego and ego.

63. See Don Browning, *Generative Man: Psychoanalytic Perspectives* (Philadelphia: Westminster Press, 1973); Browning, *Pluralism and Personality: William James and Some Contemporary Cultures of Personality* (Lewisburg, Pa.: Bucknell University Press, 1980); Browning, *Religious Thought and the Modern Psychologies: A Critical Conversation in the Theology of Culture* (Philadelphia: Fortress Press, 1987).

64. It should be noted that many of these approaches reflect the bias of the subject-object model, some falsely presuming that bracketing one's subjectivity is not only possible but ideal, others mistakenly assuming that one can and should bracket the subjectivity of the other.

65. The distinction is from Ernst A. Ticho, "Termination of Psychoanalysis: Treatment Goals, Life Goals," *Psychoanalytic Quarterly* 41 (1972):315–33.

66. Many contemporary discussions of treatment planning reflect a considerably different approach to care. Those discussions typically focus on psychopathology—independently of the self—and designate particular plans that correspond to particular manifestations of psychopathology. See, for instance, much of the literature on *The Diagnostic and Statistical Manual*. For example, a clinician-author might propose that in diagnosing depression and, checking the "menu" of therapeutic interventions, a standard plan of psychotropic medication in conjunction with psychotherapy is warranted. This approach has the advantage of working within parameters in which measurements of validity and reliability of diagnosis and treatment plans can be evaluated.

6. The Two Questions

1. Arthur Kleinman (*Rethinking Psychiatry: From Cultural Category to Personal Experience* [New York: Free Press, 1988], 110) observes that "there are hundreds of the most different kinds of practices that go by the name of psychotherapy. The term 'psychotherapist' stands for an equally bewildering array of persons. . . ."

Thinkers have identified various healing agents. Kleinman continues, "One of the more interesting controversies in the psychotherapy field is the question of whether the effects of psychotherapy are due to specific or nonspecific agents of change. Each school of psychotherapy claims that unique elements in its technique of practice are responsible for specific therapeutic effects" (112).

Judd Marmor ("Common Operational Factors in Diverse Approaches to Behavior Change," in *What Makes Behavior Change Possible?* edited by Arthur Burton [New York: Brunner/Mazel, 1976], 5) writes about "a substantial number of interacting variables" that play a part in change: "the personalities of the patient and the therapist (including both conscious and unconscious elements); the nature of the patient's problem; the degree of his or her motivation; the social role of the therapist; and the faith, hope, and expectancy that it engenders in the patient; the favorable or unfavorable potentials that the actual life situation of the patient presents; and the type of *relationship* that develops as a result of the specific patient-therapist interaction."

2. See, for example, John L. Maes, *Suffering: A Care Giver's Guide* (Nashville: Abingdon Press, 1990).

3. In this regard, I agree with Paul H. Ornstein, who writes, "My working assumption is that each patient-therapist encounter sets off a process that is characteristic, or specific, for just that treatment pair. The curative factors reside within 'the process,' which is, in a sense, automatically triggered for its unfolding by the particular encounter between therapist and patient" ("Multiple Curative Factors and Processes in the Psychoanalytic Psychotherapies," in *How Does Treatment Help? On the Modes of Therapeutic Action of Psychoanalytic Psychotherapy*, edited by Arnold Rothstein [Madison, Conn.: International Universities Press, 1988], 106).

4. A hyphen accentuates that these dimensions interpenetrate.

5. Marmor ("Common Operational Factors," 6–7) enumerates eight "operational factors" common to all psychotherapeutic approaches: a good patient-therapist relationship, release of tension, cognitive learning, operant conditioning, suggestion and persuasion, identification with the therapist, repeated reality testing, and emotional support from the therapist. Although some of this language is used, not all of his factors can be considered in the discussion.

H. Nick Higginbotham, Stephen G. West, and Donelson R. Forsyth (*Psychotherapy and Behavior Change: Social, Cultural and Methodological Perspectives* [New York: Pergamon Press, 1988], 75–76) note: "Clinicians of all persuasions adhere to the common sense belief that the quality of the client-therapist relationship is an essential, if not sufficient, ingredient in effective treatment. Widespread agreement among divergent theorists on the centrality of the therapeutic relationship was evident in . . . 1966. It is no less prominent today [1988], both in expressions of clinical intuition and in the literature evaluating clinical process and outcome. . . .

"Simply stated, this collective wisdom maintains that the quality of the therapeutic relationship inspires and constrains client change. An interpersonal bond comprised of mutual trust, liking, and respect evokes client willingness to disclose thoughts and feelings, listen carefully to therapist suggestions, and enact treatment strategies. . . . The corollary to this assumed promise is that a quality relationship will circumvent client resistance as a byproduct of the cooperation it engenders."

Focusing on the experience of being faithfully companioned is *not* limited to relationship but may take place through collaborative insight; it is not exclusive of specific factors but may be present through them; it is not restricted to the therapist's personality but may evolve through the experience of the therapist's relating through a theoretical perspective.

6. See Bibliography, s.v. Healing and Change.

7. Space does not permit any extended discussion, but I am referring her to the *developmental* level of her experience of others. Consider the following questions as illustrative: Does she convey an internal appreciation for the uniqueness of the internal life, motives, needs, aspirations of others? Is she able to approach events from another's vantage point? Does she describe people mechanically, externally, in terms of their behavior? Does she interpret relationships essentially from the point of its impact and influence on her?

8. I have amended Tillich's famous phrase, but with a variety of additional connotations. There are additional polarities relevant to this, such as autonomy-dependence and agency-communion. Of course, these various categories are more illustrative of some of the many ways in which we experience being on the boundaries.

9. See, for example, Howard Brody, "Dimensions of Sickness," chapter 2 in *Stories of Sickness* (New Haven: Yale University Press, 1987), 20–40, for a fine discussion of some of these terms. See also Arthur Kleinman's discussion of "illness" and "disease" in *The Illness Narratives* (New York: Basic Books, 1988).

10. See Ernest L. Rossi, *The Psychobiology of Mind-Body Healing* (New York: W. W. Norton, 1986) esp. 36–56.

11. See Thomas Droege's excellent discussion of self-healing and how it departs from the particular Christian theological perspective he is characterizing, in *The Faith Factor in Healing* (Philadelphia: Trinity Press International, 1991).

12. I presume that the healing of this interdimensional, multiple-identitied self takes place across "interrelated" processes. See James Lapsley's well-known text, *Salvation and Health: The Interlocking Processes of Life* (Philadelphia: Westminster Press, 1972), for a discussion of how salvation and healing are "interlocking processes."

13. As I have noted in an earlier chapter, we may use our theoretical perspective as a transitional object, a way of coping and self-soothing in the midst of the unknown and of transition.

Leston Havens says it beautifully: "Clinical theories are like the novelist's ideas and images. They allow us to vivify a patient and to become potent in understanding. It is not that the theories refer to nothing real or important to know, but every theory acts to suppress, like the novelist, the real person who consists of much else. This is a central reason for the quarrels of theorists and the terrible sectarianism that still grips us. . . . If the problem of the interview is to open our ideas to as much of the patient as possible, the problem of treatment is related: one must be able to survive the loss of either romance or theory, to find some compensation in the ordinary for what first vivified the patient and ourselves. It is like marriage: what brought us together is seldom what keeps us there" (*A Safe Place:*

Laying the Groundwork of Psychotherapy [Cambridge, Mass.: Harvard University Press, 1989], 58–59).

14. The term *collapse* is Peter Homans's in *Theology after Freud: An Interpretive Inquiry* (Indianapolis: Bobbs-Merrill, 1970), 50. One of the primary ways of collapsing mystery is to deny it entirely, or, to recast it as "placebo response."

15. In this description of conditions or contributions to healing, it should be apparent that I am focusing less on techniques or specific agents than I am on what has variously been termed nonspecific agents. Arthur Kleinman (*Rethinking Psychiatry,* 112) notes that "overall the empirical evidence fails to demonstrate specific effects of specific techniques. Rather it points to nonspecific, shared aspects of psychotherapy as the most likely chief determinants of efficacy." Jerome Frank, "Therapeutic Components," in *Effective Ingredients of Successful Psychotherapy,* edited by Jerome Frank, Rudolf Hoehn-Saric, Stanley D. Imber, Bernard L. Liberman, and Anthony R. Stone (New York: Brunner/Mazel, 1978), 19. Frank adds that "findings suggest that therapeutic features shared by all forms of psychotherapy account for a considerable portion of their effectiveness." He continues, "[T]he evidence is persuasive that personal characteristics of the therapist in interaction with those of the patient are more important than technique in determining the outcome of treatment. . . . These seem to be related to the therapist's ability to convey to the patient that he or she takes him seriously, understands him and is able to inspire the patient's hopes for improvement. Some therapists seem able to communicate these and other therapeutic attitudes to most of their patients" (21).

16. I am using the term *experiencing-reflecting* to be consistent with earlier discussions, particularly in chapter 2. The reader should be aware that I regard experiencing-reflecting, for all intents and purposes, as synonymous with the terms more common to psychoanalytic discussion, experiencing-observing.

17. Higginbotham, West, and Forsyth (*Psychotherapy and Behavior Change*) have proposed a series of hypotheses from which two are selected. "A mutually satisfying therapeutic alliance depends upon conversational cooperation that is negotiated. . . . Significantly, the clinician is constantly engaged in translating across systems of meaning. Most often, this entails translating between professional interpretive models and popular or folk models of illness and psychological dysfunction. This final assumption provides a rationale for redefining *healing,* as an outcome of the mutual interpretation or translation across systems of meaning" (90, 107–8).

18. I have proposed that these are distinguishable yet inseparable dimensions, in which we may be less influential in what we say than in what we do, and less influential in what we do than in who and how we are. To a certain degree, my approach has a basic affinity with current discussions in psychoanalysis and psychoanalytic psychotherapy that distinguish between "insight" and "relationship" but appreciate their inseparability. Consider some of these reflections.

Herbert J. Schlesinger, in an article entitled "A Historical Overview of Conceptions of the Mode of Therapeutic Action of Psychoanalytic Psychotherapy," in Rothstein, *How Does Treatment Help?* writes, "As time has passed, our thinking about the source of change has become complex. The earliest concepts of cure indicated one or two factors. More recent efforts accept the importance of multiple factors, factors that act not only singly but in patterned interaction . . . psychoanalysts have tended to favor one or another factor, and to divide sharply and ideologically as to whether insight into the nature of one's conflict or 'corrective emotional experience' is the main factor" (9–10). He continues, "[I]t is essential to our understanding of the therapeutic action of psychoanalytic psychotherapy to link the relationship factor to the interpretive process. Within the classical tradition, one might regard this factor from the positive side as standing for the patient's perhaps unverbalized awareness that conditions of respect and safety exist. From the negative side, one might regard it as a worried awareness that one's worst fears have not as yet been realized.

"In fact, it is difficult, and perhaps impossible, to distinguish the effects of correct interpretation from the effects of a good therapeutic relationship, for they are *not* separable in practice, and it is questionable if they are even separable in contemporary analytic theory" (17, emphasis added). As William Meissner (*What Is Effective in Psychoanalytic Therapy: The Move from Interpretation to Relation* [Northvale, N.J.: Jason Aronson, 1991], 59) notes, "Even if interpretation is the process by which understanding is achieved and insight generated, that process takes place within a relational matrix that both colors the interpretive process and provides those elements that make the process viable and meaningful."

Edgar Levenson, in his article, "Show and Tell: The Recursive Order of Transferences," in Rothstein, *How Does Treatment Help?* elucidates this contrast between insight and relationship: "Analysts tend to lay primary emphasis on one position or another, at least in theory. If we are impressed by the cogency of the associative flow, we tend to emphasize the neutral analyst, projection in the transference, and the role of psychic conflict. If we are impressed by the relational effect, we lean toward the active analyst, corrective experience in the transference, and the role of emotional deficit resulting from early deprivation. There is a certain symmetry: To the extent that we believe something real was done *to* the patient, we tend to believe something real must be done to correct it. To the extent we believe in the autonomy of the patient's unconscious fantasy, we tend to believe in the neutrality and inactivity of the therapist" (136–37).

See also William Meissner's excellent discussion of some of these concerns in his recent text, *What Is Effective in Psychoanalytic Psychotherapy.* He adds, "The question has become whether interpretation works because it leads to insight, or because it reflects and/or consolidates something about the analytic relationship. I have a sense that Kohut's work has had a significant impact in this regard, although he was certainly not the first to emphasize the priority of relationship over interpretation. This current of thinking is well reflected in Modell's (1984, 1986) view that, although interpretation is necessary, its content is not necessarily mutative, but that the implementation of the symbolic actualization of the holding environment in the analytic setting makes it possible for analytic interpretations to be effective.

"Thinking along this line rides on an object relations model of the analytic process that stresses the new experience of relatedness that the patient has in the analytic encounter" (183–84).

19. I emphasize again that *each client's experience of my participation will be different.* I *will* be different, not only because in the response to her "transference" (in my "countertransference") I will be enlisted to be a certain way but also because she will unconsciously evoke certain transference reactions from me, as she reminds me of people and relationships from my past. In addition, *her personal experience and history, unique as it is, will inform how she experiences and interprets* my participation.

20. Evelyne Albrecht Schwaber ("On the Mode of Therapeutic Action: A Clinical Montage" in Rothstein, *How Does Treatment Help?*) writes that "the closer we can stay to their [the client's] experience of the moment, the closer we stay with the data, the less we are tempted to teach another truth, the more deeply our patients will be able to observe and to face their own. As the patient I first described said, 'When you find the logic in my responses, when you try to understand the way my mind works without saying it should work another way, that lets me acknowledge more and experience more about how my mind works' " (92). Leston Havens (*A Safe Place*) provides a beautiful account of this kind of participation. "I wanted to be beside the patient, sitting or standing so that I could watch out of the corner of my eye while the two of us looked forward together. I didn't want to stare and embarrass, nor disappear and leave him alone. . . . So I did what Sullivan suggested. I put my chair next to his, literally side by side, not face to face but ear to ear. It represented the spatial statement of a psychological fact: I am on your side, we look out together" (51–52).

21. I am unable to locate the source. In his recent text, *Clinical Empathy*, David Berger writes, "Weiss and colleagues . . . present evidence that under 'conditions of safety' (i.e., when the patient feels secure that the therapist is trustworthy) new material emerges spontaneously" (Northvale, N.J.: Jason Aronson, 1987, 221). Leston Havens opens the preface to *A Safe Place* with these words: "The work of psychological healing begins in a safe place, to be compared with the best hospital experience or, from an earlier time, church sanctuary. The psychological safe place permits the individual to make spontaneous, forceful gestures and, at the same time, represents a community that both allows the gestures and is valued for its own sake" (vii). Arthur Modell discusses the issue of safety in his article "On the Protection and Safety of the Therapeutic Setting" in Rothstein, *How Does Treatment Help?* He also refers to the contribution of Joseph Sandler, "A Background of Safety," *International Journal of Psychoanalysis* 41 (1960):352–56.

22. This bears a family resemblance to Carl Rogers's concept of "unconditional positive regard," and to notions of "unconditional love," but is different in several crucial respects. I cannot love and do not aspire to love someone unconditionally. I do, however, intend to relate to them in ways central to my Christian identity and faith, as if they were the Christ, worthy of my reverence, respect, care, and devotion. In doing so, I regard them as mediating something through themselves. In that, I model a way for them to regard themselves and others. In that sense, I invite them to experience everyone as disclosing God's presence, love, and forgiveness.

23. Daniel Stern argues that attunement is both a capacity and a need and that words may be less important as ways of making sense than as vehicles for connection. It is difficult to say whether the goal is reassurance and relief in connection itself or in gaining mastery through that connection. I suspect some of the relief is in connecting with oneself and others and, thereby, in feeling safe and more equipped and able to survive and master. See his discussions of "Intersubjective Relatedness" and "Misattunement and Tuning" in *Interpersonal World of the Infant* (New York: Basic Books, 1985), esp. 203–20.

24. The point is worth emphasizing. If I model a kind of "empathy" with her that is exclusive of, and inconsistent with, an empathy with my self, I am conveying a mixed message. She may experience that a mature way of being in the world has to do with love of others that is competitive with and at the expense of love of the self. Much has been written, of course, about neighbor love and love of self, agape and self-sacrificial love—in theological ethics as well as in more contemporary feminist ethics and psychology.

25. Arnold Modell ("On the Protection and Safety," 101) notes, "If we are not certain what we have done right in our successful cases, our failures may point to those missing elements that are essential." In considering this notion of failure, Theodore Jacobs ("Notes on the Therapeutic Process: Working with the Young Adult," in Rothstein, *How Does Treatment Help?* 67) explains, "In reviewing my failures in analysis, I have become convinced that the problems lay not in difficulties in understanding or in technical errors, but in my inability to establish the kind of contact with these patients that would allow them to know that I was there for them and on their side."

26. Sheldon Roth suggests we regard "working-through" as "living-through." See *Psychotherapy: The Art of Wooing Nature,* 156.

27. See, for example, Paul Ricoeur, *Freud and Philosophy: An Essay on Interpretation* (New Haven: Yale University Press, 1970).

28. Freud, I think, was both ambivalent and ambiguous on this point. Through the topographic model, he indicated that the process of "making the unconscious conscious" would be like knowing the truth that would set you free. Suffering from reminiscences, identifying the deed that was in the beginning would, once and for all, free us from our past. In a sense, we could make the unconscious (entirely—or for all practical purposes, nearly entirely) conscious. We could be

"fully analyzed." At the same time, particularly by way of the structural model, he recognized later in his life that resolutions were never final. In that regard, conscious and unconscious are ontological categories, basic to our existence.

29. See Heinz Kohut, *How Does Analysis Cure?* edited by Arnold Goldberg in collaboration with Paul Stepansky (Chicago: University of Chicago Press, 1984).

30. See Droege, *The Faith Factor in Healing.*

31. Freud used the terms *repetition, recollection,* and *working through.* In this discussion, I speak about identifying and disconfirming (the repeated) patterns, and living through. My approach has affinities with Michael Franz Basch's description of the six phases of psychotherapy ("orientation, consternation, reorientation, collaboration, integration, and transformation"). *Understanding Psychotherapy: The Science behind the Art* (New York: Basic Books, 1988). "Transformation, or a permanent change in the patient's manner of coping: In some significant respect the patient is no longer the same person as before and can, as a result, now deal differently and more effectively with what bothered him than when he first came for treatment" (19–20).

32. Paul Ornstein explains one element in this, from a self psychological perspective: "Since psychopathology is in its essence the consequence of a thwarted, derailed, or arrested development, a climate in which development can be resumed, deficits can be filled in, and/or conflicts can be resolved—which in turn reopen the path for belated structure building and growth—is the basic requirement for the curative process to take place" ("Multiple Curative Factors and Processes in the Psychoanalytic Psychotherapies," in Rothstein, *How Does Treatment Help?* (109).

33. I agree with Paul H. Ornstein, who writes, "My working assumption is that each patient-therapist relationship encounter sets off a process that unfolds between them and in each of them. As far as the curative factors are concerned, these reside within 'the process,' which is triggered for its unfolding by the encounter" ("Some Curative Factors and Processes in the Psychoanalytic Therapies," in *Cures by Psychotherapy: What Effects Change?* ed. J. Martin Myers [New York: Praeger, 1984], 56).

34. This self psychological interpretation is explained further by Paul Ornstein, who writes, "In his particular near-epigrammatic formulation of the nature of cure, Kohut did not negate the contributions of the other identified factors or processes, but placed them in a subordinate role in the total therapeutic process. This is how he put it in *How Does Analysis Cure?:* While structure formation via transmuting internalization is still a major part of the developmental process toward health, and in the analytic process toward cure, we now had to recognize that 'the gradual acquisition of the ability to maintain the self within the matrix of mature selfselfobject relationships, i.e., the acquisition of empathic contact with selfobjects, is the essence of psychoanalytic cure . . .' " ("Multiple Curative Factors and Processes," 108–9).

35. See Rossi for discussions of "states," Kohut regarding selfobject relationships, Stern regarding domains of intersubjective relatedness, and Paul Pruyser for discussion of domains of experience. It is apparent that I am not focusing expressly on—but am not foreclosing awareness of—a variety of other indications, such as changes in patterns of behavior and in cognitive beliefs.

36. Carter Lindberg, "The Lutheran Tradition," in *Caring and Curing: Health and Medicine in the Western Religious Traditions*, edited by Ronald L. Numbers and Darrell W. Amundsen (New York: Macmillan, 1986), 177.

37. See the article by Stephen Toulmin, "Self-Knowledge and Knowledge of the Self," in *The Self: Psychological and Philosophical Issues*, edited by Theodore Mischel (Totowa, N.J.: Rowman and Littlefield, 1977), 291–317, in which he illumines how the self is at once psychological and ethical, and the process of psychological growth, development, healing is at the same time a process of ethical maturing.

38. William W. Meissner, in elaborating upon the impact of a comment, observes, "The words are not important here; there is no magic in the choice of words. *What is important is the attitude and set of mind with which the interpretation is given*" (*What Is Effective in Psychoanalytic Psychotherapy*, 71, emphasis added). It is this attitude that the clinician "lends" to the client, that the client "borrows."

Bibliography

Attitude

Ajzen, Icek. "Attitude, Structure, and Behavior." In *Attitude, Structure, and Function*, edited by Anthony R. Pratkanis, Steven J. Breckler, and Anthony G. Greenwald. Hillsdale, N.J.: Lawrence Erlbaum Associates, 1989.

Allport, Gordon. "Attitudes." In *A Handbook of Social Psychology*, edited by C. Murchison. Worcester, Mass.: Clark University Press, 1935.

Berger, Peter, and Hansfried Kellner. *Sociology Reinterpreted: An Essay on Method and Vocation*. Garden City, N.Y.: Anchor Press/Doubleday, 1981.

Black, Margaret J., Zenia Odes Fliegel, Lloyd Silverman, Merton M. Gill, and Marian Tolpin. "The Analyst's Stance: Transferential Implications of Technical Orientation." *The Annual of Psychoanalysis* 15 (1987):127–72.

Bloom, Allan. *The Closing of the American Mind: How Higher Education Has Failed Democracy and Impoverished the Souls of Today's Students*. New York: Simon and Schuster, 1987.

Cacioppo, John T., Richard E. Petty, and Thomas R. Green. "Attitude, Structure, and Function: From the Tripartite to the Homeostasis Model of Attitudes." In *Attitude, Structure, and Function*, edited by Anthony R. Pratkanis, Steven J. Breckler, and Anthony G. Greenwald. Hillsdale, N.J.: Lawrence Erlbaum Associates, 1989.

Ewing, James. "The Pastoral-Therapeutic Stance." In *Psychiatry, Ministry, and Pastoral Counseling*, edited by A. W. Richard Sipe and Clarence J. Rowe. Collegeville, Minn.: Liturgical Press, 1984.

Greenwald, Anthony G., "Why Are Attitudes Important?" In *Attitude, Structure, and Function*, edited by Anthony R. Pratkanis, Steven J. Breckler, and Anthony G. Greenwald. Hillsdale, N.J.: Lawrence Erlbaum Associates, 1989.

Schafer, Roy. "The Psychoanalytic Vision of Reality." In *A New Language for Psychoanalysis*. New Haven: Yale University Press, 1976.

Schlauch, Chris R. "Empathy as the Essence of Pastoral Psychotherapy." *The Journal of Pastoral Care* 44 (1990):3–17.

Tuttman, Saul. "Exploring the Analyst's Treatment Stance in Current Psychoanalytic Practice." *Journal of the American Academy of Psychoanalysis* 15 (1987):29–37.

Conversation as Metaphor

Ambrosio, Francis J. "Gadamer, Plato, and the Discipline of Dialogue." *International Philosophical Quarterly* 27 (March 1987):17–32.

Bernstein, Richard J. "Philosophy in the Conversation of Mankind." In *Hermeneu-*

tics and Praxis, edited by Robert Hollinger. Notre Dame, Ind.: University of Notre Dame Press, 1985.

Bouma-Prediger, Steve. "Rorty's Pragmatism and Gadamer's Hermeneutics." *Journal of the American Academy of Religion* 57 (1989):313–24.

Gadamer, Hans-Georg. *Dialogue and Dialectic: Eight Hermeneutical Studies in Plato*. New Haven: Yale University Press, 1980.

Neville, Robert C. *Recovery of the Measure: Interpretation and the Philosophy of Nature*. Albany: State University of New York Press, 1989.

Rorty, Richard. *Philosophy and the Mirror of Nature*. Oxford: Basil Blackwell, 1980.

————. *Contingency, Irony, and Solidarity*. Cambridge: Cambridge University Press, 1989.

————. *Objectivity, Relativism, and Truth: Philosophical Papers*, Vol. 1. Cambridge: Cambridge University Press, 1991.

Seeskin, Kenneth. *Dialogue and Discovery: A Study in Socratic Method*. Albany: State University of New York Press, 1987.

Tracy, David. *Plurality and Ambiguity: Hermeneutics, Religion, Hope*. San Francisco: Harper & Row, 1987.

————. "Hermeneutical Reflections in the New Paradigm." In *Paradigm Change in Theology*, edited by Hans Kung and David Tracy. New York: Crossroad, 1989.

Diagnosis

Draper, E. *Psychiatry and Pastoral Care*. Englewood Cliffs, N.J.: Prentice-Hall, 1965.

Draper, E., G. Myer, Z. Parzen, and G. Samuelson. "On the Diagnostic Value of Religious Ideation." *Archives of General Psychiatry* 13 (1965):202–7.

Draper, E., and B. Steadman. "Assessment in Pastoral Care." In *Clinical Handbook of Pastoral Counseling*, edited by R. J. Wicks, R. D. Parsons, and D. Capps. New York: Paulist Press, 1984.

Fowler, James. *Stages of Faith*. San Francisco: Harper & Row, 1981.

Hiltner, Seward. *Religion and Health*. New York: Macmillan, 1943.

————. *Pastoral Counseling*. Nashville: Abingdon Press, 1949.

————. *Theological Dynamics*. Nashville: Abingdon Press, 1972.

————. "Toward Autonomous Diagnosis." In *Diagnosis and the Difference It Makes*, edited by Paul Pruyser. New York: Jason Aronson, 1976.

Hobson, D. P., and M. Jacob. "Possibilities and Pitfalls in Pastoral Diagnosis." *Pastoral Psychology* 34 (1985):30–41.

Ivy, S. S. "A Model for Pastoral Assessment." *The Journal of Pastoral Care* 41 (1987):329–40.

————. "Pastoral Diagnosis as Pastoral Caring." *The Journal of Pastoral Care* 42 (1988):81–89.

Malony, H. Newton. "Making a Religious Diagnosis: The Use of Religious Assessment in Pastoral Care and Counseling." *Pastoral Psychology* 41 (4) (1993): 237–46.

Muslin, H., and E. Val. *The Psychotherapy of the Self.* New York: Brunner/Mazel, 1987.

Othmer, E., and S. C. Othmer. *The Clinical Interview Using DSM III-R.* Washington, D.C.: American Psychiatric Press, 1989.

Pruyser, Paul W. *The Minister as Diagnostician.* Philadelphia: Westminster Press, 1976.

———. *The Psychological Examination: A Guide for Clinicians.* New York: International Universities Press, 1979.

———. "The Diagnostic Process in Pastoral Care." In *Psychiatry, Ministry, and Pastoral Counseling,* edited by A. W. R. Sipe and C. J. Rowe. Collegeville, Minn.: Liturgical Press, 1984.

Pruyser, Paul W., ed. *Diagnosis and the Difference It Makes.* New York: Jason Aronson, 1976.

Roth, Sheldon. *Psychotherapy: The Art of Wooing Nature.* Northvale, N.J.: Jason Aronson, 1987.

Schlauch, Chris R. "Re-Visioning Pastoral Diagnosis." In *The Clinical Handbook of Pastoral Counseling, Volume II,* edited by Robert J. Wicks and Richard D. Parsons, 51–101. New York: Paulist Press, 1993.

Seligman, L. *Diagnosis and Treatment Planning in Counseling.* New York: Human Sciences Press, 1986.

Wolman, Benjamin. "Classification and Diagnosis of Mental Disorders." In *Clinical Diagnosis of Mental Disorders: A Handbook,* edited by B. Wolman. New York: Plenum Press, 1978.

Disciplines as Hermeneutical or Interpretive

Browning, Don. *Religious Thought and the Modern Psychologies.* Philadelphia: Fortress Press, 1987.

Capps, Donald. *Pastoral Care and Hermeneutics.* Philadelphia: Fortress Press, 1984.

Farley, Edward. *The Fragility of Knowledge: Theological Education in the Church and the University.* Philadelphia: Fortress Press, 1988.

Gerkin, Charles V. *The Living Human Document: Re-Visioning Pastoral Counseling in a Hermeneutical Mode.* Nashville: Abingdon Press, 1984.

———. "Faith and Praxis: Pastoral Counseling's Hermeneutical Problem." *Pastoral Psychology* 35 (1986):3–15.

———. *Widening the Horizons: Pastoral Responses to a Fragmented Society.* Philadelphia: Westminster Press, 1986.

Kleinman, Arthur. *The Illness Narratives.* New York: Basic Books, 1988.

Patton, John. *Pastoral Counseling: A Ministry of the Church.* Nashville: Abingdon, 1983.

———. "The New Language of Pastoral Counseling." In *Spiritual Dimensions of*

Pastoral Care: Witness to the Ministry of Wayne E. Oates, edited by G. L. Borchert and A. D. Lester. Philadelphia: Westminster Press, 1985.

Schafer, Roy. "Narration in the Psychoanalytic Dialogue." In *On Narrative,* edited W. J. T. Mitchell. Chicago: University of Chicago Press, 1981.

———. *The Analytic Attitude.* New York: Basic Books, 1983.

Spence, Donald. "Clinical Interpretation: Some Comments on the Nature of the Evidence." *Psychoanalysis and Contemporary Science* 5 (1976):367–88.

———. *Narrative Truth and Historical Truth: Meaning and Interpretation in Psychoanalysis.* New York: W. W. Norton, 1982.

Healing and Change

Berger, David M. *Clinical Empathy.* Northvale, N.J.: Jason Aronson, 1987.

Blum, Harold P., ed. *Psychoanalytic Explorations of Technique: Discourse on the Theory of Therapy.* New York: International Universities Press, 1980.

Brody, Howard. *Stories of Sickness.* New Haven: Yale University Press, 1987.

Buechner, Frederick. *Telling Secrets: A Memoir.* San Francisco: Harper Collins, 1991.

Burns, Chester. "Traditions of Healths in Western Culture." *Second Opinion: Health, Faith, and Ethics* 2 (1986):120–36.

Burton, Arthur, ed. *What Makes Behavior Change Possible?* New York: Brunner/Mazel, 1976.

Droege, Thomas A. *The Faith Factor in Healing.* Philadelphia: Trinity Press International, 1991.

Frank, Jerome, Rudolf Hoehn-Saric, Stanley D. Imber, Bernard L. Liberman, and Anthony R. Stone. *Effective Ingredients of Successful Psychotherapy.* New York: Brunner/Mazel, 1978.

Greenspan, Stanley I. "A Developmental Model of Therapeutic Change." In *The Development of the Ego: Implications for Personality Theory, Psychopathology, and the Psychotherapeutic Process.* Madison, Conn.: International Universities Press, 1989.

Higginbotham, H. Nick, Stephen G. West, and Donelson R. Forsyth, editors: *Psychotherapy and Behavior Change: Social, Cultural and Methodological Perspectives.* New York: Pergamon Press, 1988.

Kleinman, Arthur. "How Do Psychiatrists Heal?" In *Rethinking Psychiatry: From Cultural Category to Personal Experience.* New York: Free Press, 1988.

Kohut, Heinz. *How Does Analysis Cure?* edited by Arnold Goldberg in collaboration with Paul Stepansky. Chicago: University of Chicago Press, 1984.

Levenson, Edgar. *The Ambiguity of Change: An Inquiry into the Nature of Psychoanalytic Reality.* New York: Basic Books, 1983.

Lichtenberg, Joseph D. "An Application of the Self Psychological Viewpoint to Psychoanalytic Technique." In *Reflections on Self Psychology,* edited by Joseph D. Lichtenberg and Samuel Kaplan. Hillsdale, N.J.: Analytic Press, 1983.

Marty, Martin. "Religion and Healing: The Four Expectations." *Second Opinion: Health, Faith, and Ethics* 7 (1988):61–80.

Meissner, William W. *What Is Effective in Psychoanalytic Therapy: The Move from Interpretation to Relation.* Northvale, N.J.: Jason Aronson, 1991.

Modell, Arnold H. *Other Times, Other Realities: Toward a Theory of Psychoanalytic Treatment.* Cambridge, Mass.: Harvard University Press, 1990.

Myers, J. Martin, editor. *Cures by Psychotherapy: What Effects Change?* New York: Praeger, 1984.

Nouwen, Henri. *Out of Solitude.* Notre Dame, Ind.: Ave Maria Press, 1974.

Numbers, Ronald L., and Darrel W. Amundsen, ed. *Caring and Curing: Health and Medicine in Western Religious Traditions.* New York: Macmillan, 1986.

Ornstein, Paul H., and Anna Ornstein. "Clinical Understanding and Explaining: The Empathic Vantage Point." In *Progress in Self Psychology*, edited by Arnold Goldberg. New York: Guilford Press, 1985.

Pentony, Patrick, *Models of Influence in Psychotherapy.* New York: Free Press, 1981.

Pine, Fred. "Aspects of Clinical Process from a Developmental Perspective." In *Developmental Theory and Clinical Process.* New Haven: Yale University Press, 1985.

Rice, Laura N., and Leslie S. Greenberg, editors: *Patterns of Change: Intensive Analysis of Psychotherapy Process.* New York: Guilford Press, 1984.

Rosenblatt, Allan D. "Change in Psychotherapy." *The Annual of Psychoanalysis: A Publication of the Chicago Institute for Psychoanalysis* 15:175–89.

Rossi, Ernest L. *The Psychobiology of Mind-Body Healing: New Concepts of Therapeutic Hypnosis.* New York: W. W. Norton, 1986.

Rothstein, Arnold, editor: *How Does Treatment Help? On the Modes of Therapeutic Action of Psychoanalytic Psychotherapy.* Madison, Conn.: International Universities Press, 1988.

Sheikh, Anees A., and Katharina S. Sheikh, editors: *Eastern and Western Approaches to Healing: Ancient Wisdom and Modern Knowledge.* New York: John Wiley, 1989.

Shupe, Anson, and Jeffrey K. Hadden. "Understanding Unconventional Healing Models: A Progress Report." *Second Opinion: Health, Faith, and Ethics* 7 (1988):82–103.

Siegel, Bernie. *Peace, Love, and Healing: Bodymind Communication and the Path to Self-Healing: An Exploration.* New York: Harper & Row, 1989.

Sullivan, Lawrence E. *Healing and Restoration: Health and Medicine in the World's Religious Traditions.* New York: Macmillan, 1989.

Tolpin, Paul H. "Discussion: What Makes for Effective Analysis?" In *Progress in Self Psychology*, edited by Arnold Goldberg. New York: Guilford Press, 1986.

Trautmann, Joanne, editor. *Healing Arts in Dialogue: Medicine and Literature.* Carbondale and Edwardsville: Southern Illinois University Press, 1981.

Metaphor's Functions

Abrams, M. H. *The Mirror and the Lamp.* London: Oxford University Press, 1953.

Averill, James R. "Inner Feelings, Works of the Flesh, The Beast Within, Diseases of the Mind, Driving Force, and Putting on a Show: Six Metaphors of Emotion and Their Theoretical Extensions." In *Metaphors in the History of Psychology,* edited by David E. Leary. Cambridge: Cambridge University Press, 1990.

Black, Max. "Metaphor." In *Models and Metaphors: Studies in Language and Philosophy.* Ithaca, N.Y.: Cornell University Press, 1962.

———. "More about Metaphor." In *Metaphor and Thought,* edited by Andrew Ortony. Cambridge: Cambridge University Press, 1979.

Boyd, Richard. "Metaphor and Theory Change: What is 'Metaphor' a Metaphor for?" In *Metaphor and Thought,* edited by A. Ortony. Cambridge: Cambridge University Press, 1979, 356–408.

Browning, Don S. *Religious Ethics and Pastoral Care.* Philadelphia: Fortress Press, 1983.

———. *Religious Thought and the Modern Psychologies: A Critical Conversation in the Theology of Culture.* Philadelphia: Fortress Press, 1987.

Gerhart, Mary, and Allan Melvin Russell. *Metaphoric Process: The Creation of Scientific and Religious Understanding.* Fort Worth: Texas Christian University Press, 1984.

Gordon, David Cole. *Therapeutic Metaphors: Helping Others through the Looking Glass.* Cupertino, Calif.: Meta Publications, 1978.

Jaynes, Julian. *The Origin of Consciousness in the Breakdown of the Bicameral Mind.* Boston: Houghton Mifflin, 1977.

Johnson, Mark. "Introduction: Metaphor in the Philosophical Tradition." In *Philosophical Perspectives on Metaphor,* edited by Mark Johnson. Minneapolis: University of Minnesota Press, 1981.

Kuhn, Thomas S. "Metaphor in Science." In *Metaphor and Thought,* edited by A. Ortony, Cambridge: Cambridge University Press, 1979, 409–19.

Lakoff, George, and Mark Johnson. *Metaphors We Live By.* Chicago: University of Chicago Press, 1980.

Leary, David E. "Psyche's Muse: The Role of Metaphor in the History of Psychology." In *Metaphors in the History of Psychology,* edited by David E. Leary. Cambridge: Cambridge University Press, 1990.

McFague, Sallie. *Metaphorical Theology: Models of God in Religious Language.* Philadelphia: Fortress Press, 1982.

Mehrabian, Albert. *An Analysis of Personality Theories.* Englewood Cliffs, N.J.: Prentice-Hall, 1968.

Olney, James. *Metaphors of Self: The Meaning of Autobiography.* Princeton, N.J.: Princeton University Press, 1972.

Ortony, Andrew, ed. *Metaphor and Thought.* Cambridge: Cambridge University Press, 1979.

Pepper, Stephen. *World Hypothesis.* Berkeley and Los Angeles: University of California Press, 1942.

———. "The Root Metaphor Theory of Metaphysics." In *Essays on Metaphor,* edited by W. Shibles, Whitewater, Wisconsin: The Language Press, 1972, 15–26.

Ricoeur, Paul. *The Rule of Metaphor: An Interdisciplinary Study.* Toronto: University of Toronto, 1977.

Sacks, Sheldon, ed. *On Metaphor.* Chicago: University of Chicago Press, 1979.

Schafer, Roy. "Narration in the Psychoanalytic Dialogue." In *On Narrative,* edited by W. J. T. Mitchell. Chicago: University of Chicago Press, 1981.

———. *The Analytic Attitude.* New York: Basic Books, 1983.

Schlauch, Chris R. "The Intersecting-Overlapping Self: Contemporary Psychoanalysis Reconsiders Religion—Again." *Pastoral Psychology* 42 (1993):21–43.

Sewell, Elizabeth. *The Human Metaphor.* Notre Dame, Ind.: University of Notre Dame Press, 1964.

Shibles, Warren, ed. *Essays on Metaphor.* Whitewater, Wisconsin: The Language Press, 1972.

Smith, M. Brewster. "Perspectives on Selfhood." *American Psychologist* 33 (1978):1053–63.

———. "The Metaphorical Basis of Selfhood." In *Culture and Self: Asian and Western Perspectives,* edited by Anthony Marsella, George De Vos, and Francis Hsu. New York: Tavistock, 1985, 56–88.

Soskice, Janet Martin. *Metaphor and Religious Language.* Oxford: Clarendon Press, 1985.

Spence, Donald. *The Freudian Metaphor: Toward Paradigm Change in Psychoanalysis.* New York: W. W. Norton, 1987.

Tracy, David. "Metaphor and Religion: The Test Case of Christian Texts." In *On Metaphor,* edited by S. Sacks. Chicago: University of Chicago Press, 1978.

Narrative's Functions

Brody, Howard. *Stories of Sickness.* New Haven: Yale University Press, 1987.

Browning, Don S. *Religious Ethics and Pastoral Care.* Philadelphia: Fortress Press, 1983.

———. *Religious Thought and the Modern Psychologies: A Critical Conversation in the Theology of Culture.* Philadelphia: Fortress Press, 1987.

Capps, Donald. *Pastoral Counseling and Preaching.* Philadelphia: Westminster Press, 1980.

———. *Pastoral Care and Hermeneutics.* Philadelphia: Fortress Press, 1984.

Cavell, Marcia. *The Psychoanalystic Mind: From Freud to Philosophy.* Cambridge: Harvard University Press, 1993.

Crites, Stephen. "The Narrative Quality of Experience." *Journal of the American Academy of Religion* 39 (September 1971):291–311.

———. "Angels We Have Heard," In *Religion as Story,* ed. James B. Wiggins. New York: Harper & Row, Publishers, 1975, 23–63.

Crossan, John Dominic. *In Parables*. New York: Harper & Row, 1973.
———. *The Dark Interval: Towards a Theology of Story*. Allen, Tex.: Argus Communications, 1975.
Gerkin, Charles. *The Living Human Document: Re-Visioning Pastoral Counseling in a Hermeneutical Mode*. Nashville: Abingdon Press, 1984.
———. "Faith and Praxis: Pastoral Counseling's Hermeneutical Problem." *Pastoral Psychology* 35 (1986):3–15.
———. *Widening the Horizons: Pastoral Responses to a Fragmented Society*. Philadelphia: Westminster Press, 1986.
Goldberg, Arnold. *A Fresh Look at Psychoanalysis*. Hillsdale, N.J.: Analytic Press, 1988.
———. *The Prisonhouse of Psychoanalysis*. Hillsdale, N.J.: The Analytic Press, 1990.
Goldberg, Michael. *Theology and Narrative: A Critical Introduction*. Nashville: Abingdon Press, 1982.
Hauerwas, Stanley. *Character and the Christian Life: A Study in Theological Ethics*. San Antonio: Trinity University Press, 1975.
Hauerwas, Stanley, and Jones, L. Gregory, eds. *Why Narrative? Readings in Narrative Theology*. Grand Rapids, Mich.: William B. Eerdmans Publishing Company, 1989.
Hillman, James. "The Fiction of Case History: A Round," in *Religion as Story*, edited by James B. Wiggins. New York: Harper & Row, 1975, 123–72.
Kleinman, Arthur. *The Illness Narratives*. New York: Basic Books, 1988.
———. *Rethinking Psychiatry: From Cultural Category to Personal Experience*. New York: Free Press, 1988.
MacIntyre, Alisdair. *After Virtue*. Notre Dame, Ind.: University of Notre Dame Press, 1981.
Martin, Wallace. *Recent Theories of Narrative*. Ithaca, N.Y.: Cornell University Press, 1986.
McFague, Sallie. *Metaphorical Theology: Models of God in Religious Language*. Philadelphia: Fortress Press, 1982.
Mitchell, W. J. T., ed. *On Narrative*. Chicago: University of Chicago Press, 1980.
Patton, John. *Pastoral Counseling: A Ministry of the Church*. Nashville: Abingdon Press, 1983.
———. "The New Language of Pastoral Counseling." In *Spiritual Dimensions of Pastoral Care: Witness to the Ministry of Wayne E. Oates*, edited by G. L. Borchert and A. D. Lester. Philadelphia: Westminster Press, 1985.
———. *From Ministry to Theology: Pastoral Action and Reflection*. Nashville: Abingdon Press, 1990.
Polkinghorne, Donald E. *Narrative Knowing and the Human Sciences*. Albany: State University of New York Press, 1988.
Sarbin, T. R., ed. *Narrative Psychology: The Storied Nature of Human Conduct*. New York: Praeger, 1986.
Schafer, Roy. "Narration in the Psychoanalytic Dialogue." In *On Narrative*, edited by W. J. T. Mitchell. Chicago: University of Chicago Press, 1981.

————. *The Analytic Attitude.* New York: Basic Books, 1983.

————. "Narratives of the Self," In *Psychoanalysis: Toward the Second Century,* edited by Arnold M. Cooper, Otto F. Kernberg, and Ethel Spector Person. New Haven: Yale University Press, 1989, 162–63.

Spence, Donald. "Clinical Interpretation: Some Comments on the Nature of Evidence." *Psychoanalysis and Contemporary Science* 5 (1976): 367–88.

————. *Narrative Truth and Historical Truth: Meaning and Interpretation in Psychoanalysis.* New York: W. W. Norton, 1982.

————. "Narrative Smoothing and Clinical Wisdom." In *Narrative Psychology: The Storied Nature of Human Conduct,* edited by T. R. Sarbin. New York: Praeger, 1986.

————. *The Freudian Metaphor: Toward Paradigm Change in Psychoanalysis.* New York: W. W. Norton, 1987.

Stroup, George. *The Promise of Narrative Theology: Recovering the Gospel in the Church.* Atlanta: John Knox Press, 1981.

Tilley, Terrence. *Story Theology.* Wilmington, Del.: Michael Glazier, 1985.

White, Michael, and Epston, David. *Narrative Means to Therapeutic Ends.* New York: W. W. Norton and Company, 1990.

Wyatt, Frederick. "The Narrative in Psychoanalysis: Psychoanalytic Notes in Storytelling, Listening, and Interpreting." In *Narrative Psychology: The Storied Nature of Human Conduct,* edited by T. R. Sarbin. New York: Praeger, 1986.

Operationalizing Approaches

Asquith, Glenn H., Jr. "The Case Study Method of Anton T. Boisen." *The Journal of Pastoral Care* 34 (1980):84–94.

Boisen, Anton. *The Exploration of the Inner World.* New York: Harper Torchbook, 1952.

Browning, Don S. *Religious Ethics and Pastoral Care.* Philadelphia: Fortress Press, 1983.

Capps, Donald. *Biblical Approaches to Pastoral Counseling.* Philadelphia: Westminster Press, 1980.

————. *Pastoral Counseling and Preaching.* Philadelphia: Westminster Press, 1980.

————. *Pastoral Care and Hermeneutics.* Philadelphia: Fortress Press, 1984.

Draper, E. *Psychiatry and Pastoral Care.* Englewood Cliffs, N.J.: Prentice-Hall, 1965.

Draper, E., G. Myer, Z. Parzen, and G. Samuelson. "On the Diagnostic Value of Religious Ideation." *Archives of General Psychiatry* 13 (1965):202–7.

Draper, E., and B. Steadman. "Assessment in Pastoral Care." In *Clinical Handbook of Pastoral Counseling,* edited by R. J. Wicks, R. D. Parsons, and D. Capps. New York: Paulist Press, 1984.

Ellens, J. H. "Biblical Themes in Psychological Theory and Practice." In *Chris-*

tian Counseling and Psychotherapy, edited by D. G. Benner. Grand Rapids: Baker Book House, 1987.

Fairbanks, R. J. "Diagnosis in Pastoral Care." *The Journal of Pastoral Care* 6 (1952): 34–38.

Gaskill, H. S. "The Diagnostic Interview." In *Psychiatry, Ministry, and Pastoral Counseling*, edited by A. W. R. Sipe and C. J. Rowe. Collegeville, Minn.: Liturgical Press, 1984.

Gerkin, Charles. *The Living Human Document: Re-Visioning Pastoral Counseling in a Hermeneutical Mode*. Nashville: Abingdon Press, 1984.

———. "Faith and Praxis." *Pastoral Psychology* 35 (1986): 3–15.

Hiltner, Seward. *Religion and Health*. New York: Macmillan, 1943.

———. *Pastoral Counseling*. Nashville: Abingdon Press, 1949.

———. *Theological Dynamics*. Nashville: Abingdon Press, 1972.

———. "Toward Autonomous Diagnosis." In *Diagnosis and the Difference It Makes*, edited by Paul Pruyser. New York: Jason Aronson, 1976.

Hobson, D. P., and M. Jacob. "Possibilities and Pitfalls in Pastoral Diagnosis." *Pastoral Psychology* 34 (1985):30–41.

Ivy, S. S. "A Model for Pastoral Assessment." *The Journal of Pastoral Care* 41 (1987): 329–40.

———. "Pastoral Diagnosis as Pastoral Caring." *The Journal of Pastoral Care* 42 (1988):81–89.

Jordan, Merle R. *Taking on the Gods: The Task of the Pastoral Counselor*. Nashville: Abingdon Press, 1986.

Nouwen, Henry J. M. "Ronald." Unpublished article.

Patton, John. "The New Language of Pastoral Counseling." In *Spiritual Dimensions of Pastoral Care: Witness to the Ministry of Wayne E. Oates*, edited by G. L. Borchert and A. D. Lester. Philadelphia: Westminster Press, 1985.

———. *Pastoral Counseling: A Ministry of the Church*. Nashville: Abingdon, 1993.

Pruyser, Paul W., ed. *Diagnosis and the Difference It Makes*. New York: Jason Aronson, 1976.

———. *The Minister as Diagnostician*. Philadelphia: Westminster Press, 1976.

———. *The Psychological Examination: A Guide for Clinicians*. New York: International Universities Press, 1979.

———. "The Diagnostic Process in Pastoral Care." In *Psychiatry, Ministry, and Pastoral Counseling*, edited by A. W. R. Sipe and C. J. Rowe. Collegeville, Minn.: Liturgical Press, 1984.

Schlauch, Chris R. "Defining Pastoral Psychotherapy." *The Journal of Pastoral Care* 39 (1985):219–28.

———. "Defining Pastoral Psychotherapy II." *The Journal of Pastoral Care* 41 (1987):319–27.

———. "Empathy as the Essence of Pastoral Psychotherapy." *The Journal of Pastoral Care* 44 (1990):3–17.

————. "Expanding the Contexts of Pastoral Care." *The Journal of Pastoral Care* 44 (1990):359–71.

Schneider, Carl D. "Faith Development and Pastoral Diagnosis." In *Faith Development and Fowler*, edited by C. Dykstra and S. Parks. Birmingham: Religious Education Press, 1986.

Underwood, Ralph L. "Personal and Professional Integrity in Relation to Pastoral Assessment." *Pastoral Psychology* 31 (1982):109–17.

Wahking, H. "Therapy with Theological Constructs and Tactics," in *Christian Counseling and Psychotherapy*, edited by D. G. Benner. Grand Rapids: Baker Book House, 1987.

Yeomans, M., editor: *Clinical Theology*. London: Darton, Longman, and Todd, 1986.

Praxis

Bernstein, Richard. *Praxis and Action: Contemporary Philosophies of Human Activity.* Philadelphia: University of Pennsylvania Press, 1971.

————. *Beyond Objectivism and Relativism: Science, Hermeneutics, and Praxis.* Philadelphia: University of Pennsylvania Press, 1985.

Davis, Charles. "Theology and Praxis." *Cross Currents* 23 (Summer 1973):154–68.

Grant, Colin. "The Promise and Perils of Praxis." *Cross Currents* 40 (Spring 1990): 64-87.

Groome, Thomas. *Christian Religious Education: Sharing Our Story and Vision.* San Francisco: Harper & Row, 1980.

Hollinger, Robert, ed. *Hermeneutics and Praxis.* Notre Dame, Ind.: University of Notre Dame Press, 1985.

Lamb, Matthew L. *Solidarity with Victims: Toward a Theology of Social Transformation.* New York: Crossroad, 1982.

Lobkowicz, Nicholas. *Theory and Practice: History of a Concept from Aristotle to Marx.* Notre Dame, Ind.: University of Notre Dame Press, 1967.

————. "Theory and Practice." In *Marxism, Communism, and Western Society: A Comparative Encyclopedia*, edited by C. D. Kernig. New York: Herder & Herder, 1973.

McCann, Dennis P., and Charles R. Strain. *Polity and Praxis: A Program for American Practical Theology.* Minneapolis: Winston Press, 1985.

Min, Anselm K. "Praxis and Theology in Recent Debate." *Scottish Journal of Theology* 39 (1986):529–49.

————. "Praxis and Pluralism: A Liberationist Theology of Religions." *Perspectives in Religious Studies* 16 (Fall 1989):197–211.

Use at least chapters 3–6 in past. counseling Class.

Index

Attitude, 1, 77, 108, 170 n.2, n.4
  defined, 77
  internalization of, 80, 150
  polarities of, 90
Basch, M.F., 120, 171 n.14
Belenky, M., 97–98
Bernstein, R., 3, 70, 174 n.42, 177–78 n.1
Bridge discipline, 11
Bridging concepts, 14, 32–33
Browning, D., 34, 44, 70, 87
Cartesian, 3, 13, 62
Change, 92, 135–38
Collaborative translating, 76, 77, 87–89
Conversation, 1, 12, 15, 29–31, 157 n.28
Crites, S., 36, 49
Descartes, R., 3, 13, 154 n.2
Diagnosis, 105, 106, 178, n.6
  defined, 106
  diagnostic variables, 112
    content, 114–18
    affect, 118–21
    action, 122–27
  pastoral, 110–12
  revisioning, 109
Elbow, P., 100–101
Empathy, 148–49, 177 n.49
  and introspection, 58, 59, 89–90
  as tool of observation, 63
  as vicarious introspection, 59
Faithful companioning, 1, 76, 84–85, 152
Freud, S., 2, 7, 22, 40, 64, 69, 71, 72, 190 n.28, n.31
  Freudian approach, 55–58, 60
Gerkin, C., 28, 29, 41, 87
Goldberg, A., 87, 92, 93–94
Hanson, N.R., 15
Healing, 102–103, 134, 141–45, 151–52
Holland, N., 114
Holmer, P., 39, 44, 162–63 n.62
Illusion, 71
Integumentive theory, 94
Interdisciplinary, 32, 52, 53
Internal translation, 52, 166–67 n.19
Intersecting overlapping self, 66
James, W., 3, 22, 134
Kaufman, G., 43, 164 n.79
Kleinman, A., 87, 184 n.1, 186 n.15
Kohut, H., 3, 7, 55, 58, 59, 60, 61, 62, 63, 64, 65, 66, 71, 72, 80, 125, 126, 127, 148
Lakoff G. and Johnson, M., 33, 47
Limit, 39, 40
  limit situation, 39, 141
  conversation as, 41
McFague, S., 47
Meissner, W.W., 178 n.6, 188 n.18, 191 n.38
Metaphor, 1, 32, 33, 35, 46, 47–48, 81, 137
  and compound formations, 183 n.53
  defined, 33
  metaphorizing process, 47–48, 52
  root metaphor, 1, 34, 46, 108–109, 161 n.47
Narcissism, 57, 61
Narrative, 32, 33, 35–37, 46, 49, 81, 137
  defined, 35
Neville, R.C., 3, 88, 154 n.2
Nouwen, H., 93

On-the-boundary, 3, 135, 139, 144, 147–48, 150
Optimal frustration, 64–65
Pepper, S., 34, 160 n.45
Pilot and co-pilot, 86–87
Pluralism, 13, 14
Polarities
  conversing-companioning, 91–93
  doubting-believing, 100–101, 174 n.42
  experiencing-reflecting, 23–26, 32
  religion-theology, 21, 23, 24, 28
  self-experience, 90
  self-suffering, 112–13
  separate-connected, 97–99, 174 n.37
  sinful-righteous, 101–103
  subject-object, 93–97
  understanding-explanation, 96–97
Praxis, 9, 26–29, 156 n.18
Pruyser, P., 71, 107
Ricoeur, P.,101, 148
Rorty, R., 3, 31, 157 n.28, 175 n.44
Rossi, E., 141, 142, 166 n.18
Roth, S., 121
Schafer, R., 36, 79, 80, 81, 87, 155 n.9, 161–62 n.54
Self, 61, 62, 65, 139–40
  in relationships/is relationships, 65, 66, 139
  interdimensional, 139, 143
  multiple identities, 11, 89, 143
Selfobject, 62–63, 174 n.37
Spence, D., 87, 177 n.49
Stern, D., 119, 120
Suffering, 140–41
Theological anthropology, 1, 45
Theologizing, 25
  and paradox, 44
  as a critical enterprise, 42–44
  as a human enterprise, 22–23
  as experiencing-reflecting, 23–26
  as interdisciplinary, 32–38
  as practical conversation, 29–31
  as praxis, 26–29
  defined, 21
  in the territory of the big questions, 38–41
Theology, 1–2, 16, 18, 21
  and a threefold fence, 19, 40
  and practice, 18, 19
Theory and practice, 7, 8, 9, 10, 11, 12, 21, 26, 27, 32, 156 n.13
Tillich, P., 2, 15, 21, 23, 24, 75, 151, 175–76 n. 44
Toulmin, S., 27, 70–71
Tracy, D., 34, 39, 161 n. 47
Transference, 56, 60, 62, 124–27
  as a metapsychological concept, 125–26
  classical psychoanalytic, 60
  defined, 60, 125
  narcissistic, 62
  selfobject, 63
Transferencelike, 61
Transitional experiencing, 68–69
Transitional objects, 67
Transitional phenomena, 66–67
Winnicott, D.W., 3, 55, 66, 67, 68, 69, 71, 72, 74, 148